EASTERN
RELIGIONS

EASTERN RELIGIONS

Origins • Beliefs • Practices
Holy Texts • Sacred Places

General Editor Michael D. Coogan

Vasudha Narayanan
Malcolm David Eckel
Jennifer Oldstone-Moore
C. Scott Littleton

OXFORD
UNIVERSITY PRESS

Oxford University Press

Oxford University Press, Inc., publishes works that further Oxford University's
objective of excellence in research, scholarship, and education.

Oxford New York
Auckland Cape Town Dar es Salaam Hong Kong Karachi Kuala Lumpur
Madrid Melbourne Mexico City Nairobi New Delhi Shanghai Taipei Toronto

With offices in
Argentina Austria Brazil Chile Czech Republic France Greece Guatemala
Hungary Italy Japan Poland Portugal Singapore South Korea Switzerland
Thailand Turkey Ukraine Vietnam

This edition published in the United States of America by
Oxford University Press, Inc., 2005
198 Madison Avenue, New York, New York 10016
www.oup.com

Oxford is a registered trademark of Oxford University Press

Conceived, created and designed by Duncan Baird Publishers, London, England

Library of Congress Cataloging-in-Publication Data is available
ISBN-13: 978-0-19-522190-9
ISBN-10: 0-19-522190-7

Series Editor: Christopher Westhorp
Editor: Diana Loxley
Series Designer: Lloyd Tilbury at Cobalt id
Designer: Adelle Morris
Picture Researcher: Julia Ruxton

Typeset in Garamond Three
Color reproduction by Scanhouse, Malaysia
Printed in Thailand by Imago

NOTES
The abbreviations BCE and CE are used throughout this book:
BCE Before the Common Era (the equivalent of BC)
CE Common Era (the equivalent of AD)

10 9 8 7 6 5 4 3 2 1

CONTENTS

FOREWORD BY MICHAEL D. COOGAN

In the winter of 1847 in Concord, Massachusetts, Henry David Thoreau observed workers harvesting ice from Walden Pond, to be shipped to India. In his book *Walden*, Thoreau saw in this mundane if remarkable commerce a symbolic significance: "In the morning I bathe my intellect in the stupendous and cosmogonal philosophy of the Bhagvat Geeta. . . .I lay down the book and go to my well for water, and lo! there I meet the servant of Bramin, priest of Brahma and Vishnu and Indra, who still sits in his temple on the Ganges reading the Vedas . . . and our buckets as it were grate together in the same well. The pure Walden water is mixed with the sacred waters of the Ganges."

In the pages of *Walden* there are many references to the sacred texts of South and East Asia, but Thoreau was not the first Westerner to be captivated by Hindu, Buddhist, and Chinese scriptures. From Marco Polo in the thirteenth century, to traders, colonizers, and missionaries beginning in the sixteenth, to poets, musicians and actors in the modern era, eastern religions have had a compelling attraction. There is some evidence that the fascination is even older, going back at least to Hellenistic times. In fact, from Alexander the Great in the late fourth century BCE, there has been a steady stream of western visitors to South and East Asia, some of whom were more interested in learning from those who lived there than in conquering or converting them. For others, like Thoreau, the religious texts of Asia traveled to them.

The movement of ideas has not been only one direction, however. Another work of Thoreau, his short essay *Civil Disobedience*, had been largely forgotten until a lawyer named Mohandas K. Gandhi reprinted it in South Africa in 1908 and used it as a basis for his protest tactic of nonviolent resistance. And Gandhi's writings in turn influenced Martin Luther King, Jr. in his campaign for racial equality in the United States. This cross-fertilization, from the *Gita* to Thoreau to Gandhi to King, is an extension of Thoreau's conceit. Adherents to Hinduism, Buddhism, Taoism, Confucianism, and Shinto are our neighbors, not just in the global community, but more and more in our own environs as well, and the profound treasures of their religious traditions continue to influence us in innumerable ways.

In this book, we present these religious traditions— their origins, histories, beliefs, practices, sacred texts, and ethical principles—in a structured way that enhances comparison and comprehension, and ultimately contributes to increased understanding among all peoples, nations, and religions.

Michael D. Coogan
Professor of Religious Studies
Stonehill College
Easton, Massachusetts

PART ONE:

HINDUISM

INTRODUCTION

Eighty percent of India's population of almost one billion people are Hindu, and there are Hindus living in every part of the world today. Yet the term "Hinduism" is somewhat difficult to define. The religion has no single founder, creed, teacher, or prophet acknowledged by all Hindus as central to the religion, and no single holy book is universally acclaimed as being of primary importance.

The use of the word "Hindu" is itself complex. Both "India" and "Hindu" derive from Sindhu, the traditional name of the Indus River. In ancient inscriptions and documents, "Hindu" refers to the people of "Hind," the Indian subcontinent. In the Muslim-ruled empires of medieval India, it was used for many non-Muslim Indian communities. Although the term is found in Hindu literature earlier, it was only after the late eighteenth century that it became popular as a name for the dominant religion of the Indian people.

Hindus ordinarily identify themselves with reference to their caste, community, region, and language. The phrase *sanatana dharma* ("eternal faith") has become popular in the last two centuries, but it applies more to philosophical interpretations of the religion than to its colorful local manifestations. In early texts, *sanatana dharma* meant the ideal religious obligations of human beings, but it did not express the idea of a community of faith.

In Indian law, the term "Hindu" may even include those who belong to traditions usually thought of as theologically distinct from Hinduism. It is generally applied to anyone who lives in India and accepts the Hindu tradition—which is not defined—in any of its forms or developments. This therefore embraces Buddhists, Jains, and Sikhs. The term also applies to anyone else who is not a Muslim, Christian, Parsi (Zoroastrian), or Jew.

On the other hand, "Hinduism" has been a problematic label even for some traditions that many people would generally consider to be Hindu. At different times several Indian sects and movements have gone to court to argue against their official "Hindu" status.

Hinduism has been portrayed in the last two centuries as being a more or less unified religion. However, it is important to note that there are hundreds of internal divisions created by caste, community, language, and geography. Regional manifestations of a deity or a local sacred text may sometimes be more significant to a particular group of worshippers than any pan-Hindu concept. Many such groups may extensively share

*Early morning bathing at the Shivsagar tank during the
Shivaratri Festival. The tank is the most famous feature
in the city of Shivsagar, which means "the ocean of Shiva."*

common texts, deities, traditions, and patterns of
ritual, even though they interpret them variously; but
there may be other groups with whom they have very
little in common. Yet there are also threads that run
geographically throughout the subcontinent and historically across thousands of years. At certain times,
therefore, it may be more useful to talk of many Hindu
traditions, and at others, of one tradition.

Is Hinduism a religion, a culture or, as many Hindus

would say, a way of life? It is all three, but what in the West might be viewed as the boundaries between the sacred and nonsacred spheres do not apply to the Hindu traditions. While many Hindu holy texts and practices are intended to provide the devotee with spiritual paths to liberation from the repeated cycle of life and death, many other aspects of Hindu life and ritual do not lead directly to such transformation, but are perceived to enhance one's quality of life on earth. Thus such activities as tree-planting, singing, dancing, healing, archery, astrology, sculpture, architecture, and building a home might all be considered part of the religious domain.

In studying the many Hindu traditions, therefore, the words "secular" and "sacred" have to be used with caution. More meaningful terms in some Hindu contexts are *dharma* and *moksha*. *Dharma*, a Sanskrit word from a root meaning "to sustain," is truth, righteousness, duty, law, and justice. *Moksha* literally means "liberation," that is, liberation from the cycle of life and death that every soul is believed to undergo (see pp.94–99) and which is repeated endlessly, until such time as the soul achieves liberation into a state of bliss. While not unique to Hinduism, the belief in this process is perhaps one of the few concepts that most "Hindus" can be said to share.

CHAPTER ONE

ORIGINS AND HISTORICAL DEVELOPMENT

There is no specific year or even century for the beginnings of the Hindu tradition. It is a cumulative collection of communities, faiths, beliefs, and practices that have come together over the centuries, although its ancient roots are traditionally seen in the cultures of the Indus Valley, Saraswati River civilization, and Indo-European people. Sophisticated philosophies, village deities, and ethical obligations have all coexisted in pluralistic Hindu societies. Local traditions have entered Hinduism through processes of "Sanskritization," whereby a regional deity becomes identified with pan-Indian gods, and "brahminization," the adoption of "high"-caste rituals by many communities. While India is the *locus classicus* of the tradition, it has flourished in southeast Asia for more than fifteen hundred years, and now, in every part of the world.

LEFT: A woman pilgrim at Varanasi, the city on the Ganges that has for centuries been considered one of the most sacred places in Hinduism— a heavenly prototype.

The Hindu tradition has no founder figure and cannot date its origin to a particular year or century. It is generally believed that its beginnings lie in the ancient indigenous culture of India and of the Indo-European people. It is a matter of scholarly and political controversy whether the Indo-European people were the indigenous inhabitants of India or whether they migrated from outside. The stages of early Hindu history are marked not by remarkable personalities (although there have been many) and great proselytizing movements, but rather by the composition of philosophically sophisticated, edifying, or entertaining texts that were transmitted orally and through the generations primarily by means of the performing arts.

The earliest known Indian civilization existed ca. 3000–1750BCE in a broad area around the region of the Indus river and other parts of India. Entire cities have been excavated, for example, at Harappa and Mohenjo Daro. The people of this civilization (often referred to as Harappan) were literate but their script remains undeciphered. Some Harappan seals bear images of figures that share characteristics with the later Hindu deity Shiva. The huge pool complex at Mohenjo Daro known as the "Great Bath" may have possessed a religious function. From such fragmentary evidence we can tentatively state that some features of the present-day Hindu religion may be nearly five thousand years old.

The Indo-Europeans referred to themselves as "Aryans" or "Noble Ones." Their speech was the ancestor of the ancient Indian language of Sanskrit, which is closely related to all the other tongues referred to by linguists as "Indo-European," including Latin, Greek, and English. The earliest compositions in the Hindu tradition are the *Veda*s (Sanskrit, "Knowledge"), which form the core of India's ancient "proto-Hindu" religion and constitute manuals of poetry, rituals, and philosophy. A dominant feature of religious life in the Vedic period was ritual sacrifice. Most rituals involved fire and were conducted by ritual specialists and priests who also supervised the making of altars, utilizing precise mathematical measurements, and the recitation of hymns. Many sacrifices involved the use of *soma*, an intoxicating liquid.

Vedic religion perceived a delicate connection between the performance of rituals and the prevalence of *rta* ("truth," "justice," and "rightness"). *Rta* makes harmony and peace possible on earth and in the heavens and was upheld by early Vedic gods, such as Varuna. According to Vedic hymns, the world itself may have come into being through an act of cosmic sacrifice. One creation hymn explicitly mentions the beginnings of the social divisions that are referred to today as "caste" (see pp.102–107).

The sacrifice-based worldview of the early Vedic age gave way to philosophical inquiry and discussion in the later texts known as the *Aranyaka*s and *Upanishad*s (see pp.42–49). These were composed around the early sixth century BCE, a time of great intellectual speculation, when many religious leaders questioned and even rejected the authoritarian structures of traditional Indian religion, such as the religious leadership of the priestly caste (the *brahmin*s), the caste system itself, and the status of the *Veda*s.

The sophisticated philosophy of the *Upanishad*s was contemporaneous with the spirit of critical inquiry in many parts of northern India. Siddhartha Gautama (the Buddha) and Mahavira the Jina ("Victorious One," whose followers are today's Jains) both challenged the notion that the *Veda*s were divine revelation. Siddhartha and Mahavira emphasized nonviolence (*ahimsa*), and this virtue has also been very significant in Hinduism. In modern times, it informed the strategy of Mohandas Karamchand Gandhi (known as the Mahatma or "Great Soul"), who led India's struggle for independence in the twentieth century.

The *Upanishad*s sought liberation from the cycle of life and death and introduced the notion of immortality as reality. The ultimate quest of the Hindu tradition, as it subsequently developed, has been to achieve the immortality of the soul and, in this life, happiness and peace. The restless quest of these texts is seen in a line in the *Mundaka Upanishad*: "What is it that being known, all else becomes known?"

Most of the later literature in Sanskrit deals directly or indirectly with *dharma* (a word with multiple layers of meaning, including "righteous behavior," "truth," and "law"). These concepts are embedded in epic narratives called the *Ramayana* and the *Mahabharata*. The epics portray deeds of the incarnations of the deity Vishnu who is one of the prominent gods in Hinduism. The *Bhagavad Gita* ("Sacred Song") is eighteen chapters in the *Mahabharata* and emphasizes that *dharma* should be performed without expectation of reward but with devotion to one God. The "supreme being," conceived of in the *Upanishad*s as *brahman*, an abstract concept (see p.29), is referred to in the *Bhagavad Gita* as the deity Krishna or Vishnu. Devotionalism (*bhakti*)—the intensely personal worship of, and surrender to, this supreme being, whether it be manifest in the form of Vishnu, Shiva, the Goddess, or any other divine being (see pp.28–39)—has been a common feature of many Hindu communities in the last two millennia.

At least three factors contributed to the spread of such devotion. One was the use of vernacular languages, rather than Sanskrit. A second factor was its appeal across all social classes. Thirdly, from at least the fourth or fifth centuries, there was a culture of building temples. Some of the most famous devotional poet-saints, such as Nammalvar in the eighth century CE in south India, and Tukaram in the fifteenth, composed in vernacular languages and are perceived as having been from low castes. Yet their influence cut across all levels of a highly stratified society, their simplicity of worship appealing to the élite and masses alike. Other popular *bhakti* poets came from a wealthier social milieu. One of the most famous, Mira (1450?–1547CE), was a Gujarati princess who wrote passionate poetry about her love for the god Krishna. According to some legends, at the end of her life Mira merged with Krishna's icon in a temple.

Men and women built temples and endowed monies and lands to these institutions. Temples in India became the centers of devotion, rituals, poetry, music, dance, scholarship, economic distribution, as well as prestige markers for patrons. Many of the temples were centers of art, and, according to many scholars, also for astronomy.

An important development in the first millennium CE was the spread of the Hindu traditions to southeast Asia. Large temple complexes following precise ritual regulations were built in Cambodia, Indonesia and other places. Hinduism flourished in these places till about the fifteenth century CE.

Along with the devotional and temple-building movements, philosophical studies of traditional Hindu texts flourished after the seventh century CE. The *Upanishad*s, the *Bhagavad Gita*, and another text called the *Brahma Sutra* were singled out for attention and commentarial interpretation. These texts form the nexus around which philosophical traditions, generically known as Vedanta, developed. Shankara (ca. eighth century), a major philosopher, spoke about the supreme being (*brahman*) and the human soul (*atman*) as identical with each other. The phenomenal reality we live in has limited validity, like dream states. Ramanuja (eleventh century) disagreed with Shankara and argued instead that the universe—that is, all sentient and non-sentient entities—forms the body of the supreme being, whom he identifies as Vishnu. There has been a long line of Vedanta philosophers which continues to this day.

After the fifteenth century much of northern India came under Muslim rule (a dynasty known as the

The temple of Angkor Wat in modern-day Cambodia was built in the 12th century CE *by King Suryavarman II, who dedicated it to Vishnu. The building follows the groundplan of a cosmic diagram or* mandala.

Mughal, from "Mongol" due to its central Asian origins). While this led on the one hand to a meeting of cultures in art, music, and architecture, several Hindu temples were also destroyed in this period. In the sixteenth century, the Portuguese, Dutch, English, and French began to establish trading settlements in India. In time, as Mughal power disintegrated, the Europeans acquired territory, and in the eighteenth century large parts of the subcontinent became loosely unified under British control. Many social and religious practices of the Hindus—in particular "idolatry" and the caste system—came in for severe criticism from European missionaries and others. One response to external criticism came in the shape of reform movements that arose within Hinduism in the early modern period.

Ram Mohan Roy (1772–1833) and Dayanand Sarasvati (1824–1883) established movements to initiate educational, social, and religious reform. Of particular significance in the nineteenth century is Ramakrishna, whose many mystical experiences and teachings inspired leaders like Vivekananda. Vivekananda attended the First Parliament of Religions held in Chicago in 1893 and preached his experience of philosophical Hinduism in North America.

The many traditions that make up the tapestry of Hinduism continue to flourish in the diaspora. Hindus who migrated to southeast Asia in the first millennium CE sought to transmit their culture through the building of the great temples of Cambodia and Java. Similarly, Hindu émigrés to Britain and the United States in the past few decades have sought to perpetuate their culture into the next millennium through the religious and cultural nuclei of their own community temples.

In Praise of the *Bhagavata Purana*

❝ Narada asked: 'Who are you? Who are these two [men accompanying you]? And who are these women with lotus eyes?'...

The Lady replied: 'I am known as Devotion (*bhakti*). These men are Knowledge and Renunciation and are like my sons. They are old and worn out. These [women] are the rivers like Ganga and others who serve me... Listen to my story... I was born in the Dravida and came of age in Karnataka. I was respected in Maharashtra, but coming into Gujarat, I have become old and feeble. In this terrible eon called *kali*, I am crippled by heretics and their practices... It is after I reached Vrindavana that I have become young again and filled with beauty. My sons are anguished and sleep in exhaustion... they have become old and feeble.' ...

[Narada soothes Lady Devotion and assures her that this evil age has at least one advantage:]

... Narada says: 'It is only in this age of Kali that a person can attain the supreme goal by reciting the name and speaking about the glory of Vishnu. This one cannot get even with austerities, yoga or meditation.' **❞**

A *mahatmyam* ("glory") of praise introducing the *Bhagavata Purana*, translated by Vasudha Narayanan.

Commentary

This passage, possibly added to the *Bhagavata Purana* (ca. 500CE) several centuries after its composition, speaks of the spread of devotion from the south of India to the north. Although the earliest Sanskrit texts before the Common Era were composed in the north, vernacular devotional poetry became popular in the south after the sixth century CE and eventually moved north.

At least two points are significant in this passage. The first is a sectarian claim: that devotion to Vishnu is salvific in nature and devotion to Krishna (an incarnation of Vishnu), who lived in Vrindavana (in the north), is at the apex of Hindu movements. The second is the claim that the path of devotion rejuvenates itself, whereas those of knowledge and renunciation have become infirm. Although knowledge, meditation, yoga, and other forms of self-effort are lauded in texts, eventually it is devotional forms of worship that become the distinguishing characteristic of Hindu traditions—transmitted for centuries to the masses through singing and dancing lyrics of devotion.

The passage also alludes to the *kali yuga*, the worst possible era in the Hindu calculations of time. Time is cyclical, and this age of 432,000 years will be followed by the golden age. The unfolding of historical events is frequently juxtaposed against gigantic eons of time.

CHAPTER TWO

ASPECTS OF THE DIVINE

Hindus believe in many manifestations of the divine. Although most say they are monotheistic, their temples and domestic altars have multiple deities. In some Hindu texts, the supreme being is said to be ineffable and beyond name, gender, and form. Others perceive of the supreme as the perfect man or as a primordial mother. Some worship the divine being as half man, half female, or as a family of deities.

The belief that the divine is not only beyond gender and name, but also beyond number, has resulted in its manifestation in many shapes and forms: as human or animal, as trees, or as combinations of these beings. While the supreme being is beyond thought, most Hindus believe that she or he manifests him or herself periodically on earth in order to protect the good and destroy evil.

LEFT: A gilded sculpture of the popular elephant-headed deity, Ganesha, stands on the grounds of the Festival of India in Middlesex County, New Jersey, USA. Ganesha, son of Shiva and Parvati, is Hinduism's Lord of Beginnings and Remover of Obstacles. He is revered for his wisdom and courage.

The towns and cities of India may have dozens of temples and shrines dedicated to many deities. But images of gods and goddesses are also prominently displayed in stores, hospitals, government offices, and on altars and shrines in Hindu homes.

Hindus may acknowledge many deities, but consider only one to be supreme; or they may consider all gods and goddesses equal, but worship one who is their favorite. However, many Hindus consider all divinities to be manifestations of a single godhead. For some, to say that this God is male or female, one or many, is to limit it, to impose human ideas of gender and number on the divine.

The supreme being is worshipped in temples in the form of an "image," a word often used (together with "idol") to translate the Sanskrit *murti*, which, however, is more accurately rendered as "form," or "embodiment." Most Hindus think of a sacred image as an actual incarnation of the supreme being, a form taken by the godhead in order to receive worship.

During a consecration ritual called *prana pratishta* ("establishment of life"), an image ceases to be gross matter and becomes an actual presence or incarnation of divinity on earth. The divine spirit is believed to remain in the icon for as long as devotees wish. Some Hindus, however, perceive an icon as a symbol pointing to a reality external to it. Yet other communities have rejected the notion of worshipping a deity in the form of an icon.

The *Upanishad*s, Hindu sacred texts composed ca. 600BCE (see p.42), refer to the supreme being as *brahman*, which is considered to be ineffable and beyond all human comprehension. For centuries, the definition of *brahman* has been the subject of intense speculation. *Brahman*, according to the *Taittiriya Upanishad*, is truth (*satya*), knowledge (*jñana*), and infinity (*ananta*). Beyond this, all that can be expressed about *brahman* is that it is existence (*sat*), consciousness (*chit*), and bliss (*ananda*). Ultimately, brahman cannot be described, since to describe is to confine, and with the infinite, this is impossible. The sage Yajñavalkya said that, paradoxically, one may come close to describing *brahman* only by stating what it is not.

A similar difficulty surrounds any definition of the relationship between *brahman* and *atman* (the human soul). In a famous dialogue in the *Chandogya Upanishad*, a father asks his son to dissolve salt in water. The father says that *brahman* and *atman* are united in a similar manner and ends his teaching with a famous dictum: "*Tat tvam asi*" (Sanskrit, "You are that"). "That" (*tat*) refers to *brahman* and "you" (*tvam*) to *atman*. The philosopher Shankara (eighth century CE) believed this statement to imply that *brahman* and *atman* are identical. But Ramanuja (eleventh century CE) saw it as indicating that *brahman* and *atman* are inseparable, but not identical.

Although the *Upanishad*s consider *brahman* to be beyond human comprehension, the texts called the *Purana*s ("Ancient [Lore]") claim that this divine entity assumes a form and name to make itself accessible to humankind—hence Hindus speak of the supreme being as both *nirguna* ("without attributes") and *saguna* ("with attributes," such as grace and mercy). Texts identify the supreme being variously as Vishnu ("All-Pervasive"), Shiva ("Auspicious One"), or the Goddess in one of her many manifestations, such as Shakti ("Energy"), Durga, and Kali.

Hindus have continuously venerated the divine in female form—very often referred to simply as the Goddess—for more than two thousand years. The Goddess, sometimes called Devi in Sanskrit literature, is usually seen as a manifestation of Parvati, the wife of Shiva. As a beneficent deity, she is frequently called Amba or Ambika ("Little Mother"), and is widely venerated as Shri or Lakshmi (see p.32). As Kali, the Goddess is dark and awe-inspiring, garlanded with a

The god Vishnu is shown resting on the coils of a seven-headed snake symbolizing eternity in this painting in the Lakshminarayan Temple, Orchha, Madhya Pradesh, northern India. Brahma, representing Vishnu's creative energy, hovers in the center (top) while Lakshmi, Vishnu's consort, is at his feet.

necklace of skulls. Even in this form, she is called "mother" by her devotees.

As a warrior goddess, she is Durga, depicted with a smiling countenance but wielding an array of weapons. Durga, riding a tiger or lion, is one of the most popular goddesses in India. Strong and beautiful, the weapons in her hand show her readiness to assist her devotees. In one celebrated story, she manifests herself with the energies of all other deities in order to combat a buffalo-demon, Mahisa Asura. She emerges victorious after nine nights of struggle, commemorated by the festival of Navaratri ("Nine Nights") in the fall (see pp.82–83).

Perhaps the best known manifestation of the Goddess in the Hindu and Jain traditions is Shri, more popularly known as Lakshmi. She is the goddess of wealth and good fortune and her picture graces millions of homes, shops, and businesses. Shri-Lakshmi is called the mother of all creation, bestower of wisdom and salvation and grace incarnate. She brings good fortune on this earth, but above all she is instrumental in granting liberation from the cycle of life and death. Lakshmi is said to bestow wealth and saving grace just by glancing at a person. While she is depicted as an independent goddess, and has her own shrine in many temples, she is often also portrayed as the inseparable consort of Vishnu.

Shri-Lakshmi is frequently associated with the lotus. She is all-pervasive, latent in everything, but manifests herself only in auspicious places, of which the lotus is a great example. The flower (and its leaves) reminds human beings of how to regard their relationship to the world: it rises from mud and dirty water, yet is never tainted by them.

In some regions, a goddess may be known only by a local name and celebrated in stories with a local setting; elsewhere, she may be identified with a pan-Hindu goddess. In addition to the many pan-Hindu goddesses there are hundreds of regional ones worshipped by local communities. Some communities may offer animal sacrifices to their local village goddesses or Kali.

The local manifestations of the pan-Hindu gods and goddesses have distinctive histories and functions. Thus Vishnu is known in many parts of south India by specifically regional names. Lord Venkateswara, a manifestation of Vishnu in Tirupati, is one of the most popular deities in south India, and temples to him are seen in many parts of India and the United States.

Although Vishnu, Shiva, and the Goddess are the most important deities in Hindu texts, there are many other deities throughout India. The elephant-headed Ganesha (a son of Parvati), Kartikkeyya/Murugan (a son of Shiva), and Hanuman (a divine monkey-devotee of Rama, an incarnation of Vishnu), are some of the more popular deities in Hinduism. Many roadside shrines are dedicated to Ganesha and Hanuman. Ganesha is also called Vigneshwara ("He who overcomes all obstacles").

Hindus worship him before embarking on any task, project, or journey.

Gods and goddesses all have their own iconographic characteristics, and every position of the hands or feet, every associated animal, plant, or bird, has a special significance. One of Lakshmi's hands, for instance, points to the ground in what Hindus refer to as the *varada* ("giving") position. In Hindu art, she may be portrayed giving wealth to her devotees, with a shower of gold coins emanating from her hand. The other hand may be held upright, denoting her protection of the devotee. Many deities have several hands, each carrying a weapon or a flower to protect his or her devotees from harm. Some Hindus interpret the numerous arms of a deity as representing omnipotence.

Most deities are associated with one or more animals. Although sacred texts give specific mythological reasons for their presence, believers may understand them more metaphorically. Thus, Ganesha's elephant head and mouse companion are sometimes said to represent his power to overcome hindrances: an elephant crushes large obstacles, and a mouse gnaws through little ones. Like Ganesha, many deities have specific functions, so a person may worship one god or goddess in order to achieve success in their career, another to cure illness, and so on.

Devotees of a deity may perceive him or her to be the supreme being. Some early writings express the idea of a divine trinity (*trimurti*) of Brahma (the creator), Vishnu (the preserver), and Shiva (the destroyer), but this concept was never widely popular. In time, Brahma became marginal, and the functions of creation, preservation, and destruction were combined in one deity—either Vishnu, Shiva, or Devi (the Goddess), depending on the individual devotee.

The manifold aspects of Shiva's power are expressed in his often paradoxical roles: he is both fierce and benevolent, creator and destroyer, exuberant dancer and austere *yogi*, ascetic and husband of the goddess Parvati. Stories of his powers of salvation present him as granting wisdom and grace to his devotees. Iconographically, Shiva and Parvati are portrayed in the abstract form symbolizing the male and female generative powers, a shaft (*linga*) within a womb (*yoni*), which represent their spiritual and physical creative powers.

Vishnu is portrayed as having a multiplicity of incarnations (Sanskrit *avatara*, "descent"). It is believed that over the ages he has descended to earth several times in various animal and human forms to overthrow evil and establish *dharma*, or righteousness. Hindus generally consider ten incarnations to be the most important. Vishnu's first descent was as a fish that saved Manu (the progenitor of the human race), his family, and many animals from a flood. Vishnu was subsequently incarnated as a tortoise, a boar, a creature that was half lion and half man, and a dwarf-being.

The four fully human incarnations of Vishnu follow: the warrior Parasurama; Rama (the hero of a great epic, the *Ramayana*; see pp.43–45); Balarama; and Krishna. It is believed that the tenth incarnation will come at the end of the present world age, which according to some reckonings began ca. 3102BCE and will last 432,000 years. Some texts omit Balarama and introduce the Buddha as the ninth incarnation, after Krishna. The progression of the incarnations from fish to full human is understood by some Hindus today as anticipating evolutionary theory. But the more prevalent explanation is that Vishnu takes the form most suited for the crisis on hand.

Vishnu's ninth incarnation, Krishna ("the Dark One"), is one of the most popular Hindu gods. He is widely celebrated in folksongs, narratives (such as the *Bhagavad Gita*), sculpture, painting, and performance. While Krishna is generally perceived to be an incarnation of Vishnu, several traditions think of him as the supreme deity.

One such group is the International Society for Krishna Consciousness (ISKCON) which was founded in 1966 by A.C. Bhaktivedanta (born Abhaycharan De, 1896–1977) in New York. The theology of this movement (which is more popularly known as "Hare Krishna"), and its devotional chanting, may be traced back directly to the great guru Chaitanya (1486–1583). Members of ISKCON study the *Bhagavad Gita* (see pp.45–46) and the stories of Vishnu in the *Bhagavata Purana*.

To some extent, most Hindus accept Krishna's supremacy among the incarnations of Vishnu, considering him to be what is termed the "full" descent of the deity. Krishna is also the alluring lover, dancing moonlit nights away with adoring cowherd maidens. Their dances are reenacted in many communities: the Gujarati *raas lila* dances are particularly renowned.

Many Hindus attribute divine status to the Earth as well as to natural phenomena. Rivers like the Ganga (Ganges), Kaveri, Yamuna, and others, are personified and worshipped as mother goddesses. Hindus also revere heavenly bodies and propitiate the *navagraha* ("nine planets"—the sun, the moon, Venus, Mercury, Mars, Jupiter, Saturn, and two mythical entities called Rahu and Ketu) in rituals. Many temples in south India and in the diaspora incorporate images of the planets.

How Many Gods Are There?

    66 Vidagha Shakalyah asked: 'Yajnavalkya, how many gods
are there?' He answered ... in line with the ritual prayer,
'...three hundred and three, and three and three thousand.'
'Yes, but Yajnavalkya, how many gods are there, really?'
'Thirty-three.'
'Yes, but really, how many gods are there, Yajnavalkya?'
'Six.'
'Yes, but really, how many gods are there, Yajnavalkya?'
'Three.' ...
'Yes, but really, how many gods are there, Yajnavalkya?'
'One and a half.'
'Yes, but really, how many gods are there, Yajnavalkya?'
'One.'
'Yes, but who are those three hundred and three and
three thousand and three?'
'They are but the powers/greatness of the gods; but
there are only thirty-three gods.' **99**

Brihadaranyaka Upanishad III.9.1–2 (ca. 6th century BCE, Sanskrit), translated by Vasudha Narayanan.

Commentary

From a refusal to attribute gender or number to limit
the infinity of the supreme being to glowing praise for
various deities, the Hindu tradition has prose and poetry

to meet an array of philosophical and devotional aspirations. In the passage quoted, the theologian Yajnavalkya is asked how many gods there are. Replying with a formulaic number, usually given as three hundred and thirty million gods, Yajnavalkya is pressed again and again by the interrogator. His final answer seems to be "one," but he adds that all the deities are the powers of the gods and says there are thirty-three deities—an answer that is somewhat ambiguous.

Hundreds of verses in Sanskrit and vernacular languages muse at the ineffability of the supreme. Yet most Hindus also believe that the supreme being takes name and form and manifests him- or herself to devotees. Thus, the supreme power spoken of in the *Upanishad*s as "Brahman" is identified with Vishnu, Shiva, or a goddess, and in addition to these, several other gods and goddesses are also worshipped. The goddess Lakshmi, for example, is associated with salvific grace, compassion, and wealth. One of the most beloved of deities, she is worshipped in her own shrine in temples and is also seen as inseparable from Lord Vishnu. Icons of Lakshmi and the other deities were seen at home altars and in temple architecture in India and southeast Asia in the first millennium CE, and are now present all over the world.

CHAPTER THREE

SACRED TEXTS

Sacred texts in Hinduism have primarily been transmitted through music, recitation, dance, and drama. The higher castes of society consider the *Veda*s to be revealed, and in later centuries, several Sanskrit and vernacular texts were hailed as equivalent to these texts. Epic stories and narratives of deities have been conveyed through devotional poetry composed by men and women—these are popular not just in India but all over southeast Asia.

Sanskrit has been the language of the earliest texts. But many castes pay more attention to local bardic poetry and narratives. While there are several Sanskrit texts of law and ethics (*dharma*), Hindus consider custom and practice to be at least as important as these texts. In addition to Sanskrit texts, vernacular literature is beloved by all Hindus.

LEFT: The principles of many Indian classical dance forms have their origins in the Hindu sacred texts, the Vedas. For centuries, texts such as these have been transmitted to the masses via the medium of dance, which is considered a symbolic form of worship.

The Hindu traditions have a multiplicity of sacred texts in Sanskrit and regional languages. These have been commented upon, committed to memory, sung, choreographed, danced, and expressed in art and architecture. The oldest Indian sacred texts are the *Veda*s, ordinarily dated around or sometimes earlier than 1500BCE. Each of the four Vedic collections (*Rig Veda*, *Sama Veda*, *Yajur Veda*, and *Atharva Veda*) comprises hymns and ritual treatises, together with *Aranyaka*s ("Compositions for the Forest") and *Upanishad*s ("Sitting Near [the Teacher]"), philosophical works composed ca. 600BCE or a little later.

Some Hindu traditions consider the *Veda*s to be transhuman, that is, not authored by human beings. They are said to be eternal in nature and revealed in every cycle of time. The Vedic reciters, or "seers" (*rishi*s), did not invent or compose the *Veda*s; they "saw," or "envisaged," them. The seers transmitted them to their disciples, starting an oral tradition that has come down to the present. The order of the sacred words must remain fixed, and committing them to memory is a disciplined process involving the use of many mnemonic devices to ensure accurate pronunciation, rhythm, and diction.

The Vedic corpus was followed by the *smriti* or "remembered" literature. Although of human authorship, *smriti* was nonetheless considered inspired, and while of lesser authority than the *Veda*s, it has played a far more important role in the lives of the Hindus over the last two and a half millennia. The *smriti* is sometimes divided into the categories of epics, ancient stories (*Purana*s), and codes of law and ethics (*dharmashastra*s; "texts on righteous behavior;" see pp.103–104).

The two *smriti* epics, the *Ramayana* ("Story of Rama") and the *Mahabharata* ("Great Epic of India" or, alternatively, "Great Sons of Bharata"), are the best known works of the Hindu tradition. These works, with ethical, spiritual, narrative, philosophic, and cosmogonic content, have been interpreted, commented upon, and enjoyed for over two thousand years and form the heart of Hindu sacred literature. For many Hindus, the phrase "sacred books" connotes these epics in particular, and for countless Hindu children the narration of the epics is invariably their first and most lasting encounter with Hindu scripture.

The *Ramayana* focuses on the prince Rama (later portrayed as an incarnation of Vishnu), who is born in Ayodhya. On the eve of his coronation, his father Dasaratha exiles him. In the forest, Rama's wife, Sita, is captured by Ravana, the demon king of Lanka, and the epic focuses on Rama's struggle to win her back. After

An illustration, ca. 1830, depicting a scene from the Ramayana. *The epic's eponymous hero, Rama, is shown standing before kings and holy men (*rishis*) holding a bow.*

a battle, Rama kills Ravana and is reunited with Sita. They eventually return to Ayodhya and are crowned. Rama is held to be an ideal king.

There have been many vernacular versions of the *Ramayana*, and the story has been understood in various ways. In one thirteenth-century interpretation, Sita voluntarily undergoes captivity and suffering to rescue other human beings and the world from evil. In a metaphorical reading, the human soul (Sita) is captured by the material body (Ravana), which is defeated by Rama, who saves the soul from the clutches of the senses. Some versions of the tale, called the *Sitayana*, tell the story from Sita's viewpoint. The *Ramayana* is danced out and acted in places of Hindu (and Buddhist) cultural influence in southeast Asia, and its characters are well known in Cambodia, Thailand, and Indonesia.

With around one hundred thousand verses, the *Mahabharata* is considered the world's longest poem. It is the story of the great struggle among the descendants of a king called Bharata (whose name is used by many Indians to mean "India"). The main part of the poem deals with a war between two families, the Pandavas and the Kauravas. The Kauravas try to cheat the Pandavas out of their share of the kingdom, and a great battle ensues that forces every kingdom to take sides. The Pandavas emerge victorious, but at great cost—all their sons and close relatives die in the battle.

Few Hindu households will have the *Mahabharata*, but many will have a copy of a celebrated episode contained within it—the *Bhagavad Gita* ("Sacred Song"), one of the holiest books in the Hindu tradition. Just as the war of the *Mahabharata* is about to begin, Arjuna, one of the Pandava brothers (hitherto portrayed as a hero who has emerged victorious from battle), becomes distressed at the thought of having to fight his relatives.

Arjuna asks his cousin Krishna (who is portrayed as an incarnation of Vishnu) whether it is correct to fight a war in which many lives, especially of one's own kin, are to be lost. Krishna replies in the affirmative: it is correct if one fights for righteousness (*dharma*). The Pandavas had earlier tried peaceful ways of negotiation. The conversation on the field of battle between Krishna and Arjuna takes up about eighteen chapters and constitutes the *Bhagavad Gita*.

The *Gita* says one may reach Vishnu/Krishna/God through devotion, knowledge, or selfless action. Later interpreters think of these as three paths, while others consider them to be three aspects of the one path of loving surrender to the supreme being. Krishna also instructs Arjuna—who is generally understood to represent any human soul who seeks guidance—on the nature of the soul, God, and how one can reach liberation.

The epics and the *Purana*s are written in Sanskrit, the ancient "perfected" language, which, rather like Latin for many centuries in Europe, was largely the province of male members of the social élites. However, in India, men and women of other castes voiced their devotional passion and quest for divine compassion in local tongues. Today, India has over eighteen official languages and hundreds of dialects, and many of them have a long and rich history of religious literature.

The earliest Hindu religious texts in a vernacular language are in Tamil, a south Indian language spoken by more than seventy-five million people today. A sophisticated body of literature in Tamil existed two thousand years ago. The oldest works, usually referred to as *Sangam* ("Academy") poems, are secular texts about kings and chivalry or love and romance. These became the model for later devotional literature, where the deity was cast in the role of a ruler and lover.

Hindu *bhakti* (devotional) literature flourished in south India after the sixth century CE. Saints traveled from temple to temple singing hymns in Tamil in praise of Vishnu or Shiva. These hymns, which are Hinduism's earliest sacred works in the vernacular, draw on earlier Tamil poetry and address the deity in highly personal, intimate, and tender language. In the vernacular literature, Vishnu and his incarnations (see pp.35–36) and Shiva are cast in several different roles by the devotee, who considers the deity to be a father or mother, lover, bridegroom, protector, or innermost soul. Sometimes the deity is even portrayed as a young child, to whom the devotee sings with maternal love.

After the tenth century, Tamil devotional poems were introduced into temple liturgy in Tamil-speaking areas and were regarded as being equivalent in status to the Sanskrit *Veda*s. Devotionalism spread to the west and north of India after the eleventh century CE, transmitted through sacred texts such as the *Bhagavata Purana*, as well as through the figure of Ramananda (1299?–1400), a legendary devotee in Ramanuja's line. In the thirteenth century, the poet Jñaneshvar discussed the ideals of the *Bhagavad Gita* in a famous treatise that bears his name, the *Jñaneshvari*, composed in Marathi, the language of the Maharashtra region.

Several features contributed to the spread of vernacular devotion. One was the use of contemporary living languages. A second was its appeal across all social classes. A third was the building of hundreds of temples, which also increased pilgrimage traditions and supported devotional rituals. Surdas (ca. 1483–1563), a blind singer and poet, composed in a dialect of Hindi. In his *Sursagar*, the youthful Krishna is celebrated in lyrics popular among many Hindus. Another important vernacular devotional writer was Tulsidas (1543?–1623), who settled in Varanasi. His *Lake of the Deeds of Rama* was more than a recounting or translation of the *Ramayana*. Its widely known verses have their own beauty and have inspired hundreds of traditional storytellers and millions of Rama devotees in Hindi-speaking areas.

The spread of the devotional compositions all over India challenged the orthodox claim that Sanskrit was the exclusive vehicle for revelation and theological communication. While some *brahmin*s have always learned and hence kept alive large sections of the Sanskrit Vedic tradition, others may know only a few Sanskrit hymns. However, overwhelming numbers of Hindus can recite devotional verses in their own languages. The Hindi poems of Surdas on Krishna, the songs of Princess Mira, and the Tamil poems of Nammalvar and Andal (eighth–ninth centuries CE), may serve as scripture for a particular community. In this sense, vernacular poems and songs guide, inspire, console, and offer hope and wisdom to the mass of the faithful more directly than the *Veda*s and other Sanskrit writings.

This is not to say that the vernacular literature is considered to be at variance with the message of the *Veda*s. Rather, in most communities, there is a belief that the holy people who composed in the living tongues gathered the truth from the incomprehensible *Veda*s and made it accessible to everyone, inspiring devotion and hastening the attainment of divine, saving grace.

The Songs of Andal

" A thousand elephants circle,

as Narana, Lord of virtues,

walks through the town in front of me.

Golden jars brim with water;

Festive flags and pennants,

  fly through this town

eager to welcome him—

I saw this in my dream, my friend!

Drums beat happy sounds; conches were blown.

Under the canopy strung heavy with pearls,

Madhusuda, my love, filled with virtue,

came and clasped the palm of my hand.

I saw this in my dream, my friend!

Those with eloquent mouths recited the good *Veda*s.

With *mantra*s they placed

the green leaves and the grass in a circle.

The lord, strong as a raging elephant,

softly held my hand as we circled the fire.

I saw this in my dream, my friend! **"**

Nacchiyar Tirumoli 1.1 and 1.6–7, by Andal (a woman poet, ca. ninth century CE, Tamil);
translated by Vasudha Narayanan.

Commentary

Over the last four thousand years, Hindu sacred texts have been transmitted in India and southeast Asia through ritual, music, and dance, rather than through sermons—the performing arts are seen as a means to liberation. The songs of Andal are important for south Indian Vishnu devotees, in the United States as well as in India. Like many poets, she is regionally well known, and some devotees consider her poems to be as significant as the *Upanishads,* which are part of the *Veda*s.

While the most exalted texts are the *Veda*s, a great number of Hindus know their tradition through local versions of the epic narratives, and many experience devotion through the words of a local saint. In the *Nacchiyar Tirumoli* ("Sacred Words of the Lady"), Andal refuses to marry a human being and instead recounts a dream in which she marries Vishnu, whom she addresses by several other names. By the tenth century, theologians considered Andal to be a paradigmatic devotee. Every human being is considered to be like Andal and Vishnu is the bridegroom. Her icon is consecrated in Vaishnava temples and her songs are regularly recited in weddings in some communities in south India. They are also, like those of many vernacular poets in India, sung, choreographed, and danced at homes and in temples.

CHAPTER FOUR

SACRED PERSONS

In the Hindu tradition, deities descend to the earth as human beings and human beings ascend to a divine status. Salvific truth is said to be mediated by these holy persons. The earliest holy men and women who "saw" the truth and compiled the *Veda*s were called "seers." Although the many lineages of holy teachers in Hinduism were composed of men of the brahmin caste, hundreds of saints and charismatic people considered to be "*guru*s" have come from all castes of society. In many Hindu communities, the sacred teacher is considered to be as important as the deity and is venerated, and even worshipped; other communities, however, do not consider the teacher to be so significant. From the twentieth century, women *guru*s took on an increasingly significant role, and many are now viewed as deities.

LEFT:
Maharishi
Mahesh Yogi
(born 1911), the
founder of the
Transcendental
Movement, is
arguably one
of Hinduism's
most influential
figures. He is
widely accredited
with having
introduced Hindu
philosophy to
the West.

Hindus have long looked to holy men and women to instruct them on how to attain peace in this lifetime and, eventually, liberation from the endless cycle of life and death (see pp.94–95). For many Hindus, the primary religious experience is mediated by a teacher who may be called *acharya*, *guru*, or *swami*. The term *acharya* usually denotes the formal head of a monastery, sect, or subsect, or a teacher who initiates a disciple into a movement. Sometimes the word is used simply as a synonym for *guru*, which, like *swami* ("master"), is a looser and more widespread term for any religious teacher. There are also thousands of ascetics, individuals possessed by a deity or spirit, mediums, storytellers, and *sadhu*s ("holy men"), who all command the veneration of their followers.

Each of the many Hindu philosophical traditions forms a distinct sect and has its own leader. Often the leadership of Hindu groups has passed from teacher to teacher in a line of succession that has continued for centuries down to the present day. This is the case with, for example, the schools founded by Shankara (ca. eighth century), Ramanuja (eleventh century), Madhva (thirteenth century), and Chaitanya (sixteenth century). Schisms often occur in such communities, with complementary or competing leaders vying for the loyalty of the disciples. Both ascetic monastic leaders as well as married men from specific lineages have followers in many Vaishnava (devotees of Vishnu) communities.

Shankara is said to have established four or five monasteries in different parts of India: at Dvaraka (west), Puri (east), Sringeri and Kanchipuram (south), and Badrinath (north). In each of these monasteries there is a lineage of teachers, all of whom bear the title "Shankara the Teacher" (Shankaracharya). They have often engaged with social and political issues, and exercise considerable leadership among the educated urban population, as well as influencing those who adhere to the philosophy of their founder. A similar role is played by intellectual philosophical commentators such as Swami Chinmayananda, whose followers have been active in the preservation of traditional scriptures in print and electronic media. In the Ramanuja school, as part of a complex initiation ritual, the leader brands a new member lightly on the shoulders and gives him or her a new name and a personal *mantra* for meditation. However, membership in other devotional communities may be much more informal.

At any given time, there are many influential theologians, and new sects with substantial followings arise under the inspiration of charismatic *guru*s in almost every generation. Although the distinction may not be clear in the minds of followers, it is possible to distinguish between those spiritual leaders who belong to ancient or more recent lineages, and charismatic teachers who attract devotees through "supernatural" phenomena ranging from the "magical" manifestation of objects to faith healing. Such leaders defy straightforward classification, and each has a large following. Devotees sometimes consider these *guru*s to be an incarnation of a divinity, who has descended to earth in the form of their teacher for the welfare of humanity. This is the case with Sri Satya Sai Baba (born Satya Narayan Raju, 1926), a charismatic leader from Andhra Pradesh, who is believed by his followers to be an incarnation of the deities Shiva and Shakti (the Goddess).

Several female *guru*s have acquired large followings of devotees. Among the most famous are Anandamayi Ma (1896–1982), a Bengali, and Amritanandamayi Ma (born 1953). Such teachers often lead celibate lives. Many charismatic teachers who do not come from a lineage of institutionalized *guru*s are said to have been born divine. Some devotees revere their teachers simply as spiritually elevated and highly evolved souls, beings who have ascended above the cares of human life to a state of self-realization or perfection. Occasionally, a

Female devotees gather in Bhajan Ashram. Since the twentieth century, women have taken an increasingly prominent role in Hindu religion.

charismatic religious leader may have a title such as *rishi* ("seer"), like the composers of the *Veda*s. One well-known example is Mahesh Yogi (born 1911), the founder of the Transcendental Meditation movement—popularly referred to in the West as "TM"—who is known as the Maharishi, or "Great Seer."

Today, many *guru*s have internet sites maintained by devotees; their itineraries, sermons, and songs are broadcast through these web pages, creating a world-wide Hindu "cyber-community."

"Acharya devo bhava": Consider Your Teacher as God

❝ I bow to the lineage of teachers (*guru*s)

which begins with the Lord of Lakshmi

with Nathamuni and Yamuna in the middle;

I take refuge with my teacher! ❞

❝ Even if they are lower than the four castes

that uphold all clans

even outcastes to outcastes

    without a trace of virtue

if they are the servants of the servants

who have mingled in service with the Lord

    with the wheel in his right hand

    his body dark as blue sapphire

they are our masters. ❞

Laudatory invocation attributed to Kuresa (11th century CE, Sanskrit) and Nammalvar's *Tiruvaymoli* 3.7.9, translated by Vasudha Narayanan.

Commentary

Perhaps more than any other religious tradition, Hinduism recognizes divinity in human beings. Many spiritual teachers are considered to be souls who have ascended to be one with the supreme being; others think of holy men and women as the descent of the divine being to earth. For some disciples, the teachers are even more important than God. The Upanishadic dictum (*Tait-tiriya Upanishad*) to treat your teacher as God is well known by millions of Hindus.

Almost every philosophical tradition has its own set of verses celebrating holy men and women. The first, invocatory verse quoted opposite, saluting a lineage of teachers, is recited by Sri Vaishnava Hindus at the beginning of all ritual prayer; it recognizes Lakshmi as one of the first teachers then begins with the poet Nammalvar (ca. ninth century) who is lauded in other verses. Nathamuni and Yamuna (ca. ninth and tenth centuries) are seen to be in the "middle" of the spiritual chain.

One does not have to be part of a spiritual lineage to be a holy person. In the second passage, Nammalvar identifies anyone who serves Vishnu as his master, even if they are of "low" caste. Since the last century, charismatic women *guru*s have become very prominent and command large followings. Some men and women perform miracles; others interpret scripture; some keep vows of silence; others encourage service to human beings. Holy men and women come with many teachings, are of all castes, and some of the more important ones are celebrated over hundreds of years. Some are enshrined in temples; others are remembered through their holy words and works.

CHAPTER FIVE

ETHICAL PRINCIPLES

Dharma, a concept central to Hinduism, has many meanings, including "duty," "righteousness," and "ethics." There is a *dharma* common to all humanity that is evident in such virtues as non-violence, compassion, and generosity. There is also a *dharma* that is specific to one's caste and station in life, and another that leads to liberation from the cycle of life and death.

In Hinduism, *karma* has come to mean the process whereby the good and bad deeds performed by human beings in the present determine the quality of their lives both now and in future births. Some Hindus believe that through detached action, and knowledge, one may gain liberation. Others maintain that through devotion and surrender one can acquire the saving grace of the supreme being which stops the cycle of rebirth.

LEFT: *Hindu pilgrims bathing in the sacred waters of lake Pushkar, Rajasthan. The waters are believed to bring liberation from the cycle of rebirth. The town of Pushkar contains numerous Hindu temples, the most important of which is dedicated to the creator god, Brahma.*

In Hinduism, the Sanskrit word *dharma* has been used in many contexts, which include: one's duty according to one's caste, social class, or stage of life; a code of conduct which embraces, but is not limited to, regulations involving marriage, food, religious observance, and so on; virtues such as gratitude and compassion which are thought of as common to all human beings; and a path to liberation from the cycle of life and death. The texts on *dharma* also form the basis for formulating the administration of Hindu family law in India.

Hindu texts list four sources as the foundations of *dharma*: the *Veda*s (see pp.42–43); the epics—the texts of lore called the *Purana*s (see pp.42–43); the behavior and practices of the good people; and finally, the promptings of one's mind or conscience. It is most significant that in the Hindu traditions, textual norms are not the only guide to ethics—local practices and customs are extremely important in understanding what is ethical and, in Hindu family law, what is legal.

Virtues that are said to be common to all human beings are called *sadharana* (common) or *sanatana* (eternal) *dharma*. These include gratitude, non-violence, compassion, and generosity. Other forms of correct behavior depend on one's community and, sometimes, on one's stage of life, or ritual calendar. Thus most (although not all) Brahmins and Vaishnavas (followers of Vishnu) are vegetarians all the time; others eat fish, fowl, and certain kinds of meat, except during certain times in the lunar calendar.

Within Hinduism itself, among several possible routes to liberation, two broad perspectives stand out. The first characterizes Hindu traditions that believe the human soul to be identical with the supreme being. Liberation is the final experiential knowledge that we are divine. This world view, best described by the teacher Shankara (see pp.54–55), emphasizes the importance of human effort and striving in achieving the necessary transforming wisdom. The second perspective comes from the schools that speak of an ultimate distinction, however tenuous, between the human being and God. Proponents of this view advocate devotion to the supreme being and reliance on God's grace.

In the course of the *Bhagavad Gita* (see pp.45–46), Krishna describes three ways to liberation: the way of action; the way of knowledge; and the way of devotion. Some Hindus view these as multiple paths to the divine, others as aspects of one discipline. The way of action (*karma yoga*) is the path of unselfish action; a person must do his or her duty (*dharma*), such as studying or good deeds, but not out of fear of blame or punishment,

An 18th-century Indian miniature painting depicting a yogi *sitting astride an animal skin in meditation posture. In Hinduism,* yoga *is a mode of spiritual progress and a means of attaining liberation.*

or hope of praise or reward. In thus discarding the fruits of one's action, one attains abiding peace. This entails acting altruistically for the good of humanity and performing all actions in a compassionate manner.

According to the way of knowledge (*jñana yoga*), by attaining scriptural knowledge one may achieve a transforming wisdom that destroys one's past *karma* (see pp.94–97). This wisdom may be acquired through the learning of texts from a suitable teacher (*guru*), meditation, and physical and mental control in the form of the discipline of *yoga*.

The third way to liberation is that most emphasized in the *Bhagavad Gita*: the way of devotion (*bhakti yoga*). It is widely popular among Hindus of every walk of life.

The Sanskrit term *yoga* refers to the practice of various disciplines whereby a devotee "yokes" his or her spirit to the divine. It is held in high regard in Hindu texts, and has had many meanings. Patañjali's *yoga* (ca. third century BCE), as interpreted by commentators, involves moral, mental, and physical discipline, and meditation. This form of *yoga* is described as having eight "limbs," or disciplines, including restraint from violence, falsehood, and other negative practices, as well as positive practices such as equanimity and asceticism.

Patañjali also recommends bodily postures for meditation, and the practice of breath control (*pranayama*) and mental detachment from external stimuli. Concentration and meditation (*dhyana*) lead to *samadhi*, the final state of union with the divine and liberation from the cycle of life and death; it is a state that cannot be adequately described within the constraints of human language.

In the past century, a distinction has been drawn between *raja yoga* and *hatha yoga*. *Raja yoga* deals with mental discipline; occasionally, this term is used interchangeably with Patañjali's *yoga*. *Hatha yoga*, popular in the West, focuses on bodily postures and control. Final liberation can be attained only after one harmonizes different centers in the body with the cosmos.

Instructions for Students of the *Veda*

66 Speak the truth. Follow the path of righteousness. Do
not neglect your recitation of your *Veda* [or learning].
Having brought the wealth dear to your teacher, do not
cut your ties. Do not neglect truth. Do not neglect
Dharma. Do not neglect the well-being [of your body].
Do not neglect fortune and wealth. Do not neglect
study and teaching of sacred texts. Do not neglect the
rituals to honor gods and ancestors.

Consider your mother as god; consider your father
as god; consider your teacher as god; think of your
guests as gods.

Do those deeds that are without blame, not others.
Hold in esteem only the good that you have seen in us,
not other practices. ...

Give with faith; do not give without faith. Give in
plenty, give with modesty, give with fear, give with
full knowledge and compassion. 99

Taittiriya Upanishad 1.11.1–3, translated by Vasudha Narayanan.

Commentary

These words, recited by a teacher to a departing student,
are well known in many sectors of the Hindu tradition,
and even in this century, have been part of the graduation

exercises in some universities in India. The student is asked to practice daily recitation of the *Veda*—which in recent years has been interpreted loosely as "learning" something everyday. It is not just textual knowledge that is advocated; one is asked to honor one's parents, teachers, and guests. The student is specifically told to act in a manner beyond reproach and to adopt those practices that seem to be in accord with *dharma* (righteousness) and those enacted with compassion.

Wealth is not scorned or held in contempt: one is asked to take care of one's health and wealth. Hinduism is life-affirming: celibacy and rejection of wealth are recommended only for young students, or for those in the later stages of life. Those who have finished their studies, on the other hand, are encouraged to marry, earn money, and take care of the welfare of all.

Generosity has always been a virtue that is celebrated in Hindu stories; the admonition here is to give with faith, to give with trepidation and compassion, for one can be, and frequently is, indirectly on the receiving end; one is not to give with arrogance or with ego. Several narratives highlight the importance of generous giving: the history of Hindu temple-building and main-tenance is filled with the names of men and women who endowed monies with generosity.

CHAPTER SIX

SACRED SPACE

Mountains, groves, rivers, towns, cities, and forests are all considered sacred in the Hindu tradition. And although the entire south Asian sub-continent is thought to be holy, thousands of places claim a special status and have been visited by pilgrims for centuries. Many Hindus believe that they can gain liberation just by visiting a sacred place or by bathing in a holy river.

Temples were built according to strict regulations, facing specific auspicious directions. These temples and shrines display the embodied cosmologies of Hinduism, and some were built with precise astronomical coordination. The temples were centers of piety and power; they were also economic hubs and a nexus for cultural activities. The replication of holy places and sacralizing new territories have been a hallmarks of Hindu migration.

LEFT: The magnificent 8th-century Shore temple in the coastal town of Mamalla-puram is dedicated to Shiva and has been a pilgrimage destination for centuries.

Millions of Hindus regularly visit sacred towns, worship in temples, bathe in holy rivers, and climb sacred mountains, in order to pray for happiness in this life and in the next. According to some Hindu texts, all of India is holy, as it is considered to be the place where the actions that form the basis of *karma* come to fulfillment. The idea of India as a sacred land began around the beginning of the Common Era. Manu, the author of a book on *dharma* (see pp.62–63) and right behavior, defined a region south of the Himalayas and between the eastern and western oceans as the holy Aryavarta ("Country of the Noble Ones"). In time, the concept of the sacred land was extended to cover the whole subcontinent. Since the time of the early Sanskrit texts, India has been seen as a divine mother; in recent centuries, she has been hailed in many songs as "Mother India" (Bharata Mata) and as a compassionate mother goddess. This image has had political overtones: during the struggle for freedom from British rule, Mother India was portrayed as being held captive by foreign forces.

The map of India is filled with holy places. Although there are many standard Hindu pilgrimage itineraries, thousands of other towns, villages, and sites across India are also held sacred. Pilgrimage routes are often organized thematically: devotees might visit the one hundred and eight places where Shakti, or the power of the Goddess, is said to be present; the sixty-eight places where emblems of Shiva are said to have emerged "self-born;" the twelve places where he appears as the "flame of creative energies" (*jyotir linga*s); the eight places where Vishnu spontaneously manifested himself (*svayam vyakta*); and so on.

Hindu holy texts (see pp.41–51), especially the epics and the *Purana*s, extol the sanctity of many individual sites. For pious Hindus, to live in such places, or to undertake a pilgrimage to one of them, is enough to destroy one's sins and assist in the attainment of liberation from the cycle of life, death, and rebirth (see pp.93–97). A short verse known by millions of Hindus draws attention to seven of the most famous holy towns: "Ayodhya, Mathura, Maya, / Kashi, Kanchi, Avantika / And the city of Dvaraka; / These seven [cities] give us / Liberation."

Almost every holy place is associated with a *sthala purana*, a text that details the site's antiquity and sacredness. The temple itself is like a "port of transit," a place from where a human being may "cross over" (*tirtha*) the ocean of life and death. In fact, many temples and holy places are also located near the sea, a lake, a river, or a spring. When such a body of water is not close by, there is usually an artificial ritual well or pool, a feature that may date back to the time of the Harappan civilization (see p.16)—the "Great Bath" of Mohenjo Daro resembles the pools that are attached to hundreds of Hindu temples in south India today. Pilgrims cleanse themselves physically and spiritually in these pools before praying in the temple.

The Ganga (Ganges), Yamuna, Kaveri, and Narmada rivers are believed to be so holy that merely by bathing in them one's sins are said to be destroyed. Confluences of two rivers or of a river and the sea are particularly sacred. Pilgrims journey regularly to bathe at Triveni Sangama ("Confluence of Three Rivers") at Prayag (Allahabad), where the Ganga, the Yamuna, and a mythical underground river, the Sarasvati, all meet. Small sealed jars of holy water from the Ganga are kept in homes and used in domestic rituals to purify the dead and dying.

The water from the Ganga, or another holy river in the north, may be taken to a sacred site in the far south, such as the coastal town of Rameswaram, and sand from Rameswaram may be taken back to the Ganga and immersed there. This practice serves to mark the completion of a circular pilgrimage and demonstrates one way in which the various holy places and traditions of Hinduism can be interlinked.

Varanasi on the river Ganga. This sacred city, the holiest in India, is visited by thousands every year. Immersion in the holy river is considered an act of great spiritual purification.

When temples are consecrated in Hindu communities outside India, water from Indian sacred rivers is mingled with water from rivers in the host country and poured onto the new temple, physically and symbolically connecting it with the sacred motherland.

Many holy sites are situated near mountains and caves, places where Hindu deities are said to reside in *Purana* stories. For example, Shiva lives on Mount Kailasa in the Himalayas, which for the devotee is represented by every Shiva temple. In some regions, particularly in the north, large temple towers (*shikhara*s) represent these cosmic mountains. The innermost shrine of a Hindu temple is traditionally a windowless space, like the sacred caves that were among the earliest Hindu places of worship.

Although there is evidence of worship at temples dating from the beginning of the Common Era, large sacred complexes were built only after the sixth century CE. Migrants to southeast Asia also built temples to preserve and transmit their religion. Temples were major religious, cultural, and economic centers and were constructed according to elaborate rules to represent the whole cosmos. Some of the larger ones have seven enclosures, representing the seven layers of heaven present in Hindu cosmology.

Many temples, such as Angkor Wat in Cambodia, which was dedicated to Vishnu, also encoded measurements closely connected with Hindu systems of time measurement. A number of temples, of which Angkor Wat is one, were built in alignment with the position of cetain stars and planets at particular times of the year and to observe and precisely measure astronomical phenomena.

Several of the temple complexes in India are associated with the major sects—that is, they enshrine

Vishnu, Shiva, or the Goddess and their entourages. In many of them, the deities are known by their local or regional names. A typical temple may have separate shrines for the deity, his or her spouse, other divine attendants, and saints. For example, an eighth-century CE temple in Tiruvanmiyur, a suburb of Chennai (Madras), has shrines for the main god, Shiva, his wife Parvati—known locally as Tripura Sundari ("Beautiful Lady of the Three Worlds")—and their children, Ganesha and Murugan. The temple also incorporates images of other manifestations of Shiva, such as Nataraja (the cosmic dancer) and icons of his devotees. Temples in the diaspora generally cater to a broader community of worshippers and have images of Shiva, Vishnu, the Goddess, and other deities enshrined under one roof.

India's richest temple—and one of the wealthiest religious institutions in the world—is the temple of Tirumala-Tirupati in Andhra Pradesh. Referred to in ancient literature as Tiru Venkatam, it is dedicated to Vishnu, who is popularly known as Venkateshvara ("Lord of the Venkatam hills"). Devotional literature addressed to Venkateshvara dates back to the seventh century CE, but pilgrims are known to have been visiting the site of the temple for almost two millennia. The temple is located in the scenic Tirumala hills and until

1965, when the government took them over, it owned more than six hundred surrounding villages.

Tirumala-Tirupati, like many large temples in India and southeast Asia, enjoyed the patronage of Indian royalty for over a thousand years. It is now a destination of large numbers of pilgrims. Annual donations of cash by pilgrims can amount to tens of millions of dollars. The temple employs its huge financial resources to fund a range of projects and enterprises, including charities, hospitals, universities and other educational institutions, housing developments, and publications. One major objective of the temple in recent years has been to contribute to the solution of India's considerable ecological problems, to which end it has subsidized massive reforestation projects.

Most Hindus attend their local temple or other holy place that has been important to their families for generations, or they may save for an extended pilgrimage to a famous distant sacred site. Émigrés and other devotees who cannot physically go on such a pilgrimage may watch the rituals that take place there on specially commissioned television programs or videos. At all times, Hindus can also worship at home, where a special area will very often be designated as the family's domestic worship space.

The human body itself is sometimes spoken of as the "temple of the supreme being." Some Hindu traditions, such as the Virashaivas (a community organized ca. 1150CE), denounce temple worship and revere every human as the temple of the supreme being, Lord Shiva. Other traditions, for example south Indian communities that worship Vishnu and Lakshmi, uphold the practices of temple worship, but also think of the human body as divine. In one song, the eighth-century CE poet Periyalvar declared: "Build a temple in your heart. Install the lord called Krishna in it; Offer him the flower of love."

A holy space in the Hindu tradition is one in which devotees come to see the enshrined deity and hear sacred words from holy texts. In the past, religious teachers were careful about whom they imparted their teachings to, and screened their devotees carefully. But now, the Internet allows anyone to see images of deities, teachers, and gurus, and even hear the recitation and music of sacred texts and songs. Some websites call their home pages "electronic *ashram*s." An *ashram* was a traditional place of hermitage or learning. Internet images of deities are taken seriously by devotees; some websites remind Internet surfers that it would be disrespectful to download such images. The Internet may therefore be seen as the latest frontier of sacred space for many Hindus.

Heaven on Earth

66 This is the temple of him who became

the divine fish, tortoise, boar, lion and dwarf.

He became Rama in three forms, he became Kanna,

and as Kalki he will end [these worlds].

This is Srirangam, where the swan and its mate

swing on the lotus blossoms, embrace on flowery beds,

and revel in the red pollen strewn around the river. **99**

Periyalvar Tirumoli, 4.9.9 (ca. 9th century CE, Tamil), translated by Vasudha Narayanan.

66 In the beautiful city of Ayodhya, encircled by towers,

A flame that lit up all the worlds appeared in the Solar

race, and gave life to all the heavens.

This warrior, with dazzling eyes,

Rama, dark as a cloud, the First one, my only lord,

is in ... the City of Tillai.

When is the day

when my eyes behold him

and rejoice? **99**

Perumal Tirumoli, 10.1, by Kulasekhara Alvar, translated by Vasudha Narayanan.

Commentary

Many Hindu communities consider the temple and the sacred place to be an extension of heaven on earth, a place where hierophany took place. The consecrated icon of the deity is seen to be the actual body of the god or the goddess. Those in the south think of Srirangam (glorified in the first extract) as one of the most sacred places in the world. Tamil poets often sing about the natural beauty and wealth of the towns in which the deity is enshrined in a temple: here, Periyalvar, a ninth-century Tamil saint, speaks of the swans, the lush flowers, and the red pollen, all of which exemplify a fertile land. It is in a temple in this land that Vishnu is enshrined. The Srirangam temple is like a hologram, containing the deity's ten manifestations and total divinity—a place which represents the descent of the deity to earth in order to facilitate the ascent of human beings to heaven.

In the second passage, Kulasekhara, a ninth/tenth-century poet writing in Tamil, glorifies the northern city of Ayodhya, the birthplace of Rama. However, the poet conceptualizes Rama as actually being enshrined in the city of Tillai (Chidambaram) in south India. These transpositions are common in devotional poetry—consequently, thousands of places in India, as well as in other parts of the world, are seen as sacred.

CHAPTER SEVEN

SACRED TIME

The Hindu calendar is filled with auspicious and propitious times on which to embark on journeys, start new enterprises, enter homes, get married or have celebrations. Astrology is an integral part of Hindu life, and a child's horoscope is frequently cast as soon as she or he is born. There are times that are auspicious for everyone and others that are specific to individuals. Inauspicious times are also marked.

Festival days involve times of feasting and fasting. Important festivals include the birthdays of the gods Rama, Krishna, and Ganesha; Navaratri ("Nine Nights"), which marks the destruction of a demon by the goddess Durga; Dipavali ("Necklace of Lights"); and Pongal, a harvest festival in southern India. Hindus ordinarily follow a lunar calendar that is adjusted to the solar calendar.

LEFT: Sacred time in Hinduism is marked by an abundance of local festivals and rituals, many of which celebrate specific deities. At the festival shown here, a young Hindu man is dressed as Shiva, one of the tradition's most important gods (see p.35).

Hindu festivals are filled with color and joy and almost always associated with feasting and pleasure, although they usually also involve periods of ritual fasting. The birthdays of the gods Rama, Krishna, and Ganesha are widely popular throughout India, while important regional festivals include Holi (a jubilant spring festival held in parts of northern India to celebrate the new colors of the springtime flowers), Onam (a harvest festival celebrated in the southern state of Kerala between August and September in honor of the fifth incarnation of the god Vishnu (see pp.35–36), and Pongal (a mid-January harvest festival in Tamil Nadu).

The festival of Navaratri ("Nine Nights") is celebrated throughout India and begins on the new moon in the lunar month from mid-September to mid-October. In many parts of the country it is dedicated to the worship of the goddesses Sarasvati, Lakshmi, and Durga. The ninth day of Navaratri is dedicated specifically to Sarasvati, who is the patron goddess of learning and music. In south India, all the musical instruments in the house, any writing implement, and selected educational textbooks are placed before the image of the goddess in order to receive blessings for the coming year. In some regions of India, it is a time when people acknowledge with respect the tools of their trade, whatever it may be. In some areas, vehicles such as cars and buses are decorated with garlands, and in recent years, type-writers and computers have been blessed with sacred powders and allowed to "rest" for a day before being used again.

The last day of Navaratri is dedicated to Lakshmi, the goddess of good fortune (see p.32). On this day, after ritually writing the auspicious word "Shri" (a name of Lakshmi), people traditionally embark on ventures, open new business account books, and take up courses of learning. To mark the day, new prayers, pieces of music, and items of knowledge are learned, and great Hindu teachers are honored.

Dipavali ("Necklace of Lights") is probably the most widely observed Hindu festival. It falls on the new moon between mid-October and mid-November and is celebrated by decorating the home with lights, setting off fireworks, and wearing new clothes. Presents may be exchanged and festive meals are eaten. In south India, it is believed that Dipavali marks the day on which Krishna killed a demon, Narakasura, thus ensuring the triumph of light over darkness. In the north, it celebrates the return of the god Rama to Ayodhya and his coronation (see pp.43–44). In Gujarat, it heralds the beginning of the New Year.

Pilgrims gather in Allahabad during the Kumbh Mela festival. These celebrations, held every 12 years, are the largest and most spectacular in the Hindu religious calendar.

In many parts of India, people rise before dawn on Dipavali for a ritual bath, because it is believed that on this day the holy waters of the Ganga river are present in all other water.

The many Hindu calendars and systems of reckoning time are all connected with the phases of the moon. These calendars are adjusted to the solar cycle regularly so that the festivals fall within the same season every year. The different parts of India celebrate New Year at different times of the year. In the state of Gujarat, for example, it falls a day after Dipavali. Elsewhere it may fall on the new moon closest to the spring equinox, or in the middle of April.

Sacred time can also be perceived as the time when one worships in a temple or at home. Temple worship forms a key element in Hindu religious life. In most temples, worship is traditionally not congregational, in the sense that people do not gather for communal worship at fixed times. There is no seating in the temple: devotees usually stand for a few minutes while they view the deity in its shrine. The closest thing to a religious congregation in Hinduism is when people gather together to listen to a religious teacher—although in most cases, this will take place in a public hall rather than in a temple—or to sing traditional religious songs at home and in other public places. This type of group singing is a common event at homes throughout India and in the diaspora.

Footwear is always left outside the temple precincts, a custom that symbolizes the worshipper's temporary abandonment of the dust and grime of worldly thoughts, preoccupations and passions—a movement into sacred space and time. The simplest act of temple worship is to make the deity an offering of camphor, fruit, flowers, or coconut, all of which may often be bought at stalls outside the temple. In a small temple, the devotee may make the offering directly to the image of the deity, but in most places the worshipper first hands the gift to a priest, who then presents it to the god or goddess. In many north Indian temples, ordinary worshippers may enter the innermost shrines, but in the south, access to these areas is restricted to priests and other initiates.

To the devotee, the most meaningful part of temple worship is the experience of seeing the deity (in the form of an image; see p.28) and being in his or her presence. After the offering has been presented to the divine image it is considered to have been "blessed" by the deity and to contain its "favor" (*prasada*). It is then returned to the worshipper. This simple act of viewing the deity, making an offering, and getting the sanctified offering back is the most popular of all Hindu votive rituals.

As in the temple, a deity that is worshipped in the home is considered to be a royal ruler and is treated accordingly. Members of the family may regularly light an oil lamp or incense sticks before the divine image, and make offerings of fruit or other foods. An altar, a shelf, a cabinet, or even an entire room in the house, may be set apart for devotional purposes and are sometimes filled with images of gods and goddesses.

When a group of devotees prays at home or in the temple, the ritual may end with an *arati*, or "waving of lamps." The attendant priest or one of the worshippers will light a piece of camphor in a plate, and sanctify it by waving it clockwise in front of the deity. The burning camphor is then shown to the worshippers, who briefly, but reverentially, place their hands over the flame and then touch their eyelids, as if to absorb the light of spiritual knowledge emanating from the supreme deity.

Single and married women—but not widows— frequently perform special votive observances called *vrata*. Many of these rituals are domestic in nature and observed for the welfare of the husband, the extended family, or the community. Sanskrit manuals claim that these rites enable a woman to attain liberation from the cycle of birth and death, but most women perform them simply for happiness in the home. After prayers to a domestic deity, women may eat together and distribute auspicious substances, such as bananas, coconuts, turmeric, and *kum kum* (a red powder that is daubed on the forehead). A *vrata* may last from a few minutes to five days, with periods of fasting alternating with communal meals.

In northern India, many women's rites focus on the welfare of male relatives. For example, in the lunar month from mid-October to mid-November, women undertake two fasts on the fourth and eighth days of the waning moon for the benefit of their husbands and sons. In much of south India, spiritually empowering women's rituals take place in the lunar month from mid-July to mid-August. *Brahmin* women pray to the goddess Lakshmi for domestic well-being. Non-*brahmin* women may take special pots of water and milk to temples of a local goddess as offerings on behalf of their family, or they may cook rice and milk dishes to distribute. At the temples of the powerful regional goddess Draupadi Amman (a principal character in the *Mahabharata* epic), women and men alike may enter a trance and walk over hot coals in a ceremony euphemistically called "walking on flowers."

The Hindu tradition, like other religions, possesses numerous rituals marking an individual's transition from one stage of life to another. In some sacred texts, the life-cycle sacraments begin with the birth of a child, while in others they begin with marriage, for it is then that the life of a person is believed truly to begin. While some life-cycle rites are pan-Hindu, many are purely local celebrations, particularly women's rituals.

Like all significant Hindu sacraments, rites of passage must take place in the presence of a sacred fire. The importance of fire (Sanskrit: *agni*) can be traced as far back as the Vedic period. Early Vedic rituals (see p.17) were performed around an altar of fire, and fire was thought of as the master of the house. Offerings are made to the sacred fire during prenatal rites, when a child is one year old, during weddings—indeed the marriage ceremony is valid only if the couple take their vows before a fire, which is deemed to be the cosmic witness to the sacrament—and when a man reaches the ages of sixty and eighty. Finally, when a person dies, his or her body is offered up to the flames. Annual rites to commemorate one's ancestors are also performed before a fire.

Auspicious times are chosen for the conduct of all life-cycle sacraments. These times are in accordance with a person's horoscope, which is cast at birth. Almanacs also detail the auspicious dates in a calendar. These traditional almanacs are consulted regularly for scheduling all important events in one's life, including rites of passage, entering a new home, embarking on an important trip, or starting a new venture. It is believed that astrologically propitious moments maximize the possibilities of success.

The Ages of the Universe

❝ When a thousand eons are over there is a drought for many years; there are few resources and creatures starve to death… fires of destruction overcome this earth… awesome clouds rise high. At the end of time, human beings will be uncivilized and eat any flesh. … When the end of this age of time is drawing near, it will not rain, crops will not grow… **❞**

Mahabharata, translated by Vasudha Narayanan.

Commentary

While Hindus choose astrologically propitious times in which to perform their various rituals, the units of time that are spoken of in Hindu texts concerning the creation and destruction of the universe are astronomical.

One day in the life of the minor creator god Brahma lasts 4,320 million earthly years. There are distinctions between earthly years and the years of the gods, which are far longer. The total of 360 such days and 360 nights makes one Brahmic year, and Brahma lives for 100 years. This cycle is therefore 311,040,000 million years.

The end of each cycle of creation is marked by cataclysmic events, such as those described in the passage from the *Mahabharata*, above. After this period, the entire cosmos is drawn into the body of Vishnu and remains there until another Brahma has evolved.

The units of time are further subdivided into specific cycles (*yuga*s, or world ages). The first world age, the golden age, lasts for 1,728,000 earth years. During this time, *dharma*, or righteousness, reigns but thereafter a gradual deterioration of morality, righteousness and well-being takes place. When we come to the fourth, last, and most degenerate age in the cycle (the *kali yuga*, the present age in which we live), *dharma* has almost completely disappeared. This age lasts for 432,000 earth years and, according to traditional Hindu reckoning, began around 3102BCE.

At the end of the *kali yuga*—obviously, still a long time off—there will be no righteousness, no virtue, no trace of justice. When the world ends, seven scorching suns will dry up the oceans; after the drought there will be a deluge; there will be wondrously shaped clouds, torrential rains will fall and, eventually, the cosmos will be absorbed into Vishnu. While, according to many Hindu systems of thought, it is possible for a human being to end his or her cycle of birth and death and gain liberation, the cycles of creation and destruction of the universe are independent of the human being's attaining *moksha* or liberation.

CHAPTER EIGHT

DEATH AND THE AFTERLIFE

Most Hindus believe in the immortality of the soul and in reincarnation. There is also popular belief in ghosts and spirits, including those that may possess people. A person's death is followed by rebirth, and the cycle of birth and death continues until one attains liberation (*moksha*). Rebirth is perceived as suffering, and the happiness one has on earth is said to be temporary. Liberation is conceptualized in several ways, including: as ineffable and beyond words; as a loving union with the supreme being; as losing one's consciousness in the supreme being; and as being in the heavenly abode of Vishnu, called Vaikuntha. Many texts and temple sculptures (including Angkor Wat in Cambodia) present notions of a temporary paradise called *svarga*, accounts of Vaikuntha, as well as several kinds of hell.

LEFT: Mount Kailas in Tibet, the abode of the Hindu god Shiva. Emancipated souls are believed to enter this heavenly paradise after death. Some claim that, when viewed from a particular angle, the ice-covered dome of Kailas resembles a human skull.

One distinctive characteristic of the religions that began in the Indian subcontinent is the belief in *karma*, an idea first occurring around the seventh century BCE. *Karma* literally means "action," especially ritual action, but after the compilation of the *Upanishad*s (ca. 600BCE; see p.42), it came to mean the concept of rewards and punishments attached to various acts.

Underlying the theory of *karma* is the idea of the immortality of the soul. Although the early *Veda*s contain a nebulous notion of an afterlife, by the time of the *Upanishad*s it was claimed that the human soul existed forever, and that after death it underwent rebirth or reincarnation (*samsara*). The "law of *karma*" thus refers to a system of cause and effect that may span several lifetimes. It dictates that human beings gain merit (*punya*) or demerit (*papa*) from every action they perform. Good deeds and bad deeds do not simply cancel each other out; one has to experience the fruits of all actions in the course of many lives. The balance of *punya* and *papa* acquired in one lifetime determines the nature and quality of one's next existence.

Liberation (*moksha*) from this pattern, according to the *Upanishad*s, comes from a supreme, experiential wisdom. In acquiring this transforming knowledge, one has a profound insight into one's own immortality (*amrta*), from which point the soul ceases to possess the ability to be reborn. Rebirth and its connection with *karma* (notions central to the later Hindu tradition) are thus clearly articulated in the *Upanishad*s, as is the ultimate goal of every human being—liberation from the unending cycle of birth and death and from the attendant human suffering implied by experiencing multiple lifetimes (see pp.64–65).

Since the time of the *Upanishad*s, Hindus have taken the notions of *karma* and immortality for granted. However, the various Hindu traditions differ on what happens to the soul when it is ultimately liberated from the cycle of life and death. For some, the soul experiences a joyous devotional relationship with the supreme being. Other speak of an identification with the supreme being.

A number of writings describe the soul's journey after death. Although reincarnation and liberation are the most frequently discussed aspects of the afterlife in Hinduism, the *Purana*s (see p.43 and p.46) talk of many kinds of heaven and hell. In the Hindu tradition, a soul's sojourn in a hell or paradise is generally seen as being temporary. A soul is reborn in such a region if it has accumulated certain kinds of good or bad *karma*; but once this *karma* is exhausted, the soul moves on into a different form of existence.

The flower-bedecked funeral procession of Indira Gandhi
(Prime Minister of India, 1966–1977 and 1980–1984)
in Delhi, following her assassination in November 1984.
The ceremony culminated with her cremation on a pyre.

According to some texts, a soul that has attained
emancipation from the cycle of life, death, and rebirth
crosses a river called Viraja ("Without Passion") and
enters a heavenly paradise, either Vaikuntha (the abode
of Vishnu) or Kailasa (the mountain abode of Shiva
on the borders of India and Tibet). Devotees of these
gods imagine their heavenly dwellings as places filled

with other devotees singing his praises. Vaikuntha is sometimes described as a place filled with light.

As far as unemancipated souls are concerned, none of the Hindu sacred texts discuss the details of what happens immediately after death or even between lifetimes. While it is clear that one's *karma* accumulated from previous lifetimes is believed to influence what sort of life will follow, the holy books offer no theories about how long it takes before a soul is reincarnated. Nor is there any discussion or explanation of why people do not remember their past lives, although in popular belief it is claimed that many people do indeed recall small pieces of previous existences. Only the truly evolved souls, the great spiritual leaders and teachers, are said to remember all their past lives.

Many texts speak of the repellent nature of this life and urge human beings to seek everlasting "real" life through the liberation of the soul. Others, however, state that by glorifying God on earth one can achieve the experience of heaven in one's lifetime. To this end, sacred pilgrimage centers offer a break from the daily rhythms of earthly existence and the opportunity for divine revelation. Some Hindus consider that a life lived in praise of the divine is a joyful experience that is not merely an imitation of a state of liberation, but that state itself.

Salvation and Liberation

66 Words go but return without reaching it; the mind does not grasp it. One who knows the bliss of [knowing] *brahman* is not afraid.

[A person who is enlightened] does not worry: 'why did I not do the right thing?' 'Why did I do what is wrong?' A person who knows is freed... 99

Taittiriya Upanishad, 2.9.1, translated by Vasudha Narayanan.

66 Vishnu/Krishna says:

'Even if various kinds of liberation are offered to [my devotees]—

living in the same place as I do,

equality in wealth, power, and glory

being near me,

having a form like mine

and even union with the supreme,

they will still choose only to serve me. 99

Bhagavata Purana, III. 29.13, translated by Vasudha Narayanan.

Commentary

Hindu texts have conceptualized the final goal of human beings with notions of heaven and hell and as being completely beyond description. The *Upanishad*s speak about *brahman* (the supreme being), *karma*, and the afterlife. Since that time, Hindu traditions have thought of the final goal of all beings as liberation. As the first passage suggests, this superlative state involves having the bliss of *brahman* but is otherwise indescribable.

All beings are said to be born only to die again. Since all actions incur *karma*, one is born to experience the results of one's actions from lives past. One is trapped in this cycle until one's *karma* ends and one's soul is liberated. While the *Upanishad*s speak of the final state as ineffable, in texts and traditions of devotion, serving the deity—envisaged as Vishnu, Shiva, or the Goddess—is considered to be the highest goal.

In the second passage, taken from the *Bhagavata Purana*, Krishna lists several kinds of states in liberation, all of which are conceptualized in an anthropomorphic way. In some, the emancipated soul lives in the same place as Krishna, others have (almost) equal glory, some are near him and others have a form like his. Union with him is also possible, but, he says, the true devotee always seeks to serve Krishna. Occasionally, some texts speak about various kinds of hell. That these were active in the imaginations of Hindus is seen from their depictions in sculptures, as on the entire south corridor of the famous Vishnu temple at Angkor Wat in Cambodia.

CHAPTER NINE

SOCIETY AND RELIGION

Hinduism is a distinctly life-affirming religion and Hindu *dharma* speaks about the individual's obligations to the community. Hindu society is marked by different hierarchies that include caste, gender, age, and piety, and by practices that involve meditation, devotional singing, and dietary control. Although the textual sources focus on four major classes (priestly or *brahmin*; royalty and warrior; merchant and producer; and "servant") there are actually thousands of castes in Hinduism and the other religions of India.

The position of women in Hinduism has been complex: they have been both empowered and subjugated by the tradition. Powerful women poets, patrons, and philosophers have lived alongside those who have been repressed by male-dominated norms and customs.

LEFT: A Hindu bride at her marriage ceremony. In order to ensure an harmonious union, a Hindu marriage take place only after a period of prolonged matchmaking—this can often include consideration of caste, birthplace, and horoscopes.

Until recently, the word "Hindu" has seldom been used as a signifier of identity in India. A person's position in society has depended much more intimately on his or her social "class" (*varna*), birth group (*jati*), religious sectarian community, and philosophical allegiance.

While texts speak of four major *varna*s, there are hundreds of *jati*s. The earliest mention of distinct social classes within Indian society occurs in the *Veda*s. In discussing a cosmic sacrifice, in which the various elements of the universe arise from the body of a primordial cosmic man, the *Rig Veda* declares: "From his mouth came the priestly class, from his arms, the rulers. The producers came from his legs; from his feet came the servant class" (*Rig Veda* 10.90). Although some have seen these verses as the origin of what eventually came to be called the "caste system" (Portuguese *casta*, "social division"), it is probable that the stratification of Indian society had begun long before the composition of the text.

These initial four broad *varna*s were the priests (*brahmin*s), the rulers and warriors (*kshatriya*s), the merchants and producers (*vaishya*s), and the servants (*shudra*s). The latter two, at least, were always broad groupings, and while in time it came to be expected that members of all classes would, in theory, pursue the vocation associated with their particular group, it is likely that this prescription was not far-reaching. Today, while some *jati*s can be fitted loosely into the ancient fourfold division, hundreds more have an ambiguous relation to it.

Members of the priestly, warrior, and merchant groups were sometimes known as the "upper" castes, and their male members were known as the "twice born" because of their traditional initiation ritual of spiritual rebirth called *upanayana*. Through this, they become invested with a "sacred thread" that grants them the power to study the *Veda*s.

By the first centuries of the Common Era, many treatises on righteousness, moral duty, and law, known as *dharmashastra*s, were composed. The *dharmashastra*s outline the duties and privileges of the four main *varna*s (classes) of society. The *brahmin* (priestly) class retained sole authority to teach and learn the *Veda*s. Many of the *brahmin*s were teachers, priests, and ritual specialists.

The former kings and princes of India belonged to the *kshatriya* ("royal," or "warrior") class that traditionally held the reins of secular power. Many *kshatriya*s traced their ancestry back to primeval divine progenitors of humanity—in Hinduism, to this day, claimed lines of descent are highly important—and later Hindu rituals explicitly emphasized their direct connection with divine beings.

The mercantile class (*vaishya*s) were in charge of trade, commerce, and farming, and were thus potential possessors of great wealth and economic power. *Shudra*s (servants) are not allowed to accumulate wealth, even if they are able to do so. The law texts state that the duty of a *shudra* is to serve the other classes.

The caste system was—and is—far more complex and flexible than the behavior the *dharmashastra*s advocated, and historical evidence suggests that their prescriptions were probably not taken too seriously by many classes of society and apparently not followed at all in many areas. For instance, the *jati* called Vellalas were technically a *shudra* caste but in practice they were wealthy landowners who wielded considerable economic and political power in the south. The *dharmashastra* prohibitions seem to have had no effect on their fortunes.

Eventually, various groups of "outcastes" emerged who were not covered by the law codes. These arose either from mixed marriages or more often from association with professions that were deemed inferior.

While various texts and practices do clearly imply the hierarchy of the castes, some Hindus have interpreted the traditional system as an equal division of labor, with each major group being responsible for a particular area of activity essential to society.

It has been widely debated whether caste originally depended on birth or simply on a person's qualifications. The Sanskrit word *jati* implies the former, but some discussions in the epic *Mahabharata* suggest that the situation may once have been less clear-cut (see pp.108–109). This and other texts think of caste as incumbent on one's propensities. Several devotional movements in

A brahmin *priest in Bengal is shown blessing an account book.* Brahmins *(see pp.102–103) traditionally represented the intelligentsia, providing teachers and performing religious sacraments. In the Hindu caste system they are considered the highest of the four social classes.*

India have also challenged the social validity of caste and have advocated hierarchies that are based on faith alone.

To this day, people continue regularly to identify themselves by their *jati*, and the entire Indian caste system is such a strong social force that non-Hindu communities such as the Christians, Jains, and Sikhs have absorbed parts of it. For example, Nadar Christians in the south of India will only consider marrying people of the same heritage.

Sectarian, philosophical, and regional allegiances cut across caste lines and provide a different basis for social identification. Hindu sects are determined by the god they worship—Vaishnavas are devotees of Vishnu, Shaivas of Shiva, and so on. Philosophical communities—followers of such great thinkers as Shankara (eighth century CE), Ramanuja (eleventh century CE), and Chaitanya (sixteenth century CE)—also form distinct groups in many parts of India. Regional identity is important, too: as the thousands of matrimonial advertisements in weekly newspapers and the Internet suggest, Hindus tend to marry partners who not only come from the same *jati*, sectarian community, philosophical group, and geographical area, but also who possess compatible horoscopes.

On the whole, Hindu literature has expressed

paradoxical views on the role and position of women. The Laws of Manu, written at the beginning of the Common Era (see p.70), implies that contemporary women were accorded a low status.

Underlying many of the attitudes expressed by male religious writers is the concept of "auspiciousness." Essentially, a person or thing is auspicious if it promotes the three goals of *dharma* (duty), *artha* (prosperity), and *kama* (sensual pleasure). Thus, in the *dharmashastra*s, and in Hindu practice to this day, it is auspicious for a woman to be married and thus be a full partner in *dharma*, *artha*, and *kama*.

However, while Manu may have been quoted with enthusiasm by male writers on Hindu law—whose works have informed many Western notions of Indian womanhood—many Hindu women have always enjoyed, as they do today, a degree of religious and financial independence and have made an important and lasting contribution to the culture of their homeland. Even in the Vedic age, women composed hymns and took part in philosophical debates. After the eighth century CE, there were women poets, temple patrons, philosophers, religious commentators, and writers of scholarly works—such women were respected, honored, and, in some cases, even venerated.

Becoming a *Brahmin*

66 Nahusha asked Yudhishthira:

'Who can be said to be a *brahmin*, O King?'

Yudhishthira replied:

'O lord of Serpents! The one who is truthful,

is generous, is patient, is virtuous, has empathy,

is tranquil, and has compassion—such a person

is a *brahmin*.' **99**

Mahabharata Vana Parva , 177.15, translated by Vasudha Narayanan.

Commentary

As anyone reading the matrimonial advertisements in Indian newspapers or on the Internet can immediately detect, caste identity is very important for the Hindu community. Along with age, economic status, gender, and issues surrounding piety and practice, caste is one of the many factors that have determined social hierarchies in India for thousands of years.

But the concept of caste is complex. While it is almost always understood in Indian society to be incumbent on birth and birth groups, there have been many contexts in which alternative interpretations have been possible, or in which the conventional hierarchal structures have been inverted.

In the passage quoted opposite, from the *Maha-bharata* ("Great Epic of India" or, alternatively, "Great Sons of Bharata"; see pp.43–45), a serpent king interrogates Yudhishthira, the wise Pandava brother, as to who can be said to be a *brahmin*. The question comes up again later in the epic when a Yaksha, a semi-divine entity, queries Yudhishthira on the same issue: '... is a *brahmin* born or can one recognize a *brahmin* by one's propensity?' Yudhishthira's answer seems to suggest the latter, that *brahmin*-hood is determined by "propensity," or behavior. However, this issue has given rise to considerable speculation and debate in Hindu practice. The many virtues spoken of by Yudhishthira as markers of *brahmin*-hood have ordinarily been considered to be signifiers of *sanatana dharma*, or the eternal faith of the Hindus in the many Hindu texts.

At various moments in the history of Hinduism, a person of "low" caste, or sometimes even one who is beyond the pale of the caste system, is considered to be a paradigmatic devotee, thus suggesting a social revolution. But while the superiority of devotees is recognized, without heeding caste, the divisions have, on the whole, been dominant—not just in Hinduism, but also in other religions of the sub-continent, including Christianity, Jainism, and Sikhism.

PART TWO:
BUDDHISM

INTRODUCTION

Buddhism takes its name from Siddhartha Gautama, who was revered by his disciples as the Buddha, or "Awakened One." In the course of only a few centuries, his teaching spread across the Indian subcontinent and into many other parts of Asia. Although it later almost died out as a living religion in the land of its origin, Buddhism has had a profound impact on religious life and cultural development outside India, from Afghanistan in the west to China, Korea, and Japan in the east, and through southeast Asia from Myanmar (Burma) as far as the Indonesian islands of Java and Bali. Today, Buddhism is also a vibrant part of the religious landscape of Europe and North America.

According to a widely accepted scholarly chronology, Siddhartha Gautama was born in 566BCE and died aged eighty in 486BCE. Buddhist tradition reports that he was born in what is now southern Nepal to royal parents. His birth was associated with a series of omens that portended the significance of his career. According to one account of the Buddha's life, when the future Buddha was conceived, his mother, Queen Maya, dreamt that a white elephant painlessly entered her side. When the time came for the young Siddhartha to be born, he sprang from his mother's side, took seven steps, and said:

*A 19th-century Burmese manuscript painting depicts
Siddhartha Gautama meditating while being assailed by
the forces of the demon king Mara (see pp.114–115).*

"I have been born to achieve awakening (*bodhi*) for the
good of the world: this is my last birth."

Siddhartha's father asked the court sages to interpret
these marvels. The sages saw wheels on the child's hands
and feet, and predicted that he would grow up to be a
Chakravartin ("Wheel-Turner")—either a mighty conquering king or a great religious teacher.

Siddhartha was raised in his father's palace, was
married, and had a son. In his early thirties, he became

curious about life outside the palace and asked to go beyond its walls. In a garden he saw three sights that brought home the reality of human suffering: an old man, a sick man, and a corpse. On another occasion, he saw a fourth sight—a wandering ascetic (*shramana*)—and vowed that he would follow the ascetic's example and seek release from the world of suffering. His father tried to restrain him, but Siddhartha Gautama assumed the life of a wanderer. This event, known as the Pravrajya ("Going Forth"), is reenacted in Buddhist communities whenever anyone decides to take up the life of a monk or a nun.

The earliest stages of Siddhartha's withdrawal were marked by severe fasting and self-denial—so much so that he almost died. Convinced that this route to salvation was unproductive, he accepted food from a young woman and began to follow what is known in Buddhist tradition as the "Middle Way," a mode of discipline that avoids the extremes of self-indulgence and self-denial.

Siddhartha's wanderings eventually brought him to the foot of the Bodhi Tree or the "Tree of Awakening." He seated himself beneath it in a last attempt to win freedom from death and rebirth. He was assailed by the evil god Mara, who sent his daughters to seduce him and his sons to frighten him away. But Siddhartha withstood

Mara's onslaught and, during one final night of meditation, became enlightened about the Dharma ("truth" or
"law") of human existence. With this he could properly
be called a *buddha* ("awakened one").

After his awakening, the Buddha walked to a deer
park at Sarnath, near Varanasi, where he met five of his
former companions. He taught them a sermon, or discourse (*sutra*), known as the "First Turning of the Wheel
of the Dharma [Law]." The story of Buddhism as an
organized religious tradition begins with the serene and
newly wise teacher conveying the results of his awakening to a handful of companions, who formed the nucleus
of the Buddhist *samgha* ("community"). For the remaining forty-five years of his life, the Buddha wandered the
roads of northern India, preaching the Dharma and
expanding the boundaries of the community. Finally, in
the town of Kushinagari, he delivered a closing discourse to his disciples, lay down between two trees, and
died. In Buddhist terms, he achieved his "final *nirvana*"
(perfect enlightenment; *parinirvana*), never to be reborn.

The Buddhist tradition evolved in many complex
ways after the death of the Buddha, but it has retained
the same practical focus. The Buddha was not considered
to be God or a supernatural being, but a man who had
found the answer to the deepest dilemmas of human life

and had made that answer available to others. For millions of people worldwide, Buddhism conveys a sense of the sacred and a sense of social and cultural cohesion without reliance on the concept of a creator God.

About a century after the Buddha's death, the first divisions arose in the Buddhist community. Eighteen rival "schools" (*nikaya*s) emerged, of which only Theravada, the dominant tradition of present-day southeast Asia, survives. In the third century BCE, the patronage of the Indian emperor Ashoka (see p.122) brought Buddhism to Sri Lanka, whence it traveled to southeast Asia, including Indonesia. In the second century CE, monks took Buddhism along the Silk Road to China, from where it passed to Korea and thence to Japan. Tibetan Buddhism took root in the seventh century CE and today is one of the most recognizable Buddhist cultures.

The success of Buddhism in northern and eastern Asia was enhanced by the emergence of the Mahayana, or "Great Vehicle," movement in India, around the beginning of the Common Era. The Mahayana brought with it a new body of scriptures, a new emphasis on the importance of laypeople, and a new concept—the Buddha. Tantric Buddhism, an offshoot of Mahayana, appeared in the seventh century CE. With its emphasis on symbolism and ritual and its vision of *buddha*s as "wrathful" deities,

Tantra is one of the most challenging varieties of Buddhism. Schools of Tantric Buddhism are found in China, Japan, Tibet, and Nepal.

The institutional and intellectual expansion of Buddhism was fostered by several remarkable personalities, beginning with the Buddha's early followers. Both Mahayana and Theravada produced a series of scholar-monks who gave intellectual shape to the monastic tradition of southeast Asia. Buddhism has also given rise to religious and social reformers such as Shinran and Nichiren in Japan, and has a tradition of political engagement, from the emperor Ashoka to the two recent Buddhist recipients of the Nobel Peace Prize, the fourteenth Dalai Lama and Myanmar's Aung San Suu Kyi.

There have also, of course, been generations of ordinary Buddhists whose stories have not been preserved but who have given meaning to their lives through the simple gestures of Buddhist worship: by observing the "Five Precepts" (see pp.165–166); by offering food to monks; by celebrating rites of passage; by participating in celebrations of the Buddha's birthday or of Buddhist "saints"; or by going on a pilgrimage. All of these aspects of Buddhist practice seem to express, in one form or another, the same fundamental impulse—to find serenity in a world of suffering and change.

CHAPTER ONE

ORIGINS AND HISTORICAL DEVELOPMENT

The history of Buddhism as a distinct religious tradition began with the life of the Buddha, Siddhartha Gautama, also known as Shakyamuni or "the Sage of the Shakya Clan," who was born in India near the end of the sixth century BCE.

Inspired by the Buddha's teaching, Buddhism spread from India to Sri Lanka, and from there to much of southeast Asia. In the first or second century of the Common Era, it was transported north across the Silk Road to China. From China it was taken to Korea, Japan, and Vietnam. During the seventh century, Buddhist teachers moved north across the Himalayas and carried the faith to Tibet. In the modern period, Buddhism has spread far beyond its home in India to become a vital part of world civilization.

LEFT: A detail (ca. 1800) from the Vessantara Jataka—one of the most popular of the Jataka tales (see p.120)— showing Prince Vessantara, a previous incarnation of the Buddha.

From a Buddhist point of view, the story of the Buddhist tradition does not begin in the sixth century BCE with the birth of Siddhartha Gautama, but in the distant past, with the stories of his previous lives as a *bodhisattva* or "future buddha." According to the doctrine of rebirth (*samsara*), a person's life is the result of a long series of actions (*karma*) accumulated over a process of many lifetimes, and Siddhartha Gautama was no exception. A body of traditional texts known as the *Jataka* ("Birth") tales describes how he received teaching from previous *buddha*s, exhibited many of the moral virtues of the Buddhist tradition, and prepared for his final awakening.

While Buddhists view the career of Siddhartha Gautama as the result of a long process of preparation, they also see it as the beginning of a new historical process, in which others have attempted to follow his example and experience his awakening for themselves.

After the Buddha's death or "final *nirvana*" (*parinirvana*), a group of lay disciples, following his instructions, cremated his body, distributed his ashes as relics, and enshrined them in funerary mounds, or *stupa*s. The veneration of these remains provided the model for the tradition of Buddhist worship, which came to be directed not only at relics but also at other objects, images, and sites sanctified through their association with events in the Buddha's life. In Buddhist tradition, these constitute the Buddha's "Form Body," while his teaching is known as his "Dharma Body." In the two types of "body" (often understood differently in different parts of the Buddhist world), the Buddha continues to be a presence in the wider Buddhist community.

Most of the evidence for the early history of the Buddhist community, the *samgha*, comes from texts written five centuries or more after the Buddha's death. It is therefore difficult to establish for certain how the *samgha* grew from a small band of disciples around a single charismatic leader to become a major force in India and beyond. However, Buddhist tradition records several stages of institutional development that made it possible for the religion to play an important role in the growth of Asian civilization.

A short time after the Buddha's death in 486BCE, a "First Buddhist Council" is said to have been held in the city of Rajagrha. In one account, the Buddha's disciple Kashyapa was traveling with a group of monks when he heard that his master had died. One monk openly rejoiced, saying that his death freed them from the constraints of monastic rules. Fearing a breakdown in discipline, Kashyapa proposed the calling of a council to restate the Buddha's teaching and monastic regulations and set down a common body of doctrine and practice to guide the Buddhist community. The council produced what was to become the nucleus of the Buddhist canon.

Another tradition tells of a second council, called about a century later in the city of Vaishali to discuss variations to the monastic code introduced under the pressure of the community's regional expansion. However, the issues were not fully resolved and gave rise to Buddhism's first big schism, between the Sthaviras ("Elders") and Mahasamghikas ("Great Community"). This was the start of the fragmentation of the *samgha* into the Eighteen Schools (*nikaya*s), and anticipated the eventual split between Hinayana ("Lesser Vehicle") Buddhism and Mahayana ("Greater Vehicle") Buddhism.

The expansion of the early Buddhist community owed much to royal patronage, both within India and beyond. The great Mauryan emperor Ashoka (268–239BCE), who ruled northern India from his capital at Pataliputra (modern Patna), made an explicit and public conversion to Buddhism. As part of his policy of "righteous conquest" (*dharmavijaya*), he promulgated Buddhist values throughout his kingdom and actively supported the spread of the religion beyond his frontiers. For example, his son Mahendra (Pali: Mahinda) is said to have gone to Sri Lanka at the head of a mission.

At this time it seems there were also Buddhist monks in the region of Afghanistan and central Asia, where they came into contact with Hellenic kingdoms established after Alexander the Great's invasion of India in 327–325BCE. At least one Greek king, Menander (Pali: Milinda), is said to have converted to Buddhism.

The split between Hinayana and Mahayana Buddhism took place around the beginning of the Common Era, in circumstances that are still poorly understood. The Mahayana reform movement traced its history back to the Buddha himself. According to Mahayana texts, the Buddha held a special assembly at the Vulture Peak in Rajagrha and delivered a sermon known as "the Second Turning of the Wheel of the Dharma" to a select group of disciples. This teaching, it is said, remained hidden for a period and was then revealed to the rest of the Indian Buddhist community.

Whether the Mahayana emerged in one region of India or developed in several different centers is uncertain. But it is clear that its emphasis on the *bodhisattva* ideal incorporated the interests of lay Buddhists, both men and women, in a new way. A *bodhisattva* did not seek to renounce the world to attain *nirvana*, as in the traditional monastic ideal, but returned to the world out of compassion for ordinary humanity.

*One of the four carved gateways (*toranas*) to the Great Stupa
at Sanchi, which dates from the time of Ashoka and was much
embellished in later centuries.*

Tantric Buddhism—a movement that arose out of
Mahayana Buddhism in the sixth century—seemed to
challenge the most fundamental commitments of the
tradition. The term Tantra comes from the name of the
texts that convey its teachings, and is also known as the
Mantrayana ("Vehicle of Sacred Chants") and Vajrayana
("Vehicle of the Thunderbolt"). Tantric Buddhism
stresses ritual and symbolism, especially the *mandala* or
"sacred circle" (see pp.138–139), and promotes practices

aimed at achieving an immediate experience of "awakening." The radical quality of this awakening is most vividly expressed in Tantric art by the depiction of the Buddha as a "wrathful deity." A Tantric *siddha* or "saint" understands that there is no difference between peacefulness and anger, and that the awakening experience is present in even the most basic of human emotions.

For the first six or seven centuries CE, Buddhism was central to a great flowering of Indian culture, notably in the period of the Gupta dynasty (320–540CE) and the reign of King Harsha (606–646CE). Buddhist monasteries were sophisticated centers of learning, training monks in philosophy, religion, medicine, astronomy, and grammar. By the thirteenth century, however, the rise of Hindu devotionalism in India seems to have undermined the appeal of Buddhism to the common people, while centuries of Buddhist and Hindu interaction eroded the differences between the two traditions. Without strong support from India's kings and princes, Buddhist monasteries were vulnerable to persecution. When Muslim invaders destroyed the last major monasteries at the end of the thirteenth century, Buddhism's active influence on Indian culture effectively ended.

The history of Buddhism in southeast Asia goes back to Ashoka's missionaries in Sri Lanka. For a thousand years or more, the Buddhism of this region was an eclectic mix of traditions that mirrored the diversity of Indian Buddhism. From the eleventh century, when the influence of Indian monasteries began to wane, a number of Buddhist monks and kings in Myanmar and Thailand looked abroad for guidance. Following the example of Sri Lanka, they adopted the Theravada orthodoxy, and this branch of Buddhism predominates in Myanmar and Thailand to this day. In the nineteenth and twentieth centuries, southeast Asian Buddhists were confronted by European colonialism, but generations of reformers rose to the challenge and developed a distinctively "modern" form of Buddhism.

The religion came to Tibet in two waves, known as the "First" and "Second Diffusion of the Dharma." The first began in the seventh century CE, when the wives of the Tibetan king brought images of the Buddha to the capital, Lhasa. The first monastery was established at Samye in the late eighth century CE with the collaboration of the Indian scholar Shantarakshita, the Tibetan king Thrisong Detsen, and the Indian Tantric saint Padmasambhava. The history of Tibetan Buddhism is characterized by the elements that these three founders represent: monastic intellectual discipline; royal secular power; and Tantric ritual and meditation.

The "First Diffusion of the Dharma" in Tibet came to an end during a period of persecution that began in the reign of King Langdarma (838–842CE). Buddhism was reintroduced to Tibet at the end of the tenth century in what is known as the "Later Diffusion," and by the end of the eleventh century, the four main sects of Tibetan Buddhism had been clearly distinguished. One, the Nyingmapa, traced its origin back to Padmasambhava. The others—the Sakyapa, Kadampa, and Kargyupa—claimed to be rooted in the saints and scholars who came after the great persecution. From the Kadampa sect sprang the Gelukpa lineage that eventually produced the Dalai Lamas.

The title Dalai Lama (literally "Ocean Teacher," the first word presumably meaning "Ocean of Wisdom") was first given to the Tibetan monk Sonam Gyatso (1543–88CE) by the Mongol chief Altan Khan. However, Tibetan Buddhists consider Sonam Gyatso to be the third in a line of reincarnations that leads back to the monk Gendun Dup (1391–1475), who is therefore regarded as the true "first" Dalai Lama.

During the reign of the "Great Fifth" Dalai Lama, Ngawang Losang Gyatso (1617–82), the Dalai Lamas became the full secular and religious leaders of Tibet. Under their leadership, Tibetan Buddhists maintained their traditional way of life until the Chinese invasion of Tibet in 1950 forced Tenzin Gyatso, the fourteenth Dalai Lama, into exile. Since that time, he has been the focus of efforts to preserve Tibetan culture, both in Tibet and among communities of converts and exiles around the world.

Buddhism entered China in the first (or possibly second) century CE along the Silk Road. As in southeast Asia and Tibet, the religion's greatest initial challenge was how to express the richness and complexity of Indian Buddhism in an indigenous form. However, by the time of the Tang dynasty (618–907CE), Buddhism had become thoroughly acculturated and was playing an important role in Chinese civilization. This period saw the emergence of the classic Chinese Mahayana schools, including the meditation tradition of Chan (from Sanskrit *dhyana*, "meditation") and the philosophical schools of Tiantai and Huayan. Chinese Buddhism was also deeply influenced by the Mahayana tradition of celestial *buddha*s and *bodhisattva*s, especially Amitabha (Amituo Fo), Avalokiteshvara (Guanyin), and Maitreya (Mile Fo).

The Chinese variety of Buddhism was introduced to Korea in the fourth century CE and to Japan in the sixth century CE. Vietnam also came to adopt Chinese

Buddhist traditions, although the religion may originally have penetrated the region as early as the second century CE. A form of Chan Buddhism (Japanese: Zen), with its emphasis on meditation and the experience of "awakening," occurs in all three lands, as does a degree of devotion to celestial *buddha*s and *bodhisattva*s.

Scarcely known in the Western world (except to scholars) before ca. 1850, Buddhism had begun to spread actively there by 1900, due in part to an ex-US Army colonel, Henry S. Olcott (1832–1907), and a Russian mystic, Helena Blavatsky (1831–91). They took up the cause of reviving Theravada Buddhism in colonial Sri Lanka, and their Theosophical Society owed much to Buddhist precepts. The faith's profile was also raised by the World Parliament of Religions, held in Chicago in 1893, which was attended by many important Asian Buddhist figures.

By the mid-twentieth century, almost all of the major Buddhist schools and traditions had come to be represented in the West, both among immigrant communities and Western converts. In monasteries, temples, and meditation halls from Scotland to San Francisco, Buddhism has put down vigorous roots in environments quite different from that of the Ganges Basin, where it came into being.

Xuanzang's Visit to the Bodhi Tree

" The Master of the Law, when he came to worship
the Bodhi tree and the figure of Tathagata at the
time of his reaching perfect wisdom, made (*afterwards*)
by (*the interposition of*) Maitreya Bodhisattva, gazed on
these objects with the most sincere devotion, he
cast himself down with his face to the ground in
worship, and with much grief and many tears in his
self-affliction, he sighed, and said: 'At the time when
the Buddha perfected himself in wisdom, I know not
in what condition I was, in the troublous world of
birth and death; but now, in this latter time of image
(*worship*), having come to this spot and reflecting on
the depth and weight of the body of my evil deeds, I
am grieved at heart, and my eyes are filled with tears.' **"**

From *The Life of Hiuen-tsiang*, translated by Samuel Beal. Kegan, Paul, Trench, Trübner & Co. Ltd.: London,
1911, p.105.

Commentary

The travel diary of the Chinese monk and scholar
Xuanzang (596–664CE) provides one of the richest
sources of information about Buddhism in India during
its classical period (third to eighth century). Xuanzang

traveled as a pilgrim across the Silk Road, through Afghanistan, where he admired the massive, gilded, rock-cut statues of the Buddha at Bamiyan, and over the Khyber Pass to northern India.

Xuanzang spent more than ten years in India, during which time he explored Buddhist sites as far apart as the mountains of Kashmir in the north and the Tamil-speaking lands of south India. Every place he turned seemed to present a story connected with an event in the Buddha's life, the life of a previous *buddha*, or the life of a famous Buddhist saint.

In Afghanistan, he visited the cave of the Buddha's shadow and had a vision of the Buddha's body. While in Kashmir he studied Buddhist philosophy and became an expert in both the Hinayana and Mahayana intellectual traditions. A climactic moment came when he visited the site of the Buddha's awakening at Bodh Gaya, contemplated the depth of human suffering, and was reduced to tears.

When Xuanzang returned to China, he brought back many manuscripts and was recognized as one of the most learned interpreters of Buddhist philosophy. He became a great favorite in Chinese folk tradition, and the novel *Journey to the West* gives a charming, popular version of his exploits.

CHAPTER TWO

ASPECTS OF THE DIVINE

Whereas many religions focus on the worship of God or other divine beings, Buddhists focus on the figure of the Buddha—a human being who discovered how to bring suffering to an end and escape the cycle of death and rebirth. Buddhists approach the figure of the Buddha with reverence, as others might worship a divine or supernatural being. They also respect the power of local spirits or deities.

The Mahayana set itself apart from earlier traditions by developing a rich array of celestial *buddha*s and *bodhisattva*s who function as supernatural beings to guide believers on the path to salvation. Today it is just as common for a Buddhist to practice the Mahayana by chanting the name of a celestial *buddha* or invoking the compassion of a celestial *bodhisattva* as it is for them to sit alone in meditation.

LEFT: A Nepalese mandala *of 1860 depicting the celestial* buddha Vairochana *("Radiant") in the central circle and four other* buddha*s in the corners of the square. The* mandala *also depicts numerous other sacred beings.*

Theravada Buddhism insists that Siddhartha Gautama was very definitely a human being, who achieved complete *nirvana* (enlightenment; see pp.164–165) and died, never to be reborn. When a Theravada devotee makes an offering to an image of the Buddha, this is not to be understood as an act of divine worship, but a means to gain karmic merit and to be reminded of the Buddha's virtues, which one should always strive to emulate.

This does not mean, however, that Buddhism has nothing resembling the divinities of, for example, ancient Indian tradition. In the Mahayana, those who progress to the highest stages of the path to *buddha*-hood—the *bodhisattva*s ("*buddha*s-to-be," or "future *buddha*s")—are said to accumulate such power from their many works of compassion and wisdom that they are able to act as if they were gods. These extraordinary figures are known as "celestial *bodhisattva*s." They can intervene miraculously in this world, and can even create heavenly realms where people may be reborn into bliss for reasons that depend as much on the compassion of the *bodhisattva*s as on the merit of the individual worshipper. At the end of their careers as *bodhisattva*s they become "celestial *buddha*s" and attain even more remarkable powers. But many *bodhisattva*s postpone *buddha*-hood to assist ordinary devotees on the path to *nirvana*.

The line between a *bodhisattva* and a *buddha* can sometimes be indistinct. According to the Mahayana *Lotus Sutra* (see pp.148–149), the Buddha himself was merely the manifestation of a great *bodhisattva* whose long career has not yet ended. Realizing that people in this world needed an example of a fellow human being who had experienced the process of attaining *nirvana*, he manifested himself as Siddhartha Gautama and went through a show of achieving *parinirvana* (final *nirvana*). But this was not the end of his career: he continues to manifest himself in a compassionate way as long as there are others who need his help.

The concepts of celestial *bodhisattva*s and *buddha*s made it possible for Mahayana Buddhism to develop an elaborate "pantheon" of deities. One of the most important of these many deities is the *bodhisattva* Avalokiteshvara ("Lord Who Looks Down"), who has been called the personification of the compassionate gaze of the Buddha. Avalokiteshvara's compassion is invoked by pronouncing the mantra, "*Om Mani Padme Hum*" ("O Jewel in the Lotus"), which is popular as a meditation mantra. *Om* and *Hum* are untranslatable syllables— *Om* is said to be the sacred sound from which the universe was created and is believed by some to contain the essence of true knowledge.

A 19th-century gilt bronze statuette of the bodhisattva Maitreya *who features prominently in the Mahayana Buddhist traditions of Asia.*

In Indian Buddhism, Avalokiteshvara became associated with a female *bodhisattva* called Tara, who embodied the feminine aspect of his compassion. In China, where Avalokiteshvara is worshipped under the name Guanyin, the *bodhisattva*'s male and female identities became compounded, and Guanyin came to be worshipped mainly in female form. Tibetans feel a special kinship with Avalokiteshvara (whose name in Tibetan is Chenrezig). They claim that he has taken a vow to protect the nation of Tibet and is manifested in the person of every Dalai Lama.

Important celestial *bodhisattva*s also include Maitreya, the *buddha* of the future age, who will be the next *bodhisattva* to enter the world and become a *buddha*. Like Avalokiteshvara, Maitreya is said to rescue people in danger: in China, where he is called Mile Fo, messianic movements have at times proclaimed his imminent arrival and the transformation of society according to Buddhist principles. Other celestial *bodhisattva*s are Manjushri, the *bodhisattva* of wisdom, and Kshitigarbha, the consoler of the dead and protector of travelers, pilgrims, and children.

The best known celestial *buddha* is Amitabha ("Infinite Light"), who is said to have established a paradise, the "Pure Land," on becoming a *buddha* (see pp.196 and 198). Anyone who remembers the name of Amitabha, especially at the moment of death, will be reborn in the Pure Land and come face to face with Amitabha himself. The worship of Amitabha Buddha had great impact in China and Japan, where he is called Amituo Fo and Amida Butsu respectively (*fo* and *butsu* = *buddha*). Indeed, during the social and political turmoil of the Kamakura Period (1185–1333), the worship of Amida became one of the most important elements in Japanese Buddhist life. The Buddhist reformer Honen (1133–1212) made the worship of Amida accessible to people who had no specialized training in Buddhism, and Shinran (1173–1263)—the founder of Japan's Jodo

Shinshu, the "True Pure Land Sect"—insisted that salvation depended only on the grace of Amida rather than on one's own efforts. The traditions founded by Honen and Shinran continue to be the most popular form of Buddhism in Japan and are represented in North America by the Buddhist Churches of America.

Other important celestial *buddha*s include the physician-*buddha* Bhaishajyaguru ("Teacher of Healing") and the "Sun Buddha" Vairochana ("Radiant"), the central *buddha* in many of the *mandala*s, or "sacred circles," of Tantric Buddhism. The *mandala* symbolizes the relationship between the macrocosm and the microcosm: it represents the entirety of the cosmos and also the mind and body of the practitioner. *Mandala*s are used in Tantric ritual and meditation to help the devotee unify his or her vision of the cosmos; to contemplate the integration of the self and the world; and to overcome the distinction between *nirvana* and the realm of death and rebirth.

One of the most common of these sacred images is known as the "*Mandala* of the Five Buddhas" and plays a central role in the Tantric Buddhism of Tibet and in the Shingon tradition of Japan. It takes as its starting point a configuration of five celestial *buddha*s: Vairochana in the center, Amitabha in the west, Amoghasiddhi in the north, Akshobhya in the east, and Ratnasambhava in the south. The *mandala* is expanded and elaborated by a process of symbolic association to include five colors, five personality traits, five wisdoms, and so on, with each element of every pentad associated with one of the five *buddha*s. The *buddha*s are also associated with five goddesses located at the center of the *mandala* and at the four intermediate points of the compass.

As well as appearing at the centre of many *mandala*s, Vairochana, who is identified with the sun, was also important in the acculturation of Buddhism to Japan, where Vairochana was identified with Amaterasu, the sun goddess who heads the Shinto pantheon.

In addition to this host of widely worshipped celestial beings, Buddhism has also always found room for the reverence of local deities and spirits. The Buddha himself is said to have been protected by a *naga* (in Indian tradition, a *naga* is a snake deity that controls the rain; in Buddhism, *naga*s also guard the treasures of the tradition). *Stupa*s (funerary mounds; see pp.172–173) are often associated with *yaksha*s (gods of wealth and good fortune) and *yakshi*s (fertility goddesses). In southeast Asia, Hindu gods such as Indra and Vishnu function as important Buddhist guardian figures, and the faith embraces many local and regional deities in China, Korea, Japan, and Tibet.

The Land of Bliss

" Then the Blessed One said to Shariputra: 'In the west, Shariputra, many hundreds of thousands of *buddha*-fields from here, there is a *buddha*-field called the Land of Bliss. A perfectly awakened *buddha*, by the name of Infinite Life (Amitayus), dwells in that land and preaches the Dharma. Why do you think it is called the Land of Bliss? In the Land of Bliss no living beings suffer any pain in body or mind, and they have immeasurable reasons for pleasure. . . .

'When any sons or daughters of good family hear the name of the Blessed Tathagata (or Buddha) of Infinite Life and keep it in mind without distraction for one, two, three, four, five, six, or seven nights, then, at the moment of death, the Buddha of Infinite Life will stand before them, leading a group of *bodhisattva*s and surrounded by a crowd of disciples, and those sons or daughters of good family will die with minds secure. After their death, they will be born in the Land of Bliss, the *buddha*-field of the Tathagata of Infinite Life.

'This is what I have in mind, Shariputra, when I say that sons or daughters of good family should respectfully aspire for that *buddha*-field.' **"**

From the *Shorter Sukhavativyuha Sutra*, translated by Malcolm David Eckel.

Commentary

The *Shorter Sukhavativyuha Sutra* (Discourse on the Land of Bliss) gives a vivid picture of devotion to Amitabha Buddha (here known as Amitayus, the Buddha of Infinite Life). This *sutra* was composed in India in the early centuries of the Common Era and had immense influence on the practice of Mahayana Buddhism in India and in the Buddhist countries of north and east Asia.

According to the tradition that surrounded this text, a *bodhisattva* named Dharmakara promised long ago that, when he attained awakening and became Amitabha Buddha or Amitayus, he would create a blissful land to save living beings from suffering. This land is depicted as a celestial paradise, full of beautiful trees, lotus ponds, and the sounds of birds proclaiming the virtues of the Buddha. Anyone who recalls the name of Amitabha Buddha is to be reborn in this land and proceed irreversibly to supreme awakening.

The key to salvation in this tradition is the power of Dharmakara's promise or "vow." The vow becomes effective at the moment of his awakening and acts as the grace of the Buddha to lift people to rebirth in the blissful land. When believers "respectfully aspire for this *buddha*-field" they bring their own aspirations into harmony with the vow that created Amitabha's paradise.

CHAPTER THREE

SACRED TEXTS

According to tradition, the Buddha achieved his awakening under the Bodhi Tree in silence, and many Buddhists say that the content of his awakening can never be expressed in words. But this has not prevented the development of a complex and elaborate scriptural tradition to transmit his words to subsequent generations.

Each of the early Schools developed a distinctive body of canonical literature. Of these, only the Pali canon of the Theravada now survives. With the rise of the Mahayana came new scriptural texts and new problems of interpretation. In India, the corpus of authoritative Mahayana literature expanded with relatively few limitations. Today, the Chinese and Tibetan canons provide an enormous treasure trove of Buddhist tradition and an eloquent testimony to the power of the Buddha's awakening.

LEFT: A Buddhist devotee turns a "prayer wheel" in a temple at Kyicho, Bhutan. Each "wheel" is a cylinder containing sacred prayer texts, which are believed to be activated when the cylinder is spun by the worshiper.

After the Buddha's death, his followers are said to have called the First Buddhist Council to recite the content of his teaching (see p.121). The council established a procedure for memorization that allowed the teaching to be transmitted orally for almost five centuries before it was committed to writing. Written versions of the canonical collections exist in all Buddhist cultures and are often treated with great reverence, but the oral tradition is still of central importance. Owing in part to this practice of oral transmission, Buddhism has no single canon of scripture—different schools and traditions regard different collections of texts as authoritative.

While Buddhist canonical literature is variable and new texts have often been added, it is still considered a source of authority, not only because it provides a record of the Buddha's teaching but because it provides access, in a certain sense, to the Buddha himself. Buddhist sacred texts represent the most important, enduring aspects of the Buddha, what Buddhists refer to as his "Dharma Body" (see p.121). A line in the Pali *Samyutta Nikaya* says: "What is there, Vakkali, in seeing this vile body? He who sees the Dhamma [Pali for "Dharma"] sees me; he who sees me sees the Dhamma." The Dharma/Dhamma functions as the continuing presence of the Buddha in the Buddhist community, and is as worthy of respect as the Buddha himself. Buddhist texts are often recited or copied as acts of devotion, and it is not uncommon, especially in the Mahayana tradition, for texts to be placed on altars as objects of worship, along-side, or even instead of, images of the Buddha.

The most conservative canon of Buddhist writings is the *Tipitaka* ("Three Baskets") of the Theravada tradition. Written in Pali, it is often referred to simply as the Pali Canon and contains ancient material from the earliest stages of the oral tradition alongside texts possibly composed in the second century BCE. The *Tipitaka* (Sanskrit, *Tripitaka*) is said to have been written down in 29BCE under King Vattagamani of Sri Lanka.

The three "baskets" are the three sections of the Pali canon: the *Sutta* (Sanskrit, *Sutra*) *Pitaka*, *Vinaya Pitaka*, and *Abhidhamma* (Sanskrit, *Abhidharma*) *Pitaka*. The *Sutta Pitaka* generally consists of the Buddha's doctrinal discourses and ranges from short poems to long prose narratives about the Buddha's previous lives. The *Vinaya Pitaka* is concerned with rules of discipline and includes stories that illustrate Buddhist moral principles. The *Abhidhamma Pitaka* provides a systematic analysis of the categories of Buddhist thought.

The traditional interpretation of the Pali canon owes a great deal to the monk Buddhaghosa, who came to Sri

Lanka from India in the fifth century CE. He collected and translated a large body of Sinhalese commentaries on the Pali texts and his most important work, the *Visuddhimagga* ("Path to Purification"), is an authoritative guide to the practice of Theravada Buddhism.

The development of the Mahayana tradition is intimately connected with the evolution and dissemination of its scriptures. The earliest Mahayana texts can be dated to the first century BCE. Important Mahayana writings were translated into Chinese as early as the second century CE, and texts that came to assume canonical status were produced in India after 1100. India never produced a Mahayana canon that was as clearly fixed as the Pali canon, although informal Mahayana collections existed as early as the second century CE.

The oldest extant catalog of Chinese Buddhist canonical literature dates from 518CE. The first printed version of the Chinese *Tripitaka* (as it is referred to there, using the Sanskrit form of the Pali word *Tipitaka*) was made during 972–983CE, at the beginning of the Song dynasty. The Tibetan canon was collected by the scholar Buton (1290–1364) and was first printed in its entirety in Beijing in the early fifteenth century.

The Chinese and Tibetan canons each give the impression of being a codification of a monastic library.

These 12th-century "Perfection of Wisdom" sutras are written on palm leaves which have been threaded together ("thread" is the literal meaning of sutra).

Clearly, for both canons, the concept of "canonicity" was quite loose. There was a core of literature (known in Sanskrit as *sutra* and in Tibetan as *ka*) that bore the direct authority of the *buddha*s and *bodhisattva*s. These *sutra* portions of the Chinese and Tibetan canons both include a section called the "Perfection of Wisdom" (Sanskrit, *Prajnaparamita*), which provides some of the most basic accounts of the *bodhisattva* ideal and the concept of "emptiness." Taking a fairly short text as their starting point, the Perfection of Wisdom *sutra*s grew to include as many as one hundred thousand lines and were condensed into brief texts such as the *Diamond* and *Heart* *sutra*s. Around these core *sutra* portions of the Chinese and Tibetan canons accumulated a body of doctrinal, philosophical, and interpretive literature known in Sanskrit as *shastra* and in Tibetan as *ten*, or "teaching."

The most extensive collection of Tantric texts is found in the Tibetan canon. Like other Buddhist canonical literature, it ranges widely in form, from the simple songs of the Indian Tantric saints to elaborate commentaries on Tantric ritual, meditation, and symbolism. The Tibetan tradition generally classifies Tantric texts in four categories: ritual (*kriya*), practice (*charya*), discipline (*yoga*), and highest discipline (*anuttarayoga*). The *Mahavairochana Tantra* ("Tantra of the Great Vairochana"), a text that had central significance in Chinese and Japanese Tantra, belongs to the *charya* category. To the *anuttarayoga* category belong texts such as the *Hevajra Tantra* and *Guhyasamaja Tantra* that focus on the immediate realization of "emptiness." Buddhist Tantric literature in India evolved gradually from the seventh to the twelfth centuries CE.

The *Lotus Sutra* has functioned in East Asia almost as a compendium of Mahayana doctrine and has had wide impact on the religious and philosophical development of the Mahayana tradition. The *sutra* is the source of a famous parable in which the Buddha is represented as a father who lures his children out of a burning house by promising them different "vehicles." When the children get outside, he gives them the "great vehicle" of the Mahayana. The parable points to the relationship between Mahayana teaching and that of the "lesser" vehicles associated with the earlier schools.

The enormous variety of Buddhist scriptures has led to many controversies about scriptural authority and interpretation. Members of the Eighteen Schools (*nikaya*s; see p.122) attacked the Mahayana by claiming that its *sutra*s were not the actual teaching of the Buddha. The Mahayana responded by saying that the teaching of the Schools was merely a preparatory teaching, which the Mahayana superseded. Within the Mahayana, the Madhyamaka School argued that only certain Mahayana texts were definitive in meaning (*nitartha*), while others had a meaning that required interpretation (*neyartha*). The Chinese and Tibetan traditions produced several complex schemes of classification to reconcile contradictions and determine which texts could be relied on for the most definitive teaching. The Tantric tradition dealt with issues of interpretation by insisting that the meaning of the *tantra*s was deliberately veiled and could be correctly interpreted only by a qualified teacher (Sanskrit *guru*; Tibetan *lama*).

The Discourse on Turning the Wheel of the Dharma

66 Thus have I heard. At one time the Lord was staying in the Deer Park at Isipatana, near Banaras. There the Lord spoke to a group of five monks: 'O monks, someone who has gone forth into the monastic life should avoid two extremes. What are the two? One is devotion to passions and worldly pleasures. This is inferior, common, ordinary, unworthy, and unprofitable. The other is devotion to self-mortification. This is painful, unworthy, and unprofitable. By avoiding these two extremes, O monks, the Tahatagata has realized the Middle Path. It gives vision, it gives knowledge, and it leads to calm, superior insight, awakening, and *nirvana*.

'And what, O monks, is the Middle Path? It is the Noble Eightfold Path: right views, right thoughts, right speech, right action, right livelihood, right effort, right mindfulness, and right concentration. This, O monks, is the Middle Path realized by the Tathagata. It gives vision, it gives knowledge, and it leads to calm, superior insight, awakening, and *nirvana*.' 99

From the *Samyutta Nikaya* LVI.11, translated by Malcolm David Eckel.

Commentary

The Buddhist scriptural tradition traces its origin to the Buddha's first sermon, or the first turning of the wheel of the Dharma. The Pali version of this sermon gives a concise summary of basic Buddhist doctrine, including the Middle Path. Buddhist scripture carries great authority, and prodigious effort has gone into the memorization, copying, transmission, and preservation of the Buddha's words. But it is wrong to equate the authority of the Buddha with any particular formulation of his teaching. The Buddha's teaching has been compared to a raft—when people use a raft to cross a river, they leave the raft behind and go on their way. When someone uses the Dharma to cross the river of suffering, the words of the Dharma can be left behind.

With its practical approach toward the authority of scripture, the Buddhist tradition has been remarkably flexible about developing new scriptures to respond to new cultural situations. The *sutra*s of the Mahayana constituted a "second turning of the wheel of the Dharma" to introduce the *bodhisattva* ideal. The *tantra*s of the Vajrayana introduced another body of scripture to express a new method of awakening. New scriptures have played a role in Chinese Buddhism, and they have often contributed to the vitality of Buddhism in Tibet.

CHAPTER FOUR

SACRED PERSONS

If the goal of Buddhist life is to follow the example of the Buddha, it should be no surprise that the tradition has produced many remarkable figures. During the Buddha's lifetime, several monks and nuns followed in his footsteps and, according to tradition, attained *nirvana* (see p.196). As monastic communities became sophisticated centers of learning and meditation, they continued to play a formative role in the development of the Indian tradition, as well as throughout the rest of Asia.

With the appearance of the Mahayana, the *bodhisattva* ideal meant that it was no longer necessary to be a monk or nun to follow the example of the Buddha. In the Mahayana tradition, there are many who have achieved a special degree of sanctity or authority outside the structure of a monastic community.

LEFT: Tibetan Buddhist nuns participate in a debating session in the courtyard of Dolma Ling nunnery, Dharamsala, India.

To be a "sacred person" in the Buddhist tradition is, above all, to imitate the example of the Buddha. The most basic way to do this is to embark on a monastic life in pursuit of *nirvana* (perfect enlightenment). The greatest exemplars of the monastic ideal were the Buddha's first followers, such as his chief disciple, Shariputra (in Pali, Sariputta). Shortly after his conversion by the Buddha, he became an *arhant*, or "worthy one"—one who, like his master, had attained *nirvana*. Converted at the same time was his friend Maudgalyayana (Pali, Moggallana), who was reputed to possess the magical ability to quell the hostile forces of nature and to travel at will to the highest levels of the cosmos. He became popular in Chinese Buddhist legend as Mulian, who journeyed to Hell to intercede for his mother.

One of the most remarkable of the Buddha's early disciples was Angulimala ("Garland of Fingers") who, before he met the Buddha, is said to have been a mass murderer who wore his victims' fingers as a necklace. However, after meeting the Buddha, he was so moved by his account of the Dharma that he became a monk and eventually attained *nirvana*.

The Indian monasteries of later centuries also produced personalities renowned for their courage, learning, or meditative attainments. The great Chinese monk Xuanzang (596–664CE) visited India in the early part of the seventh century, studied philosophy in the Indian monasteries, and left us an account of scholar-monks who vied for royal patronage in public debate. Among the products of the sophisticated monastic world were the Mahayana philosophers Shantarakshita and Kamalashila, who presided over the foundation of the first Buddhist monastery in Tibet, and Atisha, who helped reintroduce Buddhism to Tibet during the "Later Diffusion."

The roster of monastic figures in east and southeast Asia and Tibet who helped shape the religion is almost inexhaustible. In Sri Lanka, for example, the Indian monk Buddhaghosa (fifth century CE) collected the indigenous commentaries and gave definitive shape to the Theravada tradition in southeast Asia. In China, the monk Huineng (638–713CE) became the Sixth Patriarch and founder of the Southern school of Chan ("Meditation")—his iconoclastic version of Chan eventually became the dominant tradition in China and the source of Japanese Zen.

The Japanese monk Kukai or Kobo Daishi (774–835CE), traveled to China and brought back a form of Chinese Tantric Buddhism that was known in Japan as the Shingon ("True Word") School. He also introduced the phonetic writing system that is used in Japan today to supplement the use of Chinese characters. In the Kamakura period, the monk Dogen (1200–1253) followed Kukai's path to China and brought back a new and vigorous form of meditation to create the Soto school of Zen. In fourteenth-century Tibet, the monk Tsong kha pa (1357–1419) performed an extraordinary feat of intellectual synthesis to produce the Gelukpa tradition and the school of the Dalai Lamas.

The monastic practice of Buddhism continues today with such widely revered figures as Thich Nhat Hanh (1926–), a Vietnamese monk who headed the Buddhist Peace Delegation during the Vietnam War and preaches the Buddhist virtue of "mindfulness" in the West. For many, Buddhists and non-Buddhists alike, perhaps the most visible living example of the "Buddha ideal" is Tenzin Gyatso, the fourteenth Dalai Lama (see p.205).

In the Tantric tradition, especially in Tibet, there has been a complicated interaction between the ideal of the scholar-monk in a monastic community and that of the solitary *siddha* or "saint." The Indian Tantric tradition describes *siddha*s, such as Maitrigupta (or Maitripa), who achieved their meditative breakthroughs on the fringes of civilization, in the forests or cremation grounds, working with unconventional and charismatic teachers.

A Japanese monk collecting alms. The words bhikshu
("monk") and bhikshuni *("nun") come from a Sanskrit
root that means "to beg."*

Padmasambhava, the Indian Tantric saint who shared in the foundation of the first Tibetan monastery, is pictured as a solitary figure with extraordinary powers. His consort, Yeshe Tsogyal, was a powerful figure in her own right.

The Tibetan "saint" Milarepa (1040–1123) worked for many years with the irascible guru Marpa before he was given his initiation and retired into the mountains to live as a solitary *siddha*.

One of the most important institutional developments of the *bodhisattva* ideal was its extension to include a form of sacral kingship, a tradition that has existed in Buddhism since the third century BCE and the time of the emperor Ashoka, who assumed a special status as a Dhamma-raja (Sanskrit, *Dharma-raja*, "Righteous King") for his policy of protecting and promoting the Dharma (see p.122).

As the Mahayana tradition developed, revered Buddhist princes and kings came to be regarded as *bodhisattva*s. Such figures include Prince Shotoku, who played a crucial role in the introduction of Buddhism to Japan, and the Dalai Lamas of Tibet, whom Tibetan Buddhists venerated as the incarnation of the celestial *bodhisattva* Avalokiteshvara. The respect accorded to their status as *bodhisattva*s enabled the Dalai Lamas to assume responsibility for the secular as well as the religious governance of Tibet.

Not all examples of the monastic ideal have been men. During his lifetime, the Buddha agreed to ordain his aunt and create an order of nuns. The Pali canon contains a text, known as the *Therigatha* ("The Eldresses' Verses"), which contains many eloquent songs that have been attributed to this first group of nuns. Today, the lineage of nuns has died out in many Buddhist countries, but there are active female orders in Tibet and China, and movements are afoot to revive orders in other countries.

During the Kamakura Period in Japan, several major movements broke with the monastic ideal and allowed their leaders to be married. This pattern has continued to the present day. The leadership of the Jodo Shinshu ("True Pure Land Sect"), which traces its origin to Shinran, now has a married clergy and does not attempt to abide by the rules of monastic life. The same is true of the Japanese denominations, such as the Soka Gakkai and Rissho Kosei-kai, that trace their origin to the charismatic Japanese reformer Nichiren (1222–81). Nichiren brought a prophetic message to Japan and called upon the nation to return to the true practice of Buddhism.

Milarepa Meets His Teacher

❝ By the side of the road, a large, corpulent monk with sparkling eyes was plowing a field. As soon as I saw him, I felt inexpressible and inconceivable bliss. For a moment, his appearance stopped me in my tracks. Then I said: 'Sir, I have been told that Marpa the translator, direct disciple of the glorious Naropa, lives in this place. Where is his house?'

For a long time he looked me up and down. Then he said: 'Where are you from?'

I said: 'I am a great sinner from upper Tsang. He is so famous that I have come to ask him for the true Dharma.'

He said: 'I will introduce you to Marpa, but now plow this field.'

From the ground he pulled some beer that had been hidden under a hat, and he gave it to me. It was good beer, and it tasted great.

He said, 'plow hard,' and he went away. **❞**

From *Mi la ras pa'i rnam thar*, translated by Malcolm David Eckel.

Commentary

There are few more dramatic moments in the story of the Tibetan saint Milarepa (1040–1123) than his first encounter with Marpa, the man who was to become his teacher. Milarepa had studied black magic, and then he practiced it in order to wreak revenge on a group of hostile relatives. Tormented by his crime, he sought out a teacher who could help him escape from the weight of his sin. Marpa accepted the challenge, and put Milarepa through a process of severe punishment and discipline before he gave him the initiation that set him free. Milarepa's humility and his willingness to accept extreme hardship in pursuit of the truth have made him one of Tibet's most beloved saints.

The student-teacher relationship is a crucial part of practice in many Buddhist traditions. Stories of the Buddha often emphasize his "skillful means," by which he perceived the distinctive needs of his disciples and developed a teaching that would be effective for them. For students of Tantric Buddhism, the teacher functions as a representative of the Buddha to guide the student through the dangers of the path. In Chan or Zen Buddhism, the master transmits a lineage of teaching "outside words and letters" that goes back to the Buddha himself.

CHAPTER FIVE

ETHICAL PRINCIPLES

Traditional accounts of Buddhist ethics focus on the "Noble Eightfold Path" that leads from the world of suffering to the achievement of *nirvana*. To follow this path, a person must avoid the evil actions, such as killing and stealing, that lead to negative consequences in this life and the next. A person also has to discipline the mind through meditation and to develop an awareness of the nature of reality.

The practical details of Buddhist ethics have been negotiated differently in different parts of the Buddhist world, particularly in the Mahayana countries where the active ideal of the compassionate *bodhisattva* tended to replace the more contemplative ideal of a solitary seeker of *nirvana*. But Buddhist ethics has never lost its practical concern for the development of the total personality.

LEFT: A 12th-century Chinese painting depicting the Buddha giving alms to the poor—an example of a "good action" that will aid the soul's progress toward the attainment of nirvana.

The spirit of Buddhist ethics is expressed in the story of a man named Malunkyaputta, who tells the Buddha that he will not listen to his teaching until he has answered a series of questions, such as "How was the world created?" and "Will the Buddha exist after death?" The Buddha responds by comparing Malunkyaputta to a man who has been shot by a poisoned arrow but refuses to let it be pulled out until the physician can tell him what the arrow is made of, who shot it, and so on. For Buddhists, all speculation is subject to one practical principle: it is valuable only if it can directly help a person to remove the "arrow of suffering" and find the way to *nirvana*. Any other type of speculation, like Malunkyaputta's questioning, is incidental.

In the Mahayana lands of north and east Asia, the ethical ideal of the *bodhisattva* became the central principle of moral practice for Buddhist monks and nuns as well as laypeople. The *bodhisattva* cultivates the virtues of compassion (*karuna*) and wisdom (*prajna*). These two principles are expressed in the "*bodhisattva* vow": "May I attain *buddha*-hood for the sake of all other beings!"

The virtue of compassion is an active ideal, centered on relieving the suffering of others. This includes helping others to attain *nirvana*, even to the extent of postponing one's own entry into *nirvana* in order to do so.

Wisdom is more contemplative. It focuses on seeing through the "veil of illusion" that clouds ordinary experience, thereby becoming free from suffering oneself.

The basic guide to the attainment of *nirvana* is the "Noble Eightfold Path," a process of discipline with eight components: "right understanding," "right thought," "right speech," "right action," "right livelihood," "right effort," "right mindfulness," and "right concentration." Alternatively, the fundamental prerequisites for *nirvana* can be expressed as three principles: abstention from harmful actions (*shila*, "moral conduct"); a disciplined mind (*samadhi*, "mental concentration"); and a proper understanding of the self and the world (*prajna*, "wisdom").

These principles are related to the traditional Buddhist understanding of the law of *karma*, or moral retribution, that governs the process of death and rebirth. A person should abstain from harmful actions because they will lead to punishment in a future life and thus make it doubly difficult to escape the cycle of death and rebirth. "Mental concentration" helps remove the desire and hatred that lead to harmful actions. And "wisdom" removes the false sense of self that feeds the whole process of desire, hatred, and harmful action.

For Theravada Buddhist laity, and indeed most other

Buddhists, "moral conduct" is summarized in the Five Precepts: no killing, no stealing, no abusive sex, no lying, and no intoxicating beverages. Novice Theravada monks observe five further precepts: no eating after midday, no use of ornaments, no attending entertainments or shows, no use of money, and no use of soft beds. However, once fully ordained, monks are bound by more than two hundred rules found in the *Vinaya Pitaka*.

The practice of "mental concentration" (*samadhi*) can take many different forms in the Buddhist tradition. One of the most basic techniques is to sit with a straight back and crossed legs, and cultivate "mindfulness" (Sanskrit *smrti*, Pali *sati*) of one's breathing. The purpose is to calm the mind, diminish harmful emotions, and become more fully aware of the flow of reality that makes up the self and the world. Other forms of meditation involve a deliberate cultivation of mental images, often of *buddha*s or *bodhisattva*s, to serve as the focus of worship.

The cultivation of "wisdom" (*prajna*) also takes many forms. In the Theravada tradition it is associated with the study of the *Abhidhamma*, the third section of the Pali canon, and its key concept is the doctrine of "No-Self." To be wise (or, in the words of the Noble Eightfold Path, to have "right views") is to see that the self changes at every moment and has no permanent identity.

In the Mahayana tradition, the understanding of "No-Self" is expressed in the doctrine of "emptiness." For many practitioners of the Mahayana, all things are seen as "empty" of identity. *Nirvana* is not simply a goal to be sought at the end of a long process of discipline—it can be experienced in the emptiness of the present moment.

A monk sits in contemplation of Buddhist scriptures at the great temple complex of Angkor Thom, Cambodia.

The Foundations of Mindfulness

66 At one time the Lord was staying at Uruvela, under a
fig tree on the bank of the Neranjara River, having just
become awakened. As the Lord was isolated and
secluded, he had the following thought: 'This is the
only way for living beings to become pure, to overcome
grief and pain, to end suffering and sadness, to attain
the right path, and to realize *nirvana*, namely, the four
foundations of mindfulness.'

What are these four? A monk should live in such a
way that he practices body-contemplation with regard
to the body. He should be energetic, attentive, and
mindful, and he should restrain ordinary covetousness
and discontent. A monk should do the same with
regard to the feelings, the mind, and mental states.
This is the only way for living beings to become pure,
to overcome grief and pain, to end suffering and sadness, to attain the right path, and to realize *nirvana*,
namely, the four foundations of mindfulness. 99

From the *Samyutta Nikaya* XLVII.18, translated by Malcolm David Eckel.

Commentary

An essential prerequisite for the attainment of *nirvana* is the facility to calm the mind and allow its passions to cool. In the Mahayana tradition, this "mindfulness" is often viewed as an essential prerequisite for compassion as well: as the mind becomes focused and calm, it is more possible to be attentive to the suffering of others.

Buddhists often begin their meditation with a simple exercise of mindfulness. Sometimes a person practices mindfulness in a formal way by sitting with his or her legs crossed, in a traditional meditative posture, and being attentive to the movement of the breath. But the same form of mindfulness can be extended to every kind of human activity. When one is lying down, one should be aware that one is lying down. When one is sitting, one should be aware that one is sitting. When one is walking, one should be aware that one is walking.

At its most basic level, this practice is meant to cultivate clarity of mind: for one to become aware of the thoughts and feelings that flood the mind in the process of everyday experience. But mindfulness also allows the mind to become calm, just as a lake becomes calm when there is no longer any wind to stir up its waters into waves, or as a fire begins to cool and go out when it is no longer stoked by fuel.

CHAPTER SIX

SACRED SPACE

In the Buddhist tradition, spaces become sacred by their association with the Buddha or with other sacred persons. Historically, the prototype of a Buddhist shrine was a *stupa*, or funerary mound, that contained the relics of the Buddha's cremated remains. *Stupa*s continue to function as important focal points for worship, not only in northern India but across the Buddhist world, as do temples dedicated to the worship of particular *buddha*s or *bodhisattva*s.

As the seat where the Buddha achieved his awakening, the cosmos itself can be considered sacred. The same can be true of particular countries, like Tibet, or particular geographical sites, such as mountains, that are associated with Buddhist deities. Even the seat of a practitioner's meditation, as a replica of the thrones of the *buddha*s, may be viewed as sacred.

LEFT: Master Soen Ozeki raking gravel in the Zen garden at Daisen-in, Kyoto, Japan. The white gravel represents the purity of the mind. The tree represents the Buddha's awakening.

In his final instructions to his disciples, as recorded in the Pali *Mahaparinibbana Sutta*, the Buddha requested that his body should be cremated and the remains enshrined in a series of *stupa*s, or funerary mounds, to serve as focal points for worship and meditation. The basic form of a Buddhist shrine replicates one of these early *stupa*s, with a large central mound surrounded by a railing and topped by a square structure with a central post holding a series of parasols. In the earliest *stupa*s, the relics of the Buddha were housed in the square structure, but later they were enshrined inside the central mound. As the form of the *stupa* evolved in India, the mound came to be decorated with representations of the Buddha, events of his life, or important stories from Buddhist texts. To pay homage to the Buddha at one of these traditional shrines, a worshipper could make offerings in the same way a Hindu devotee might make offerings to an image of a Hindu god, with flowers, candles, incense, and so on; or a person might walk around the *stupa* in an act of ritual circumambulation.

The basic *stupa* was elaborated in many different ways in different lands. In southeast Asia, shrines commonly retain the low, rounded shape of a traditional *stupa*. In Tibet, the structure has been elongated vertically into the shape of a *chorten* or "offering place." In

China, Korea, and Japan, the soaring shape of a pagoda is derived from the graceful parasols that used to adorn the top of *stupa*s in India.

At the great Buddhist temple at Borobudur in Java, the simple path of circumambulation has been elaborated into a series of ascending galleries, decorated with the story of Sudhana, a young Mahayana pilgrim in search of enlightenment. On the top of the structure, the worshipper is confronted by an open platform with an array of individual *stupa*s, each revealing an image of the seated Buddha. In the center of the platform stands a large, vacant *stupa* representing, it seems, the empty clarity of the Buddha's awareness—there are few more elegant and powerful representations of the Buddha's awakening in all of the Buddhist world.

Indian Buddhists established a tradition of temple-building following the Hindu style. The earliest Buddhist temples were created in caves in western India. Typically, the cave entrance led into a large open space where worshippers could sit or stand in front of a small *stupa* or an image of the Buddha. Sometimes the Buddha-image was in a separate room similar to the *garbha-grha* or "womb-house" of a Hindu temple. In recent years, there have been efforts to rebuild some of the important Indian Buddhist temples that were destroyed in the twelfth and thirteenth centuries. For example, a Buddhist organization called the Mahabodhi ("Great Awakening") Society has led the restoration of the temple at Bodh Gaya, on the site where the Buddha achieved his awakening.

Indian Buddhist temple architecture was highly influential throughout the Buddhist world. The Temple of the Tooth in Kandy, Sri Lanka, and the Temple of

The Buddhist temple of Borobudur on the island of Java, Indonesia. This remarkable transformation of the traditional stupa is a representation of the cosmos in three dimensions.

the Emerald Buddha in Bangkok, Thailand, are sacred to the royalty of both countries and have served as symbols of royal power. The Jokhang in Lhasa is said to house the oldest image of the Buddha in Tibet and has functioned for centuries as an active center of Buddhist pilgrimage. The great temple at Nara, Japan, played a decisive role in establishing the relationship between Buddhism and the Japanese imperial dynasty.

In the twentieth and twenty-first centuries, Buddhist temples have become common sights in Europe and North America. Los Angeles is sometimes called the most complex and varied Buddhist city in the world, and its many sacred sites include the sprawling Hsi Lai temple complex, established by a thriving Taiwanese Buddhist community.

The holy space created by Buddhist sacred architecture can be understood on a cosmic scale. For example, the central dome of a *stupa* stands for Mount Meru, the Buddhist cosmic mountain that marks the center of the world, and the parasols that rise above the *stupa*'s central axis represent the levels of heaven occupied by different categories of gods in ancient Indian tradition. Above the parasols, in the empty space of the sky, lies the formless realm attained by Buddhist "saints" in the highest levels of meditation, and the "*buddha*-fields"—

the dwelling places of celestial *buddha*s and *bodhisattva*s of Mahayana tradition. Thus, to perform a ritual circumambulation of a *stupa* is not simply to recall and venerate the life of the Buddha, but also to orient oneself firmly at the center of the cosmos.

In Indian tradition, the concept of the sacred center was particularly associated with the throne of the Buddha's awakening, or *bodhimanda*, at Bodh Gaya. According to Indian popular legends, all *buddha*s come to the same throne to achieve their awakening. The stone structure now visible under the Bodhi Tree at Bodh Gaya was said to be the top of a diamond throne extending down to the middle of the earth. The concept of the sacred "seat of enlightenment" can also be applied to sacred mountains, such as Mount Kailasa in Tibet and Mount Wutai in China, which are revered as the thrones of powerful *buddha*s or *bodhisattva*s.

Conversely, the idea of the sacred seat also serves to sanctify the simple space in which the ordinary Buddhist sits to meditate. Devotees of Zen remind themselves that the spot upon which they sit for meditation is the throne of all the *buddha*s of the past and future.

In the Buddhist tradition, the bodily relics and physical images of the Buddha that are venerated in shrines constitute his "Form Body." His teaching, known as his

"Dharma Body," is also the object of veneration, often quite literally. Some of the early Mahayana *sutra*s say that any place where the Dharma is expounded should be treated as a "shrine" (*chaitya*) of the Buddha, and classical Indian writings describe shrines where a copy of a Mahayana scripture is set up with great pomp and ceremony to serve as the focus of worship. Many Indian *stupas* contained sacred texts in place of the relics of the Buddha. Reverence for the physical scripture is also seen in Tibetan temples, where copies of the Mahayana *sutra*s lie on or around the altars, and in the esteem accorded to the *Lotus Sutra* by the Japanese sects tracing their origins to the social and religious reformer Nichiren.

In India and elsewhere the definition of a Buddhist temple or shrine could be quite fluid, and a place that was sacred on account of its association with the Buddha did not have to be marked by a major architectural monument. Many travelers' tales from ancient India tell of small but unusual features of the landscape that were linked with the life of the Buddha. It was claimed that marks on rocks in a stream near Sarnath had been made by the Buddha's robe as he crossed the stream. A ravine in a town near Shravasti had opened up, it was said, to swallow one of the Buddha's enemies. In many places there has been a lively cult of the Buddha's supposed footprints, most notably perhaps at Adam's Peak in Sri Lanka. According to Theravada tradition, the Buddha used his magical power to fly to Sri Lanka, and left the footprints as a mark of his visit.

For centuries, the sacred sites of the Buddhist tradition have also been the focus of pilgrimage. As indicated by the Chinese story *The Journey to the West*, places in northern India associated with the Buddha's life attracted pilgrims from as far away as China until the destruction of Indian Buddhism made such journeys impossible. Buddhists throughout southeast Asia make pilgrimages to sites sacred in their tradition, including Adam's Peak. Tibetans travel to central Tibet to the holy sites of Lhasa, and they make the grueling journey to the west of the country to circumambulate Mount Kailasa. Other mountains are also regular pilgrimage destinations. Chinese Buddhists make a journey to Mount Putuo on a small island off the coast of Zhejiang Province to pay homage to the *bodhisattva* Guanyin, who is said to reside there, and seek her favor. In Japan, Mount Fuji is venerated by many Buddhist sects.

The history of Japanese Buddhism is rich with the recollections of well-known pilgrims. Some, like the Zen founders Eisai and Dogen, traveled to China to pursue their quest for the Dharma. Others, like the poet

Matsuo Basho (1644–94), lived out their quest for awakening on the roads of Japan.

Buddhist sacred places may even by invisible. The apocalyptic *Kalachakra* ("Wheel of Time") *Tantra*, one of the last Tantric texts to appear in India, tells the story of a mythical kingdom named Shambhala, which lies hidden in the mountains to the north of India and is ruled by a righteous Buddhist king. The text prophesies a time when the forces of evil have conquered the world. Shambhala will then become visible and the righteous king will emerge from his citadel, surrounded by his armies, to defeat the forces of evil and reestablish the rule of the Dharma.

The prophecy of the *Kalachakra* represents a type of messianic speculation that has had important influence at certain stages of Buddhist history. For Tibetans, it serves not just as an image of an ideal Buddhist kingdom but also as an idealized symbolic goal for a *yogi* to attain through the process of meditation.

As the utopia of "Shangri-la," Shambhala has become bound up in the Western imagination with the idea of Tibet itself as an idealized Buddhist paradise, its ancient and sacred way of life preserved for centuries from outside influence by the impregnable mountain barrier of the Himalayas.

Guanyin's Home on Mount Putuo

" With brows of new moon shape

And eyes like two bright stars,

Her jadelike face beams natural joy,

And her ruddy lips seem a flash of red.

Her immaculate vase overflows with nectar from year

to year,

Holding sprigs of weeping willow green from age.

She disperses the eight woes;

She redeems the multitude;

She has great compassion;

Thus she rules on T'ai Mountain,

And lives in the South Sea.

She saves the good, searching for their voices,

Ever heedful and solicitous,

Ever wise and efficacious.

Here orchid heart delights in great bamboos;

Her chaste nature loves the wistaria.

She is merciful ruler of the Potalaka Mountain,

The Living Kuan-yin [Guanyin] from the Cave

of Tidal Sound. **"**

From *The Journey to the West*, Vol 1, translated by Anthony C. Yu. University of Chicago Press: Chicago, 1977, p.185.

Commentary

These lines from *The Journey to the West*, the sixteenth-century novel about the travels of the Chinese monk Xuanzang, show the connection between the *bodhisattva* Guanyin and the pilgrimage site at Mount Putuo, an island off the coast of southern China.

Buddhist sacred geography in China associates three mountains with three major *bodhisattva*s: Mount Wutai in Shanxi province is the home of Wenshu (Sanskrit, Manjushri), the *bodhisattva* of wisdom; Mount Emei in Sichuan is the home of Puxian (Sanskrit, Samantabhadra), the *bodhisattva* of virtuous action; and Mount Putuo in Zhejiang is the home of Guanyin (Sanskrit, Avalokiteshvara), the *bodhisattva* of compassion. Mount Putuo has come to be linked with Potalaka, the island home of Guanyin or Avalokiteshvara in Indian tradition.

One of the founding legends about Mount Putuo tells of a Japanese monk named Egaku who was sailing back home with an image of Guanyin. As his boat neared Mount Putuo, it became stuck. He prayed to Guanyin for help, and the boat was drawn to a cave on the shore known as the Cave of Tidal Sound. There Egaku established a shrine to the Guanyin "who refused to leave." Today, pilgrims come to Mount Putuo from all over China to seek the *bodhisattva*'s blessing.

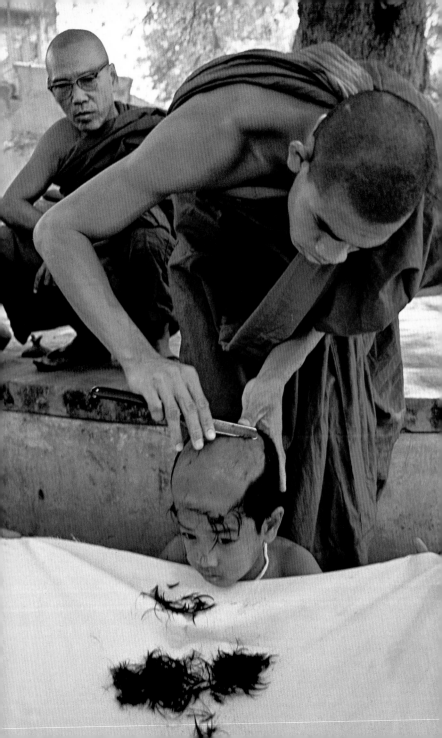

CHAPTER SEVEN

SACRED TIME

Buddhists mark the movements of the seasons and the stages of human life in many different ways. Some festivals and rituals are tied explicitly to events in the life of the Buddha, the preaching of the Dharma, or the practice of the monastic community, but some of the most important events, such as New Year celebrations and marriage ceremonies, are tied only loosely to Buddhist traditions.

On a larger scale, Buddhists have sometimes been influenced by a theory of historical stages, in which the present is believed to be a "degenerate age" and requires a simpler, more direct approach to the practice of the Dharma. Some Buddhists insist that the distinction between different moments in time is insignificant, and reality can only be experienced by absorption in the sacrality of the present.

LEFT: A Burmese boy has his head shaved prior to entering a monastery for a period of training as a novice monk.

For many Buddhists, the most significant festivals in the course of the year reflect stories about the life of the Buddha. In Sri Lanka and other Theravada countries of southeast Asia, the most important Buddhist holiday is "Buddha's Day," or Visakha Puja, which falls on the day of the full moon in the lunar month of Visakha (April–May). This festival commemorates the birth, enlightenment, and death of the Buddha. Devotees mark the occasion by visiting monasteries, venerating shrines or images of the Buddha, and listening to traditional sermons about his life. Tibetans also celebrate the key events of the Buddha's life, but on separate occasions at different times of the year. Most significant is the festival of the Buddha's conception, or incarnation, on the fifteenth day of the first lunar month, one of a range of events that mark the Tibetan New Year.

Celebrations may also center on personal relics of the Buddha. At Kandy, Sri Lanka, Buddhists turn out in July or August to witness the procession of what is believed to be one of the Buddha's teeth in a great festival that is more than a thousand years old. Faxian, a ninth-century Chinese pilgrim, wrote one of the earliest eyewitness accounts of this ancient celebration.

There are festivals in many Buddhist countries to honor important Buddhist teachings or scriptures.

Theravada devotees celebrate the Buddha's first sermon on the full moon of the eighth lunar month, a date that coincides with the beginning of the monsoon season, when monks go on an annual retreat. In Laos, the story of Prince Vessantara, one of the Buddha's previous incarnations (see illustration, p.118), is celebrated annually. Tibet commemorates the *Kalachakra Tantra* every year (see p.179), and Chinese and Japanese Buddhists have annual festivals in honor of Buddhist *sutra*s, most notably the *Lotus Sutra*.

In Theravada countries, the beginning of the *samgha*, or Buddhist community, is celebrated on the full moon of the third lunar month. Celebrants circumambulate Buddhist shrines and listen to sermons that praise the monks as a source of merit for their lay devotees. Individual countries commemorate the arrival of the monastic community on their own shores, and many monasteries honor the date of their foundation.

In south and southeast Asia, the monastic communities observe the custom of the "rain retreat" during the months of the monsoon (July to October). This custom goes back to the earliest days of Buddhism, when the rains made the roads impassable for wandering monks and they had to settle in monasteries for the duration of the season. For monks, the rain retreat is a time for focused study and meditation; for laypeople, its conclusion has become a time for lively celebration, when they join the monks in elaborate processions and make offerings of clothing and other necessities to sustain the monastic community for the coming year.

Worshippers in Kandy, Sri Lanka, celebrate during the annual festival in which the sacred relic of a tooth allegedly belonging to the Buddha is paraded through the streets.

One of the most important seasonal celebrations in Buddhist cultures, especially in East Asia, marks the coming of the New Year. In China and Japan the New Year celebration is connected only tangentially with Buddhist themes. The Tibetan New Year celebration includes a reference to some of the miraculous events in the Buddha's life, but its main ritual function is to exorcise the evil influences from the past year in order to bring prosperity and good fortune to the community.

An East Asian festival with more explicit Buddhist content is the Festival of the Dead. Celebrated in Japan in mid-July, the O-bon Festival commemorates the efforts of Maudgalyayana, one of the Buddha's first disciples, to save his deceased mother.

Rites of passage are as important to Buddhists as they are to other religious traditions. Buddhists in Theravada countries observe a series of rituals as a child moves from birth to adulthood. In Myanmar, special childhood rites include a pregnancy ceremony, a birth ceremony, a naming ceremony, an ear-piercing ceremony for girls, and a hair-tying ceremony for boys. Frequently there is little in such ceremonies that owes its origin directly to Buddhism (although Buddhist monks are often present to recite chants or prayers). However, once a boy reaches his early teens, monastic ordination often serves as a rite of passage to symbolize his transition from childhood to adulthood. Once ordained, a youth may spend only long enough in the monastery to learn the rules of monastic practice or how to read and write. However, he may decide to take the necessary vows and become a permanent member. The ordination ritual reenacts the events of the Buddha's own renunciation. The young man has his head shaved, dons monastic robes, and pronounces the phrases that indicate his entry into the order. (In the Mahayana lands, there is less stress on ordination as a coming-of-age ritual. But for the few young men or women who choose the monastic path, it is an equally decisive transition into another way of life.)

The same ambiguity that permeates childhood rites in Theravada countries often pertains to "Buddhist" weddings. The Buddha himself hardly serves as an affirmative model of marriage, since he left his family to become a wandering monk. In southeast Asia, Buddhist monks are often invited to weddings to receive offerings and chant auspicious texts, but the Buddhist element in the ceremonies seems only peripheral. In China, even for Buddhists, the ritual of marriage is traditionally governed by Chinese values of filial piety and respect for ancestors. In Japan, traditional weddings usually take place in a Shinto, rather than Buddhist, context.

However, funerals are a different matter. The Buddha's renunciation of his home and earthly comforts was provoked by a vision of old age, sickness, and death, and the rituals surrounding death are decisively linked to Buddhist values. In China, Korea, and Japan, people turn to Buddhist monks and priests to perform their funerals, and family ties with particular temples are often reinforced by yearly acts of offering and remembrance in honor of the deceased. In southeast Asia, funerals frequently last for several days and involve offerings and the chanting of *sutra*s. These are intended to bestow extra merit on the deceased for their benefit in the next life.

Buddhist views of sacred time are not limited to the movements of a single season or to the events of a single life. There is also a Buddhist tradition that relates to the decline of the Dharma from a golden age, that which existed during the life of the Buddha, to a degenerate age in which it is difficult to practice the Dharma in a traditional way. This concept had a profound influence on Japanese Buddhism during the Kamakura Period (1192–1333). Finally, it is important to recognize that for many Buddhists, distinctions in time are unimportant and awakening can occur at any moment.

The Degenerate Age of the Dharma

❝ The Lord Shakya proclaimed to all celestial beings
that when, in the fifth five hundred years after his
death, all the truths should be shrouded in darkness,
the Bodhisattva of Superb Action should be commissioned to save the most wicked of men who were
degrading the truth, curing the hopeless lepers by the
mysterious medicine of the adoration of the Lotus of
the Perfect Truth. Can this proclamation be a falsehood? If this promise be not in vain, how can the rulers
of the people of Japan remain in safety, who, being
plunged in the whirlpool of strife and malice, have
rebuked, reviled, struck, and banished the messengers
of the Tathagata and his followers commissioned by
Buddha to propagate the Lotus of Truth?

People will say that it is a curse; yet those who propagate the Lotus of Truth are indeed the parents of all
men living in Japan. . . . I, Nichiren, am the master and
lord of the sovereign, as well as of the Buddhists of other
schools. Notwithstanding this, the rulers and the people
treat us maliciously. . . . Therefore, also, the Mongols are
coming to chastise them. . . . It is decreed that all the
inhabitants of Japan shall suffer from the invaders. ❞

From "Nichiren's Account of the Degenerate Age of the Dharma" cited in Wm. Theodore de Bary, ed., *Sources of Japanese Tradition.* Columbia University Press: New York, 1958, pp.225–26.

Commentary

In common with the first few generations of many religions, early Buddhists had a sense that life was better when the founder of their tradition was still alive. From this idea grew a theory about the decline of the Dharma: for the first five hundred years after the Buddha's *parinirvana* it was possible to practice the true Dharma (*saddharma*); for the next five hundred years it was possible to have access only to a shadow of the true Dharma. In the "last days" (Chinese *mo-fa*, Japanese *mappo*), even this shadowy Dharma had begun to disappear.

This model of historical decline had significant influence on Buddhist practice in India, China, and Tibet, but its most striking impact came during the Kamakura Period (1192–1333) in Japan. There was social turmoil; the country was plagued by incessant warfare; and a Mongol invasion fleet threatened imminent catastrophe. Shinran and Nichiren, a pair of remarkable reformers, preached that the degenerate times called for a fundamental reorientation of Buddhist practice. For Shinran the solution was to trust in the saving grave of Amida Buddha; for Nichiren it was to rely on the power of the *Lotus Sutra*. Both reformers challenged prevailing religious authorities and spawned mass movements that changed the face of Buddhism in Japan.

CHAPTER EIGHT

DEATH AND THE AFTERLIFE

According to the traditional account of the Buddha's life, Siddhartha Gautama, the young man who was to become the Buddha, visited a park outside his palace. In this park, he saw three sights which confronted him with the problem of death: a sick man, an old man, and a corpse. On a later trip outside the palace, he encountered a wandering ascetic who had renounced ordinary life to escape the cycle of death and rebirth. These "Four Sights" inspired Siddhartha to follow the path of renunciation.

Like the Buddha, Buddhists share a keen awareness of death, and cultivate strategies to deal with its challenge—from the moral and spiritual disciplines that insure a favorable rebirth to the meditation and study that allow a person to be released from *samsara*, the endless cycle of death and rebirth.

LEFT: A Tibetan thangka (devotional painting) of the "Wheel of Life," which depicts the human cycle of death and rebirth. There are six realms of rebirth, and it is a person's actions in previous lives that determine which one he or she will enter.

Traditional Buddhist ideas about death are based on the ancient Indian doctrine of *samsara*, variously translated as "reincarnation," "transmigration," or simply "rebirth," but literally meaning "wandering"—from one lifetime to another. By the time of the Buddha, Indian religion had come to assume that life is cyclical: a person is born, grows old, dies, and is then reborn in another body to begin the process again. Rebirth can occur as a human being, deity, ghost, or animal; or else a person may be reborn to punishment in Hell.

The nature of an individual's reincarnation depends on *karma* or moral "action." Someone who accumulates merit or good *karma* in the course of a life will be reborn in a more favorable situation in a future life, perhaps even as a god. The reverse applies to those who perform bad actions. Before they can be reincarnated in a different form, the worst offenders have to eradicate their demerits by suffering in one of the layers of Hell, which are ranked according to the severity of their punishments. The lowest and worst level is reserved for people who have killed their parents or teacher. Just as the inhabitants of Hell can wipe out their sins and be reborn as humans once more, those who rise to divinity can exhaust their merit and slip back into the human realm. No matter how high a person rises on the scale of reincarnation, there is always a danger of slipping back down. No state of reincarnation is permanent.

Traditionally, people endeavor to avoid evil deeds and accumulate merit through acts of worship or donations to monks, in the hope of receiving a better birth in the next life. But Siddhartha Gautama saw *samsara* as an eternal grind of deaths and potential suffering and set out to break the cycle. According to Buddhist tradition, the moment of Siddhartha's "awakening" was under the tree at Bodh Gaya. After he had overcome the temptations of Mara, he entered a state of concentration and resolved that he would not get up until he had attained release from the cycle of death and rebirth.

The first of his insights was the knowledge of his previous births. This was followed by the knowledge of the births of others, and finally by the knowledge of the "Four Noble Truths": the "truth of suffering," the "truth of the origin of suffering," the "truth of the cessation of suffering," and the "truth of the Path." This can be explained as follows. The Buddha's "awakening" began with the realization that all life is filled with suffering, in particular the suffering that comes from seeing a beloved person, object, or experience pass away, as it inevitably must. He perceived that the origin of suffering lies in desire, and that desire comes from a misconception about the nature of things, in particular the nature of the self. By removing this ignorance, Siddhartha was able to bring suffering to an end in the experience that Buddhists call *nirvana*—a word which means literally to "blow out" the fire of ignorance and desire, states which the Buddha perceived to be the "fuel" of *samsara* and the source of suffering.

The Buddha achieved *nirvana* in two stages. At the moment of his "awakening", he realized that he was no longer fueling *samsara* by performing karmic actions—in other words, all desire in him had ceased. Decades later, at the moment of his death, known as his *parinirvana* or "final (or 'complete') *nirvana*," all the Buddha's residual *karma* was exhausted and he was completely released from *samsara*, never to be reincarnated.

Monks and nuns have attempted to follow the Buddha's example and achieve the same liberation from rebirth by renouncing their own attachment to the pleasures and responsibilities of lay life and practicing meditation and good moral conduct. For all Buddhists, the way to *nirvana* involves following precepts such as the "Noble Eightfold Path" (see p.165).

The tradition of Pure Land Buddhism, a form of Mahayana Buddhism that is found principally in China, Japan, and Tibet, holds that if a believer chants with

A 17th-century Japanese hanging scroll that depicts Amida Butsu (Amitabha, top left) surrounded by the faithful.

faith the name of the celestial *buddha* Amitabha (Chinese, Amituo; Japanese, Amida), the latter will visit the believer at the moment of death and convey him or her to rebirth in Sukhavati, the heavenly "Pure Land," or "Western Paradise." Here, free from earthly distractions, the devotee can prepare for *nirvana*, which is guaranteed to all who attain the Pure Land.

The practice of Pure Land Buddhism, or Amidism, has its roots in the ancient Indian idea that meditation on a particular deity at the moment of death will help ensure rebirth in that deity's celestial domain. Amidism continues to dominate the understanding of death in some of the most popular forms of Japanese Buddhism, particularly in the Jodoshu ("Pure Land School") and Jodo Shinshu ("True Pure Land School") movements in Japan and in the Buddhist Churches of America.

In Japanese Zen Buddhism, there is a tradition of composing a poem at the moment of death. These poems often give powerful expression to the sense of detachment that infuses the story of the Buddha's own *parinirvana*. One Zen warrior, who was forced to commit suicide out of loyalty to his feudal lord, wrote of death as a sharp-edged sword that cut through the void, and compared it to a cool wind blowing in a raging fire. It was as if his own sword were the sword of the Buddha's wisdom that cut through the illusions of life and blew out the fire of existence.

Buddhist funerals are intended to assist the deceased into a better birth. Tibetan funerals go a step further, aiming to ensure the person's liberation from *samsara*. The Tibetan *Book of the Dead* is one of the best-known Buddhist funeral texts. Over a period of as long as forty-nine days—said to be the length of time it takes for a person to be reborn in another life—a *lama* chants the words of the text, at first in the presence of the corpse and later before a picture of the deceased.

The text describes an array of benevolent and wrathful *buddha*s who will appear to the deceased in the "intermediate realm" (*bardo*) between death and rebirth, and explains that a person should recognize these forms as nothing but manifestations of his or her own mind. According to the text, it is possible for the deceased to unite with these forms and thereby be liberated from the cycle of death and rebirth. For those who are not successful in uniting with the *buddha* forms, the *Book of the Dead* goes on to explain how to achieve a positive incarnation in the next life. This practice seems to be directed as much at the living as the dead—it helps mourners to come to terms gradually with their loss, and to prepare themselves for their own transition out of this life.

Japanese Poems on the Moment of Death

⟦ The sharp-edged sword, unsheathed,

Cuts through the void—

Within the raging fire

A cool wind blows. ⟧   By Shiaku Sho'on

⟦ Throughout the frosty night

I lay awake. When morning bells

rang out, my heart grew clear—

upon this fleeting dream-world

dawn is waking. ⟧   By Hasegawa Shume

⟦ On a journey, ill:

my dream goes wandering

over withered fields. ⟧   By Matsuo Basho

⟦ Mt. Fuji's melting snow

is the ink

with which I sign

my life's scroll,

'Yours sincerely.' ⟧   By Kashiku

From *Japanese Death Poems*, compiled by Yoel Hoffmann. Charles E. Tuttle, Co.: Boston 1986, pp.51, 67, 85, 82.

Commentary

The religious traditions of ancient India put special emphasis on composing the mind at the moment of death, for that was the moment that prepared the way for rebirth in another life. Also, it was the moment when the personality or soul could become free from the rebirth altogether. The same emphasis is reflected in the Japanese tradition of writing poems when close to death.

The Japanese often make eloquent use of Buddhist images that express the fleeting, dreamlike, and sorrowful quality of experience in this world. They also reflect a longing for the incisive insight that will cut through the suffering of life and lead to an experience of detachment and peace. However, many Zen poets and practitioners insisted that it is misleading to focus solely on the moment of death—in their view, because every aspect of life is impermanent, there is no moment that does not share in the experience of death.

When the poet Matsuo Basho lay on his deathbed and his pupils hinted that he should leave them a death poem, he said that any of his poems could be considered a meditation on death. His response reflected the insight of the Zen master Dogen, who said: "Each moment is all being, is the entire world. Reflect now whether any world or any being is left out of the present moment."

CHAPTER NINE

SOCIETY AND RELIGION

The Buddhist community, or *samgha*, has four divisions: monks, nuns, laymen, and laywomen. The monks and nuns renounce the duties of ordinary lay people and live lives of simplicity. The laity marry, have families, grow crops, accumulate and distribute wealth, maintain order, and do everything to enable the inhabitants of the monasteries to pursue *nirvana*.

However, the simple divisions of Buddhist society are made more complex by the different roles that exist within the monastic community —by the complexity of occupations and functions within the lay community, and by the shifting relationships that bind the two orders of society, monastic and lay, together. In recent years, Buddhist communities have expressed Buddhist social teachings in new ways in order to respond to the challenge of modernity.

LEFT: His Holiness Tenzin Gyatso (1935–), the 14th Dalai Lama. Largely due to his influence, Tibetan Buddhism is one of the most prominent Buddhist cultures in the world today.

The Buddhist monastic community began as a group of wanderers who followed the Buddha through the towns and villages of northern India. As time went on, the monks and nuns adopted a more settled lifestyle. During the months of July and August, the monsoon rains forced them to stay in a fixed location. Out of this practice grew the institution of the monastery (*vihara*), which in time became the central institution in Buddhist life. Supported by the patronage of kings and wealthy donors, the great Indian monasteries became centers of learning, not just in Buddhist philosophy and ritual, but in secular arts such as literature, medicine, and astrology. Buddhist lands in southeast Asia in particular developed sophisticated monastic traditions that often were closely linked to royal power.

The tradition of Buddhist kingship looks back to Ashoka, a ruler of the Maurya empire in northern India in the third century BCE (see p.122), as the ideal *dharmaraja* or "righteous king." Ashoka converted to Buddhism after a particularly bloody military campaign and he attempted to promote a policy of *dharmavijaya*, "righteous conquest" by means of the Dharma rather than by force of arms. Buddhist monarchs have traditionally viewed themselves as "righteous rulers" in the style of Ashoka and have protected the monasteries in their domains in return for monastic recognition of their own legitimacy as rulers.

The most unusual variant of the institution of Buddhist kingship occurred in Tibet, where the "Great Fifth" Dalai Lama took advantage of the weakness of his rivals to become the country's full secular *and* religious leader. Tibet was governed by this distinctive combination of monastic and secular leadership for centuries until 1950, when the newly founded People's Republic of China invaded the country to enforce its claims to hegemony. The fourteenth Dalai Lama, Tenzin Gyatso, a youth of fifteen, remained in office but was forced to acknowledge Chinese overlordship.

In 1959 an uprising against Chinese rule provoked harsh intervention and the Dalai Lama fled to India. From this time, the Tibetan monasteries suffered severe persecution and many were destroyed, especially during the Cultural Revolution (1966–76). However, in the 1980s, controls on religious activities were relaxed and monastic life began again in some of its traditional centers. From exile in India, the Dalai Lama has continued to call for peaceful efforts to preserve Tibet's culture and autonomy. He was awarded the Nobel Peace Prize in 1989. But China has been unreceptive to his appeals and seeks to control Tibetan religious affairs.

Aung San Suu Kyi (1945–) reads a statement at the gate of her home, to which she has been mainly confined by the Burmese military because of her pro-democracy activities.

Buddhists around the world, while respecting the large and socially influential monasteries, also retain a reverence for the individual "saint" who retires in solitude or with a small group of companions to seek *nirvana* away from the affairs of society. The forest-saints of Sri Lanka or Thailand are often treated as the great heroes of the tradition and provide an important counterweight to, and critique of, life in the major monasteries and society as a whole. When Dogen, the founder of the Soto Zen sect in Japan, rejected the requests of an imperial envoy to involve himself in the life of the Japanese court, and threw the envoy out of his monastery, he was enacting an ancient Buddhist ideal of withdrawal from the affairs of state.

The relationship between monks and ordinary laypeople is best seen in the ancient practice of the morning begging round, still observed in southeast Asia. Each day, monks leave the monastery and go from house to house to beg their food for that day. This simple ritual ties the monks and laity together in a network of mutual support. The monks receive the alms that aid their quest for *nirvana*, and laypeople are offered a daily opportunity to practice generosity and thereby accumulate merit that will lead them to a better rebirth in the next life. This reflects the broader idea of "interdependent causation" taught by the Buddha. According to this, every person has a distinct role to play in the framework of Buddhist society, but all are bound together in a network of mutual dependence.

In the nineteenth and twentieth centuries, the traditional structures of Buddhist society in southeast Asia have been shaken by the challenges of European colonialism, secularism, Communism, and modern science. Under the influence of the modernist and scientific vision of Buddhism developed by the Theosophical Society, the Sri Lankan monk Anagarika Dharmapala (1864–1933) led an important movement to rationalize Buddhist practice, strip away "superstitious" aspects, and mobilize the Buddhist community in a struggle against British colonial rule. Since Sri Lanka (as Ceylon) gained independence in 1948, Buddhist institutions have flourished there, but not without struggle. Ethnic violence between Buddhist Sinhalese and Hindu Tamils has introduced an element of religious conflict into Sri Lankan society that seems difficult to reconcile with the image of Buddhist tolerance and peacefulness.

Myanmar is particularly notable for its distinctive vision of the active relationship between Buddhism and politics. After independence (as Burma) from Britain in 1948, the first prime minister, U Nu (1907–95), promulgated a program of reform referred to as "Buddhist Socialism." U Nu said that a true socialist state should promote equality, discourage acquisitive instincts, and provide enough leisure so that the people may devote time to meditation and the pursuit of *nirvana*. Ousted by the military in 1962, U Nu lived in exile in India for a number of years before returning to Myanmar in 1980 and becoming a Buddhist monk.

In other parts of southeast Asia, Buddhists have faced the challenge of living under secularizing Communist regimes. In Vietnam, for example, Buddhist institutions have remained fairly active, but in Cambodia they suffered massively from the devastation wrought nationally by the Khmer Rouge government of 1975–79 and are still recovering.

The twentieth century also saw an attempt to revive Buddhism in its homeland of India as part of a critique of the traditional caste system. Dr. Bhimrao Ramji Ambedkar (1891–1956), an "Untouchable" from the Indian state of Maharashtra, saw in Buddhism an ideal of equality and social justice that could relieve the oppression of the disadvantaged castes in Indian society. He created an important social movement based on Buddhist principles that continues to play a role in Indian religious life and politics.

A Spiritual Revolution

❝ The quintessential revolution is that of the spirit, born of an intellectual conviction of a need for change in those mental attitudes and values which shape the course of a nation's development. A revolution which aims merely at changing official policies and institutions with a view to improvement in material conditions has little chance of genuine success. Without a revolution of the spirit, the forces which produce the iniquities of the old order would continue to be operative. . . . It is not enough merely to call for freedom, democracy and human rights. There has to be a united determination . . . to make sacrifices in the name of enduring truths, to resist the corrupting influence of desire, ill will, ignorance, and fear.

Saints, it has been said, are the sinners who keep on trying. So free men are the oppressed who go on trying and who in the process make themselves fit to bear the responsibilities . . . which will maintain a free society . . . . A people who would build a nation in which strong, democratic institutions are firmly established as a guarantee against state-induced power must first learn to liberate their own minds from apathy and fear. ❞

From *Freedom From Fear and Other Writings* by Aung San Suu Kyi. Penguin: London, 1991, p.183.

Commentary

In July 1988, the Burmese ruler General Ne Win, head of the Myanmar Socialist Programme Party, held a national referendum on the country's political future. Popular opposition to authoritarian military rule crystallized around the figure of Aung San Suu Kyi, who has become one of the most celebrated examples of a person who brings Buddhist religious values to bear on secular affairs. Her father, Aung San, was a colleague of U Nu and had led the movement for national independence until his assassination in 1947.

Aung San Suu Kyi's political writings, gathered in a collection called *Freedom From Fear*, speak eloquently about a modern quest for democracy and human rights, about the traditional Buddhist values of truth, fearlessness, and loving kindness, and about the connection between spiritual and political forms of liberation. In recognition of her campaign for peaceful democratic reforms, she was awarded the Nobel Peace Prize in 1991.

As Aung San Suu Kyi's career demonstrates, it is possible for women to play an important role in the political life of the modern Buddhist countries of southeast Asia. But it cannot be denied that traditional ideas of male dominance are still deeply rooted in the culture of this and other regions.

PART THREE:

TAOISM

INTRODUCTION

The principal focus of Taoism is the Tao (meaning "Way," or "path"), which refers to a nameless, formless, all-pervasive power which brings all things into being and reverts them back into non-being in an eternal cycle. The tradition stresses the importance of following the way of the Tao—that is, of taking no action that is contrary to nature, and of finding one's place in the natural order of things. Understanding the pattern of the Tao includes the ability of trained specialists to control spiritual powers, which are either inferior to the Tao or emanations of it. Overall, the concept of the Tao provides a structure for making sense of the change of seasons, the life-cycle of creation, and the individual's place in the world.

Taoism has had a significant impact on the development of Chinese civilization and its ideas pervade virtually all aspects of the culture (see pp.305–311). Some of Taoism's most surprising contributions to Chinese and world civilization have been scientific. In the course of deciphering the pattern of the natural world in order to benefit humankind, a number of important discoveries were made. For example, the search for the "elixir of immortality" led not only to the invention of gunpowder (see p.308), but also to notable advances in Chinese medicine (see p.244 and pp.298–299). In the effort to align human life with cosmic energy, the magnetic compass was also devised—its first use was in *fengshui*, the art of fixing the most auspicious site for buildings and structures.

Despite its influence on Chinese civilization, Taoism has been notoriously difficult to define—this is largely attributable to the many different and distinctive forms the tradition has adopted throughout its history (see pp.222–226). This historical complexity is partly due to the fact that Taoists have always been willing to absorb new ideas, personalities, and practices, including philosophical discourses, fresh revelations, the activities and techniques of shamans and makers of elixirs, and various deities. The schools of Taoism have never been united under a central authority, and the development of systematic teachings has not been an overriding concern, although

An early 18th-century jade statuette depicting Taoist deities being worshipped by pilgrims.

there is an organic unity in the various expressions of Taoism, particularly in the quest for longevity.

The Taoist contribution to Chinese religious practice and belief has been both overt and subtle. It is highly visible in some of the most important rituals, notably healing rites and funerals, and in techniques to attain immortality. However, in most other areas of religious practice its presence is less obvious. Chinese religion is an amalgam of the "Three Teachings" (Confucianism, Taoism, Buddhism) and the folk tradition. All three formal teachings provide methods for self-cultivation and transformation, but have different approaches which reflect concerns specific to each. Confucianism primarily addresses matters of government and social behavior. Buddhism provides an elaborate cosmology, a structured priesthood, and a detailed theory of the afterlife. Taoism meets other needs, and offers methods of spiritual and physical healing, a means of commerce with the spirit world, and securing blessings and protection. The popular tradition is typified by practices that vary by region; the worship, both locally and nationally, of hosts of deities; and by folk beliefs that cannot be categorized as coming from any of the formal traditions. Of the three major teachings, Taoism is the most closely linked to the popular tradition, but has remained distinct from it.

Relatively few people identify themselves as exclusively Taoist or Confucian, and there is considerable evidence to suggest that many members of the historic Confucian literati were also practitioners of Taoist arts. In the modern era, just as in the past, rather than professing a single doctrinal affiliation most Chinese people draw simultaneously from elements of all the teachings. Religious holidays reflect this syncretism— few of them can be identified as belonging specifically to any one tradition and most reveal influences from all the traditions. Taoist concerns and practices are clearly expressed in the quest for longevity and in sensitivity toward the seasonal patterns of change in nature.

Historically, Confucianism and Taoism have always served as foils for each other, and are examples of *yin-yang* complementarity in Chinese religion: the image of the worldly Confucian is contrasted with the Taoist recluse seeking an escape from human concerns; and the Confucian observance of the rules of etiquette is set against the Taoist's frequent flouting of social convention. Similar divisions were, and still are, often apparent within individuals: for example, a person may exhibit Confucian values in their professional life, but express Taoist qualities when retired or relaxing with friends—particular modes of being are chosen when considered most appropriate.

Despite the fact that Taoism is an essential element of East Asian culture, with an extensive literature and significant history, knowledge of Taoism has been, until recently, largely limited to a few philosophical texts. This is partly due to the nature of the Taoist canon itself—the abstruseness of many of the texts made them extremely difficult to decipher. As a rule, the canon was not studied by the Confucian élite who, for political reasons, were sometimes at odds with Taoist clergy. Additionally, very few copies of the canon were available until the twentieth century. Western scholars were also slow to begin serious study of Taoism, in comparison with Buddhism and Confucianism. Influenced by the biases of some prominent Chinese scholars, many of the first Western scholars of Chinese religion were missionaries who were appalled by the Taoist magical and exorcistic traditions. To their eyes, Taoism, as practiced by priests and people, seemed to be a debased and superstitious version of the lofty and philosophical tradition of antiquity. It was only in the latter half of the twentieth century that Taoism's complex, elaborate religious tradition began to be plumbed and appreciated—this process was assisted by recent archeological discoveries in tombs at Mawangdui and Guodian.

In addition to being a major component of Chinese society, Taoism also made an impact on Korean, Japanese, and Vietnamese civilizations, all of which were influenced by Chinese culture in the early centuries of the Common Era. Taoism's presence was relatively understated in these countries, and the tradition was integrated unobtrusively with local religious practices, especially nature cults, geomancy, divination, and shamanism. This influence became increasingly diffuse in later centuries. Many practices affiliated with Taoism, such as *taiji quan*, *qigong*, acupuncture, and traditional Chinese medicine, continue to thrive, not only within East Asia, but outside the region as well.

The Taoist priesthood is strong in Taiwan, and Taoist communities have reappeared in mainland China in recent decades. Taoism has made inroads in the West too, where the availability of numerous translations of the *Tao Te Ching* have helped to boost its popularity and contributed to the establishment of a few nascent Taoist organizations and religious communities. There has also been a move to develop a Taoist-inspired ecology. Part of Taoism's appeal to Westerners undoubtedly lies in its naturalistic mysticism and in its concept of a universe in which humans and the natural world are integrated.

CHAPTER ONE

ORIGINS AND HISTORICAL DEVELOPMENT

Taoism has a complex history, established over several centuries. Traditionally, a distinction has been made between "philosophical" Taoism, identified as one of many strands of thought that arose during the Late Warring States Period (403–221BCE), and "religious" Taoism, which denotes a variety of religious movements, communities, scriptures, and practices, the first of which appeared at the end of the Han dynasty (206BCE–220CE).

The tradition has proved difficult to define because it draws on a wide range of apparently divergent ideas and practices. However, there is continuity between both the religious and philosophical traditions, particularly in the quest for longevity, the use of quiescence as a mode of being and cultivation, and identification of the Tao ("Way") as the source of all things.

LEFT:
A 17th-century Chinese painting depicting three Taoist deities, associated with long life, wealth and good fortune, studying a yin-yang banner.

Studies of Taoism usually begin with the figure of Laozi (see pp.232–233) and his text, the *Tao Te Ching* (the *Classic of the Way and its Power,* also known as the *Laozi*), traditionally dated to the sixth century BCE, but now thought to be a later text (see p.242). However, it is clear that the teachings contained in the text were developed in the context of ideas that were established well before the sixth century. These include divination, especially as articulated in the *Yijing* (*Book* or *Classic of Changes*); the theory of the complementary forces of *yin* and *yang*; the mutually engendering, mutually destroying "Five Phases" (see pp.272–273); and the notion of *ch'i*, the vital matter or life energy of which all things are made. Other early influences on the tradition included the shamans who commanded spirits, related ecstatic spirit journeys, and engaged in exercises that induced mysticism and deep, contemplative states. All these elements were key to the development of Taoism.

In addition to the *Tao Te Ching*, the classic works of philosophical Taoism are the *Zhuangzi* (fourth century BCE), the *Huainanzi* (second century BCE), and the *Liezi* (ca. third to fourth century CE; see pp.242–243). These texts stress mysticism, the virtue of performing no action (*wu-wei*) that is contrary to nature, and learning and following the mysterious, constantly changing pattern of the cosmos, the Tao. There are also references in the first and last texts to meditative practices, to "perfected beings" who fly among the stars, to developing the capacity to "nourish life," to the limitations of human knowledge, and speculation concerning the relationship between the cosmos and humanity. Although each text is distinctive, commonality in subject matter created a loosely identifiable school of thought.

At the time of the first school of religious Taoism at the end of the Han dynasty, the spiritual landscape of China had developed in several important ways. By the third century BCE, individuals knowledgeable in techniques for achieving immortality—the *fangshi*, or "gentlemen with recipes" (see pp.254–256)—were hired by imperial courts to reveal their secrets. By the beginning of the Common Era, Laozi had been elevated to the status of a god, Taishang Laojun, or Most High Lord Lao. The introduction of Buddhism to China brought the concepts of retribution and reincarnation, as well as an elaborate pantheon and a highly organized religious tradition. The chaos at the end of the Han saw a rise in millenarian and messianic hopes, some by groups claiming revelation from the deified Laozi.

One such group, the Yellow Turbans, preached the coming of a golden age and emphasized therapeutic practices to increase one's lifespan and bring about spiritual purity. The Yellow Turbans rebelled in eastern China in 184CE, declaring the founding of a new state and a new era. The rebellion was quashed, but another group, the Way of the Celestial Masters, was established in Szechwan in the same year. The founder, Zhang Daoling, established himself as Celestial Master, the head of a theocracy with an elaborately ordered hierarchy. Confession and repentance, including expiation of sin through public works, were offered as the means to healing and salvation (for one's ancestors as well as for oneself). In 215CE, the grandson of Zhang Daoling relinquished authority to the new political order; in return, the school received royal patronage.

The Celestial Masters moved south in the beginning of the fourth century as political vicissitudes destabilized the north. There the school encountered another current of religious practice which focused on the achievement of longevity through medicinal, alchemical, and magical pursuits. The coming together of these two distinctive traditions, one with an elaborate communal structure, the other with a focus on individual perfection and salvation, resulted in a new Taoist sect, Shangqing (Highest Purity) Taoism. Based on Mount Mao, the movement was also known as the Mao Shan school.

Shangqing was initiated between 364 and 370CE by a series of revelations from a group of spirit beings from the Heaven of Highest Purity. The school emphasized interiorization and visual meditation, viewing the interior of the body as a microcosm of the universe. Scriptures were considered especially holy, and were carefully guarded from the uninitiated; Shangqing thus flourished among the élite. Another school of the south, Lingbao (Numinous Jewel), drew from the Celestial Masters' practices, Shangqing's revelations, and the Mahayana Buddhist idea of universal salvation. The Lingbao school elaborated and systematized liturgy and rituals—these are still practiced today.

The Lingbao connection with Mahayana Buddhism reflects a larger trend at this time. The Period of Disunity (265–589CE) saw tremendous growth and popularity in Buddhism. Buddhists and Taoists vied for royal patronage with varied success. Both were changed as a result, most famously in the development of Chan (Zen) Buddhism, an amalgam of Taoist and Buddhist ideas.

Taoism enjoyed tremendous support during the Tang dynasty (618–907CE). The imperial family shared Laozi's surname, Li, and traced its lineage to him. The dynasty supported monasteries and temples, established Laozi's birthday as a national holiday, and decreed that each family was to have a copy of the *Tao Te Ching*. It became compulsory reading in the civil service exams, which traditionally had used only Confucian texts. The Song dynasty (960–1279CE) also traced its lineage to an important god of the Taoist pantheon. The Taoist canon was first printed in the twelfth century.

Of the many new schools that emerged in the Song and Yuan (1279–1368CE) dynasties, two have remained active to this day—the Quanzhen (Complete Perfection) and Zhengyi (Orthodox Unity), whose main temples are in Beijing. The Quanzhen founder, Wang Zhe, supported a syncretic religion of the "Three Teachings" (Confucianism, Taoism, and Buddhism), and demanded the study of their respective classics. It was the first school to mandate celibacy for adepts. When Wang Zhe's disciple Qiu

A bronze statuette depicting Laozi as an old man mounted on a buffalo, the animal that was said to have carried him out of China across the western border.

Changchun was summoned to court by Genghis Khan to reveal the secrets of longevity, Qiu recommended sleeping apart from the imperial harem for one night, which would be "more beneficial than taking elixirs for 1,000 days." Quanzhen emphasized interior alchemy (see p.298) as part of its method for internal purification. The Zhengyi (Orthodox Unity) was the restored Celestial Masters school. Unlike the celibate Quanzhen practitioners, Zhengyi priests marry and pass on the lineage to their descendants. The patriarchs of this school are believed to be descendants of Zhang Daoling. The 64th Celestial Master resides today in Taiwan.

In the twentieth century, Taoism suffered many setbacks. Religious freedom is guaranteed in the People's Republic, but "superstition" is to be eradicated—the practices of priests have sometimes been defined thus and suppressed. Considerable disruption took place during the Cultural Revolution (1966–1976), including the destruction of temples and texts. Today, Taoists operate under the auspices of the National Taoist Association, and there is some indication of renewed growth. The situation in Taiwan and some overseas communities is, however, quite different: the demand for the services of Taoist priests is great, and they are hired for festivals, funerals, and rituals at community temples.

Tao: The Origin of Creation

❝ There is a thing chaotic yet formed,

It was born before Heaven and Earth.

Silent.

Empty.

It is self-sufficient; it does not change.

It goes in all directions, but is not exhausted.

It could be considered the mother of all creation.

I do not know its name; I call it Tao.

If forced to name it, I would call it Great.

Being great, it fades away.

Fading away, it becomes distant.

Becoming distant, it reverses.

Therefore,

Tao is great.

Heaven is great.

Earth is great.

The king is great.

Within the boundaries of the land there are four great

things, and the king is one.

The person follows the pattern of earth.

Earth follows the pattern of Heaven.

Heaven follows the pattern of Tao.

And Tao follows the pattern of Nature. **❞**

From Laozi's *Tao Te Ching*, Chapter 25, translated by Jennifer Oldstone-Moore.

Commentary

Much is disputed about the *Tao Te Ching*—its authorship, dating, and meaning—but what is clear is that
it has been foundational to the Taoist tradition, a source
of great inspiration throughout history (see p.242).
The text is about *Tao*, the "Way," and *Te* (or *de*), "virtue"
or "power," which is the activated power of Tao in
manifest creation.

Taoists identify the origins of the cosmos as the Tao,
a nameless, formless power and pattern which effort-
lessly and spontaneously brings all things into being.
After fruition, it reverts to its origins where the cycle
begins again. The *Tao Te Ching* advises quiescence, and
wu-wei, or taking no action that is contrary to nature. It
also exalts the humble and lowly with the compelling
image of water that always moves to the lowest place,
and yet can wear away stone.

This chapter relates several of the Tao's key attributes:
undifferentiated yet complete, formless and nameless, the
source of all things, one with the movement and changes
of Nature, eternal. The mystical oneness of the Tao is at
the heart of the manifold practices and thoughts of the
Taoist tradition, which themselves change and mutate
into variety and color, but which nevertheless ultimately
depend on the ineffable and colorless Origin.

CHAPTER TWO

ASPECTS OF THE DIVINE

The divine manifests in a variety of ways in Taoism. In one sense, all creation is an expression of the divine, as all things come from the Tao ("Way"), and all eventually return to it. But Tao is not a supreme being, it is a cosmic principle, permeating and infusing all aspects of creation with vitality.

In seeming contradiction to this unity is the vast number of gods and deities who inhabit the cosmos. First there are divinities that are manifestations of primordial energy. Then there are gods of the created world: some are ancient deities adopted by Taoism, others are gods of the popular tradition, powerful figures promoted to the celestial bureaucracy after death. The contrast between the One and the many is appropriate: Tao is the cosmic principle that describes the unity behind myriad creation.

LEFT: This Ming dynasty (1454) hanging scroll depicts Fuxing, Luxing, and Shouxing, three popular deities, who were associated with conferring happiness, high salaries, and longevity. Their attendant holds a parasol with banners aloft.

In Taoism, the source of the divine is the Tao. Originally meaning "road" or "way" in the texts of Chinese philosophy, in Taoism it becomes the cosmic principle that permeates and transcends all things. The Tao informs the pattern by which things become manifest, and is thus the Way of transformation and nature. It gives each creature its *de*, or distinctive power, once creation is brought forth. Formless, timeless, and limitless, the Tao, which begins as primordial chaos, gives rise to primordial or original *qi*, then *yin* and *yang*, then myriad creation. Tao generates and sustains all things in an eternal ebb and flow from chaos to form and back to elemental chaos.

The Tao is known in the human realm through gods and divinities who have manifested themselves throughout history. One of the most important is the deified Laozi, Taishang Laojun, Lord Lao Most High (see pp. 222–223). By the Han era, Laozi was firmly established as a god; over time, he was considered coeval with primordial Tao from which he emerged prior to the formation of the universe. Scriptures describe a series of incarnations and metamorphoses during which he "waxed and waned with the seasons" before his miraculous conception by a virgin, eighty-one year gestation and birth through his mother's armpit. Lord Lao is the source of many Taoist revelations, including those in 142CE to Zhang Daoling (see p.234).

There are descriptions and illustrations of Lord Lao's many incarnations, including his role as advisor to the sage kings of antiquity. In some texts, he is a messianic savior to the masses who will bring an era of great peace. According to the *Huahu jing* (*Scripture of the Conversion of the Barbarians,* written around 300CE), after Laozi left China he continued his journey to India, where he became incarnate as the Buddha, seeking to bring the Way to those outside China. In the seventh century, Laozi was canonized as the "Sovereign Ancestor of the Most High Mysterious Origin," and worship of him was officially mandated. Through example, scripture, revelation, and incarnation, Laozi and his divine manifestations are key sources for understanding the Tao.

There are a number of other divinities that are emanations of the Tao; many are grouped in triads. They are from the remote heavens, pure and untouched by the created world. T'ai-i, the Supreme One, is understood cosmologically as the first stirring of the Tao, and also as a personified deity. As a deity, Taiyi is a part of a triad, the Three Ones, which plays an important role in the microcosmic/macrocosmic scheme of Taoism, whereby all the gods of the cosmos are found in the body. The Three Ones reside not only in the cosmos but also in the three "cinnabar fields," or vital centers, of the body.

A Ming dynasty shrine showing the Taoist god Zhenwu (top) riding a mythical beast. The middle grotto is occupied by the Three Pure Ones. At the bottom (center) sits the Jade Emperor.

Moreover, they have come to refer to the three vital forces of the body: breath, essence (or semen), and spirit. In practices of internal alchemy, these forces are cultivated to create an "embryo of immortality," the foundation of an immortal body (see p.299).

Another important triad is the Three Pure Ones: the Heavenly Worthy of the Original Beginning, the Heavenly Worthy of the Numinous Jewel, and the Heavenly Worthy of Tao and Te, who is none other than Laozi. The Three Pure Ones are rarely worshipped by the general populace; they are representations of the abstract power of the Tao. Instead of granting favors, they are invoked by Taoist priests in liturgies of cosmic renewal, such as the great *jiao* ritual (see p.267), bringing the creative energy of the Tao to renew community bonds.

Gods are understood and addressed as administrators and bureaucrats. The oral and ritual language used to address them follows the protocol of the Chinese imperial court. It was necessary to name and visualize these gods accurately, and an important part of training included revealing to the adept, in careful detail in documents called registers, how to do this. In visualization exercises, adepts work to establish and maintain the Three Ones in their bodies, thereby cultivating the vital forces to ensure longevity and immortality.

The Taoist pantheon includes many astral gods, and gods of natural formations, such as important rivers and sacred mountains. Gods who were popular before the development of religious Taoism were, over time, absorbed into an ever-growing Taoist pantheon. Examples include the Yellow Emperor (Huang Di) and the Queen Mother of the West (Xiwang mu). The Yellow Emperor is a ruler of antiquity, revered in the Confucian as well as Taoist tradition. He is considered to be an ideal ruler; the ancestor of all Chinese people, he was an adept in the arts of self-cultivation and longevity. One of Lord Lao's incarnations was as the Yellow Emperor's advisor, and together they signify the ideal relationship between ruler and advisor.

The Queen Mother of the West is referred to in the *Zhuangzi* (see pp.242–243) as one who has "obtained the Tao," and is thus immortal. One of the most popular deities of the Han dynasty, she was worshipped by royalty and common folk alike. In 3BCE veneration of her inspired a millenarian movement in which large groups of people traveled west or waited in expectation of her imminent arrival to bring about a new age of peace and prosperity. She advised ancient rulers on leadership and self-cultivation and is particularly revered in Taoism for her techniques of immortality. (See also pp.238–239.)

Over the centuries, Taoism also absorbed the gods of the popular pantheon. These gods have human origins and gain their rank as gods when promoted to the celestial bureaucracy after death. At the apex of the celestial bureaucracy is the Jade Emperor. Sometimes identified as the younger brother of the Heavenly Worthy of the Original Beginning, he is the link between the pure Taoist heavens and the gods of the bureaucracies. He oversees the numerous gods of the popular tradition and is the celestial counterpart of the terrestrial emperor.

The gods of the popular tradition include a variety of personages, some of whom are widely worshipped today. Mazu, for example, was officially recognized as a goddess after two centuries of popular veneration, and was promoted in the celestial hierarchy. Finally, in the seventeenth century, she became Empress of Heaven, a consort of the Jade Emperor. Another popular god, Guandi, was a historical folk hero. He was known for his ferocity, courage, and unswerving loyalty to his blood brothers and to his king. He was captured and executed in 219CE—his story is told in the *Romance of the Three Kingdoms*, a famous novel from the Ming dynasty. Like Mazu, his popular following grew until it gained imperial recognition, and he was granted titles by the emperor for his exemplary work as a god.

The Queen Mother of the West Visits Emperor Wu

" The host of transcendents numbered several tens of
thousands. Their glow made the courtyard resplendent
all the way to the eaves. Once she had arrived, one did
not know their whereabouts, one only saw the Queen
Mother, riding a Purple Cloud sedan yoked to a nine-
colored striped dragon. Set apart on the side were fifty
heavenly transcendents ... The Queen Mother ascended
the royal audience hall, faced east and sat down. She
wore a full-length, lined, yellow damask gown. The
pattern and color of the gown were fresh and bright,
and her luminous bearing was pure and solemn. As her
belt she wore the Numinous Flying Great Sash. Slung
from her waist was the two-edged Image Separating
sword, and her hair was dressed with the Great Flower
hair knot. She wore on her head the headdress of the
Grand Perfected Dawn Infant; on her feet she wore
slippers with the Primal Gem Phoenix pattern. When
one looked at her, one could guess her age to be about
thirty; her height was perfect. Her heavenly demeanor
veiled the bright, lush carpet of flowers. Her visage
eclipsed the beauties of the age. She was truly a divine,
numinous personage. "

From the *Han Wudi neizhuan*, translated by Jennifer Oldstone-Moore.

Commentary

One of the most important goddesses, Xiwang mu, the Queen Mother of the West (see p.236), is "the queen of immortals and a symbol of the highest *yin*." At her abode on sacred Kunlun mountain grow various herbs and fruits that can promote longevity, including the famous peaches of immortality which ripen every 3,000 years and grant those fortunate enough to eat them 3,000 years of extended life. Legend has it that she visited the Han ruler Wu in 110BCE on the seventh day of the seventh month, gracing him with immortality peaches, sacred texts, and powerful talismans—a story first told in the *Han Wudi neizhuan* (*Inner Story of the Han Emperor Wu*), dating from the fourth or fifth century CE.

In early references, she is dangerous and wild—a human with dishevelled hair and tiger fangs. But she is later described as a beautiful goddess who greets suppliants with the splendor appropriate to a queen. Her youthfulness was attributed, in part, to her artful sexual practices. The Queen Mother of the West was sought out by adepts seeking immortality and a divine audience. Mount Kunlun was understood to be a pivot between Heaven and Earth, a place visited by gods. Ascending this sacred mountain was considered to be both a literal and symbolic progression through immortality practices.

務成子

老君扵夏禹時師務成子說開天經教以理化
之道帝行之治滔滔之水鑿龍門導九河手足
胼胝唁呱呱而泣三度過門不顧功成得天錫

CHAPTER THREE

SACRED TEXTS

The literature of Taoism includes a vast collection of works, from revelations, genealogies, and codes of conduct to sacred diagrams. The Taoist canon, currently in its 1445 edition, runs to 1,120 volumes. Few copies were to be seen outside of Taoist temples and monasteries until it became widely available after reprinting in 1926—and its unexplored depths are now the focus of considerable scholarly inquiry.

There are non-canonical texts too. Archives have yielded collections of scriptures, as have such archeological finds as the Dunhuang caves, which were sealed in the eleventh century and only reopened in 1900. Other works have been discovered inscribed on stone and bronze. Most Taoist scriptures are regarded as verbal articulations of the Tao, made accessible for moral, spiritual, and physical cultivation.

LEFT: An early 12th-century silk handscroll depicting the ninth of ten manifestations of Laozi (see pp. 24–5). In this incarnation, he appears as an imperial instructor, guiding the development of Chinese civilization.

At the heart of Taoism is the *Tao Te Ching* (the *Classic of the Way and its Power*). Tradition has it that these teachings were written in the sixth century BCE by Lao-tzu, a royal archivist. Disillusioned with court life, he set off for the western mountains mounted on an ox. At the Chinese frontier a guard asked him for his teachings—the result of this request was the *Tao Te Ching*, a brief text of just over 5,000 Chinese characters. It is written in mystical and allusive language, addresses the importance of taking no action contrary to nature (*wu-wei*); makes reference to methods and attitudes for preserving one's life; and gives examples of the Way of the sage ruler. Also known as the *Laozi*, the text is now thought to be the work of several people and to date from the fourth century BCE; it is likely that Laozi is a mythological figure.

The second great work of philosophical Taoism is the *Zhuangzi*, named for its fourth-century BCE author, Zhuangzi (Master Zhuang), otherwise called Zhuang Zhou. His work is addressed to the private individual rather than to the ruler. Zhuangzi delights in the infinite manifestations of the Tao and in its imperviousness to human values. He considers the nature of reality and reflects on the endless variations and transformations that occur in life and also in death, which he sees as a blending with the Tao. Zhuangzi speaks of Immortals—perfected individuals who live on mountains, feed on the wind, sip the dew, and experience ecstatic flight. All these ideas became central to the tradition of religious Taoism. It is thought that Zhuangzi wrote seven of the chapters; the other twenty-six were perhaps the work of his students.

Two other great works of philosophical Taoism are the second-century BCE *Huainanzi* (*Master of Huainan*) and the *Liezi* (ca. third to fourth century CE; and, like the *Zhuangzi*, named after its author). The *Huainanzi* demonstrates how time, cosmos, and human action are mutually responsive and connected. The *Liezi* describes the Tao and its changes in a variety of stories indicating the marvels found in creation.

There are thousands of texts from the schools and practices that emerged in the Common Era. One of the most important was the *Bao Puzi* (the *Master who Embraces Simplicity*) by Ge Hong, dated to 320CE. Ge Hong was a member of a southern aristocratic family connected with the Shangqing school. His text addresses the form of meditation of that time and the practice of alchemy; it shows influence from the *fangshi*, or "gentlemen with recipes" (see pp.254–256), and the shamanistic tradition of south China. The *Bao Puzi* is divided into "inner" (esoteric, Taoist) and "outer" (ethical, Confucian) chapters. The inner chapters relate secret methods and techniques for gaining immortality, including the creation of elixirs of immortality from mineral substances. The outer chapters are concerned with customs for ordering society and regulating human behavior. Morality, wisdom, and physical cultivation are all deemed central to the pursuit of immortality; one must be dedicated and faithful in practice, receive help from the gods, and have a skilled and trustworthy teacher.

These texts are included in the vast Taoist canon (*Tao-tsang*). The first attempt to collect and organize all Taoist works took place in the fifth century CE; periodically thereafter works were collected with new materials added to form new versions of the canon. With occasional proscriptions on Taoist material and the disruption to the Chinese heartland caused by foreign invaders and domestic rebels, early versions of the canon were destroyed, with some of the works lost entirely. Under the Mongol rulers of the Yüan dynasty, a version of the canon was produced with 7,000 chapters. Kubilai Khan later ordered all Taoist texts except the *Tao Te Ching* to be burnt after a dispute between Buddhists and Taoists.

The fifth-century canon was organized into three sections, the "Three Caverns," perhaps to echo the canon of Buddhism, which was growing rapidly in popularity at that time. The divisions reflect three Taoist revelatory traditions of the time: the Shangqing, Lingbao, and Sanhuang (Three Sovereigns) schools. Other divisions, incorporating works of other schools, including those from the Celestial Masters, were added later. The Three Caverns are further subdivided by subject matter, which is wide ranging. One includes original revelations; another exegeses. Others are grouped around genealogy and

A painting, from the Sui dynasty (581–618CE), of Taoist masters presenting the emperor with a new edition of the Tao Te Ching, *the central text of Taoism.*

stories of the lives of Taoist luminaries. Charts, diagrams, and sacred talismans are organized; some sections have ethical prescriptions and sacred songs; and there are manuals for practices such as alchemy and geomancy.

Religious Taoism is a revealed religion. Its scriptures are emanations from the beginning of creation, formed by the primordial breath (*yuanqi*) that existed at the first stirring of the Tao. Thus the schools of religious Taoism, beginning with the Celestial Masters (see p.224), viewed scripture as the manifestation of the Tao on earth. The *Tao Te Ching* was understood to be a revelation by Lord Lao, the divinized Laozi. He also revealed sacred registers of divine guardians—knowledge that enabled priests to summon and command gods. A famous recipient of revelations was Yang Xi, who was visited by a number of Taoist spirits between 364 and 370 CE. The resulting scriptures were said to be from the uppermost heaven of all, that of the Highest Purity (Shangqing), and became the basis for the Shangqing school. The scriptures are highly literary in style, and Yang Xi's elegant calligraphy lent them further prestige. Other texts, such as the *Classic of Great Peace* (*Taiping jing*) of the Yellow Turbans (see pp.223–224), infused Taoism with messianic expectations whereby Lord Lao, or a representative, would usher in an era of peace, prosperity, and longevity.

Many Taoist texts are written in obscure or coded language to prevent information from falling into the hands of the uninitiated. Adepts were trained by masters who withheld complete teachings until they were convinced that the adepts were worthy to receive them. The final teaching would often be orally transmitted and was the key to the veiled and symbolic language that could only be understood by the fully initiated.

Hagiographies in the canon described the lives of Taoist worthies and Immortals and gave guidance on and examples of the path to transcendence. They also included the lives of divine transcendents, Taoist patriarchs, and a number of figures in local cults. Other texts related the teachings and writings of important figures in Taoist schools, such as Lu Dongbin and Wang Zhe.

One unusual and important body of works in the canon charted sacred space. Many discussed the Five Sacred Mountains, including shrines and temples, and noted the Immortals or gods who have been seen or met there. A central assertion of Taoism is that the macrocosm is an exact parallel of the microcosm of the body. Thus, topographical texts contained maps of heaven, earth, and subterranean grottoes, important not only for traversing, making pilgrimages, and observing nature, but also for mapping the cosmos of one's own body.

A Passage from "Autumn Floods" in the *Zhuangzi*

❝ The god of the North Sea said, 'You can't discuss the ocean with a frog in a well—it is trapped by a confined space. You can't speak of ice to a summer insect—it is bound by one season. You can't speak of the Way with a biased scholar—he is limited by partiality. You have come out through the cliffs and banks and gazed at the great sea and know your relative insignificance; now it is possible to talk to you of the great underlying pattern.

Of all the waters under heaven, none is greater than the sea. The myriad streams return to it, the rivers ever flow into it, and yet it does not fill; it ever drains at the end of the world and yet it does not empty. Spring and autumn do not change it; flood and drought have no effect on it; it is immeasurably greater than the Yellow River and Yangtze.

Yet I never once took this greatness to make much of myself. I take my form from Heaven and Earth and receive vital breath from *yin* and *yang*. My place between Heaven and Earth is like that of a small stone or tree on a large mountain. I see that I am small—on what account would I regard myself as great?' **❞**

From the *Zhuangzi*, translated by Jennifer Oldstone-Moore.

Commentary

The works of philosophical Taoism are cherished in the Chinese literary tradition for their mystical vision, arresting images, and outstanding literary beauty. This is especially true of the eponymous work of Zhuangzi (ca. 369–286BCE), whose text is typified by fantastic conversations and playful yet profound and poignant observations.

Zhuangzi affirms the eternal flux of nature, the ever-shifting shapes and manifestations of the natural world that are part of a glorious whole, where nothing is ever lost and from whose vantage point all things must be considered as being equally precious and significant. The central goal for humans is to learn the impartiality and all-encompassing nature of the Tao, and, like the Tao, to understand creation and experience from an ultimate perspective, rather than from a selfish and limited vantage point.

The featured passage from "Autumn Floods" demonstrates this idea. The river god had been boasting of his greatness, until he was humbled by his encounter with the vast sea. The god of the sea reflects on the necessarily limited perspective of any creature in the cosmos; he then embraces the philosophy of the Tao and observes that even the sea must be considered tiny in the great scheme of Heaven and Earth.

CHAPTER FOUR

SACRED PERSONS

The history of Taoism is filled with illustrious figures. Many famous Taoists—frequently those who experienced revelations from divinities—are founders of schools of Taoism. Such notables often received royal patronage and enjoyed prestige at court. Local priests were the most visible representatives of Taoism and were hired for healing, exorcisms, and rituals; their various powers inspired awe and fear.

Other Taoists, such as Lao-tzu and Chuang-tzu, are renowned for their rejection of society and worldly ambition. There are many stories of Immortals who have transcended both human and divine existence. Some Taoists, like the Seven Sages of the Bamboo Grove, revelled in their freedom from society's constraints, and spent their time appreciating nature and the virtues of wine and good conversation.

LEFT:
The Eight Immortals and the son of the Jade Emperor are represented on this large joss stick. Joss is made from the trunk of the cinnamon tree. Ground into powder, and mixed with sawdust and water, it is molded into shape, painted with symbolic colors, and then burned as an offering.

Taoist priests, ordained members of the clergy, are able to summon and command the multitude of beings that make up the spirit world. Such awesome power commands great respect. Through training and memorization of esoteric scriptures, they have the ability to call and direct supernatural forces, to confer benefits, and to fight demons. They are commonly employed as exorcists—for example, to appease earth spirits inhabiting the site of a planned new building, to remove ghosts, or to dispel demons who may be causing mental or physical distress.

A priest summons the spirits by making magical gestures and reciting chants and scriptures. Holy water and, sometimes, flaming alcohol are also used, either sprinkled or sprayed through the mouth over a written spell. Other ritual techniques include the "Dance of Yü," a dance patterned on the gait of the legendary ruler. This command of spirits enables Taoist priests to play key roles at funerals. As masters of the celestial and infernal bureaucracies of the world of spirits, they know how to compose writs of pardon and perform the rituals that will speed the soul through the afterlife.

Taoist clergy follow a variety of paths. Some withdraw from the community to live as hermits or monastics and practice self-cultivation, while others are "fire-dwellers" who marry and live with their families, performing rites of healing and exorcism in the community. Of the priests who work in the community, there is a distinction between the "blackheaded" and "redheaded" Taoists, referring to the distinctive headdress of each. Redheaded Taoists are, in effect, shamans who can access the local spirits and perform dramatic exorcisms. Blackheaded priests are orthodox: they are literate and have received extensive training. Rather than managing a mere handful of gods, they are able to control celestial hosts as well as to summon the divinities who are pure emanations of Tao. Contemporary fire-dwelling priests are from the (blackheaded) Orthodox Unity, or Zhengyi, school and they claim lineage with the Celestial Masters of the Han dynasty. Their order is hereditary: sons learn rituals as they grow up, they are initiated into secret lore, and inherit family ceremonial robes and texts. It is the blackheaded priests who perform elaborate rituals of penitence and renewal such as the *jiao* (see p.267). Both blackheaded and redheaded priests may be hired at a community temple where they may perform their services side-by-side and in the company of other religious specialists.

Historically, those who became monastic Taoists were typically novices between the ages of twelve and twenty and began monastic life with menial labor, in addition to the daily practice of devotions. Some monasteries were open to Taoists of all schools, as well as to individuals who wished to pursue Taoist practices of self-cultivation. The Complete Perfection, or Quanzhen, school is the main monastic school to have survived to the present day; it is unusual in that it is a celibate, vegetarian order.

Many famous Taoists cultivated connections at court. Beginning in 215CE with the ceding of power by Celestial Master Zhang Lu to the ruler of the new Wei dynasty, Taoists have used political authority to enjoy the favor of temporal rulers and to grant a special legitimacy to their own teachings. Another Celestial Master, Kou Qianzhi (365–448CE), both reformed the Celestial Master school, ending sexual rites which had by this time become infamous, and convinced the emperor to prohibit Buddhism.

Several illustrious Taoists were advisors to emperors, such as Du Guangting (850–933CE), a Taoist scholar of the Tang Court. Some rulers received religious titles from these high ranking Taoists, including Song emperor Huizong (r. 1101–1125CE), who set up a theocracy, placing himself at the apex of the Taoist pantheon. The Taoist as advisor and teacher to the emperor had antecedents in the *fangshi*, the "gentlemen with recipes"

The Seven Sages of the Bamboo Grove *by Fu Pao-shih (1904–1965). This group of 3rd-century* CE *scholars rejected worldly ambition for a life in pursuit of the Tao.*

who flourished before the Common Era. The *fangshi* were the emperor's official magicians and performed a wide range of functions, which were later continued in various forms by priests. These included communicating with ghosts and spirits, performing exorcisms, and practicing various types of divination. They also performed acupuncture and moxibustion, prescribed special regimes of hygiene, diet and medication, and techniques for sexual vitality.

Stories of Immortals date from Chinese antiquity. Taoist texts described their various forms and characteristics. There are accounts of Immortals who do not experience hunger or cold, who are able to "enter fire without burning and water without getting wet," who have feathers and are as light as birds, and who transform their old bodies into young ones. Some ride dragons, cranes, or phoenixes. Immortals are able to soar through the vastness of space in the twinkling of an eye; they can disappear into a gourd, within which one finds whole kingdoms. They have the ability to appear and disappear and to change their shape. Their flesh is as smooth as ice, they have snow white skin and jet black hair, and strange features such as square pupils. Immortals live in remote mountains and caves, or in magic places, such as Penglai Island off the Chinese mainland. They walk among the stars and planets, occasionally visiting the earth incognito to grant immortality to deserving mortals.

Immortals occupy a unique place in the hierarchy of beings. They are humans who have realized the Tao and are free from the concerns of both humans and the gods, beyond the anxieties and distractions of either the terrestrial or celestial bureaucracies.

Many Chinese folk stories tell of the Eight Immortals—a group of "perfected persons" who attained immortality. They are a diverse group, associated with blessings and happiness and the "Eight Conditions of Life" (youth, age, poverty, wealth, high rank, common rank, femininity, and masculinity). Their varied experiences, status, and methods for immortality represent the accessibility of perfection to any who choose to pursue it.

One of the Eight Immortals, Lu Dongbin, is credited with establishing the Complete Perfection school, and co-authoring texts on alchemy with his master Zhongli Quan. Upon meeting Zhongli for the first time, Lu magically experienced an entire lifetime of worldly achievements and disasters in the few minutes it took him to prepare a pot of millet. Awakening to his meal and to the folly of mundane pursuits, he abandoned a conventional life to become an itinerant Taoist.

In literature and fable, Immortals and other Taoist heroes exemplify those who practice intense self-cultivation to absorb the teachings of Taoism in order to acquire magical powers and, above all, achieve immortality. Although admired, these figures are often unconventional. The ragged Taoist monk, free from society's bonds, laughing uproariously and irreverently, is a recurrent literary image.

"In Praise of the Virtues of Wine" by Liu Ling

  ❝ There is Mr Great Man:

He takes Heaven and Earth to be one day,

Ten thousand years to be one moment

The sun and moon are his windows;

The eight barren places are his palaces.

He travels without tracks or traces

He lives without room or cottage

Heaven is his curtain, the earth his mat

Self-indulgent, he does what he pleases...

No worries, no brooding,

He is content and well pleased.

He becomes intoxicated without moving;

All of a sudden, he awakens from his drunkenness...

He doesn't know the feeling of flesh hurt by bitter cold

or searing heat,

Or the sensations of covetousness

Gazing down, he watches the rest of the world

agitated and unsettled

    like bits of duckweed borne on the Yangtze and

    Han rivers... **❞**

From Liu Ling's "Qiute song," in the *Wenxuan*, translated by Jennifer Oldstone-Moore.

Commentary

The Seven Sages of the Bamboo Grove were a group of friends living in the third century CE during a time of dynastic collapse—a period of great anxiety and uncertainty. They eschewed the court and worldly ambition for a carefree and elegant life in pursuit of the Tao. Their lives combined erudition with highly unconventional behavior: one of the seven is said to have given up using cups—instead, he drank his wine from a communal bowl which was placed on the ground and sometimes shared by the family pigs.

Liu Ling, the author of this poem, "Qiute Song" ("In Praise of the Virtues of Wine"), was famous for his uninhibited behavior and freedom from the rules and mores of polite society. Sometimes, having drunk much wine, he would take off his clothes and sit naked in his room. When criticized for doing this by one of his visitors, Liu responded, "The universe is my home; the room my trousers—what are you doing in my trousers?"

Liu's poem describes the existence of the Taoist who retreats from the world and views it with detached amusement. Down through the centuries, a disregard for the niceties of etiquette, together with a love of poetry, wine, and music, all became attributes of Taoist eccentrics and sages.

CHAPTER FIVE

ETHICAL PRINCIPLES

The ethics of the earliest texts of Taoism take the perspective of the Tao, which creates, nurtures, destroys, and embraces all things. Human conventions, which privilege human concerns and divide the world into opposites, such as good and bad, are not to be trusted, for they make following the pattern of the Tao impossible.

By the Common Era, more conventional ethical principles were added to the earlier ideals—all emphasized the pursuit of longevity. Distinctly Taoist ethics—such as flexibility, humility, embracing the feminine side, and, above all, taking no action contrary to nature (wu-wei)—were gradually and harmoniously combined with ethical principles drawn from the varied traditions of other Chinese religions, in particular, from Confucianism and Buddhism.

LEFT:
Charms on a souvenir stall at the entrance to the Temple of Wong Tai Sin in Kowloon, Hong Kong. Wong Tai Sin is a local deity renowned for the accuracy of his predictions. These charms are worn as jewelry or placed in the home to bring good luck.

A striking passage from the *Tao Te Ching* states that neither Heaven and Earth nor the sage are benevolent. Heaven and Earth treat all things as "straw dogs," as implements to be discarded after they are used; the sage treats the people in the same way. This rather startling doctrine of non-preference, and of taking the priorities of nature rather than society, informs the ethics of the earliest Taoist writings. According to this worldview, conventional morality—which is based on distinctions between good and bad, beauty and ugliness, value and worthlessness—is dangerous as well as irrelevant. It is only when people become aware of distinctions between things that they learn to covet and desire; any statements advocating a specific virtue, such as beauty or goodness, will imply and even create its opposite.

At the core of the ethics of philosophical Taoism is *wu-wei*, or "noninterference," which demands that one submit to and move with, rather than against, natural processes and change. Just as the Tao shows no favorites among creatures, the sage human privileges no particular mode or outcome, but rather follows this pattern itself, gaining the power of the force of nature.

The rejection of conventional modes is demonstrated in the story of Hundun, the cosmic gourd. The gourd, a favorite symbol of Taoists, is a lumpy and irregularly shaped container of seeds that symbolizes the creative potential of undifferentiated Tao. In the story, the cosmic gourd Hundun is the king of the center, who naturally and generously bestows gifts on the kings of the north and south. These kings do not react spontaneously, but fret about proper protocol in gift-giving. Their response is to bore seven holes into Hundun, to provide him with human orifices and thus give him the prestige of a human face. But when they have finished their drilling, he dies. The story illustrates the dangers of assuming human-oriented bias, and the ideal of natural and spontaneous action which existed in the Taoist golden age, before the advent of the destructive and perverting rules and protocols of civilization.

Return to the boundless potential and undifferentiated perfection of the primal state continued to be the goal in religious Taoism and the quest for immortality. By the Common Era, however, the prescriptions of Taoist teachings reflected a more conventional ethic. This is demonstrated in the *Xiang'er*, an early commentary on the *Tao Te Ching* that interprets the lack of benevolence of Heaven, Earth, and the sage to mean that Heaven, Earth, and the sage are benevolent to the good and not to the wicked. This and other texts affirmed the importance of following earlier ethics while at the same time incorporating new behavior. Adherents were to practice *wu-wei*; be weak (yielding) and supple; maintain their feminine nature; practice humility; and attain contentment and non-desire. Significantly, texts advocated filiality, loyalty, and benevolence—all Confucian virtues—and also prohibited curses, insults, breaking promises, theft, fornication, greed, hardheartedness, curiosity, gossip, and anger.

Ethical behavior was considered important for health and to ensure that rituals and practices of self-cultivation would be efficacious. Many ideas and aspects of the rituals from the early schools continue today. The Celestial Masters identified sin of both the individual and the individual's ancestors as the cause of illness and a shortened life-span. Rituals were believed to remove the stain of sin and encourage healing and longevity. Following rites of confession and repentance, transgressions were pardoned by works of community service, which included repairing roads and providing food for the needy. Three times a year there were celebrations of the "Three Officials" (San Guan), the deities of Heaven, Earth, and Water, who both recorded and forgave sins. Penitents confessed their sins on slips of paper which were then burned for the Official of Heaven, buried for the Official of Earth, and submerged for the Official of Water. Another rite, the Fast of Mud and Charcoal, extended its benefits universally: penitents asked for forgiveness for sins committed by themselves and all creatures: living and dead family members, other people, and animals. Participants showed remorse by signs of physical humiliation, smearing mud and charcoal on their bodies, assuming the attitude of accused criminals, and beating their heads on the ground.

The development of techniques of self-cultivation enhanced the importance of ethical principles. Ge Hong, whose fourth-century work includes recipes for achieving immortality through the ingestion of alchemical elixirs (see pp.243–244), assumed that one must be morally and ritually pure for the substances and techniques to be effective. He held a common Taoist view that the "Three Worms," agents in the body that sap vitality, were spies that reported one's sins to Heaven, with every sin resulting in a predetermined reduction of life span. Wang Zhe, the founder of the Complete Perfection monastic order in the twelfth century (see p.226), emphasized the importance of the ethics of the "Three Teachings"—Confucianism, Taoism, and Buddhism—in the pursuit of immortality through interior alchemy. He also prohibited sexual activity, alcohol, anger and desire for wealth.

欺火含雷速大皺當雷大作折樹誅妖孽兩傾盆

This illustration from a 19th-century Taoist weather manual depicts fire (yang) and cloud (yin) combined in a phase of evolving qi, or vital energy. Ink and cinnabar on paper.

Admonitions for ethical behavior were also linked to recurrent millenarian expectations. Good works and confession for the forgiveness of sins were believed to hasten the coming of a perfect world. Believers antici- pated that a cataclysm would result from accumulated evil, and that this would be followed by the appearance of a savior, often identified as Lord Lao. After the destruction of all non-believers, there would be an era of peace, prosperity, and longevity. Good works and ethical behavior were thus linked to bringing about a perfected world as well as perfected individuals.

The basic themes of early Taoist ethics are still expressed today. The practices of self-cultivation are continued by priests, who bring renewal and healing to communities as well as to individuals. The benefit conferred on the community by priestly ritual is most eloquently expressed in the great *jiao* ceremony. Dating from the fifth century CE, the *jiao* is known for its beautiful vestments, elaborate altarpieces, and powerful music. It is usually performed around the time of the winter solstice, when the creative *yang* force is believed to be on the verge of renewal. Priests involved in the *jiao* must be ritually pure to ensure that the cosmic powers, envisioned as the Three Pure Ones (see p.235), will descend.

In the sacred space of the *jiao*, the priest reconstructs the universe through ritual acts. During the ceremony itself, the energies of the cosmos are realized in the high priest's body. The Taoist theme of returning to the origin in order to achieve renewal is central to the ceremony: the priest aims to bring about the replenishment of the forces of light, life, blessing, growth, and *yang* for the entire community, both living and dead.

Precepts for Becoming an Immortal

❝ Do not permit your heart to contain wicked and jealous feelings. Do not allow crafty and treacherous thoughts to grow and come forth from you. ...

Preserve your humaneness, and do not kill. ... Have compassion and love for all. ...

Preserve your purity, and expound on righteousness. Do not engage in debauchery, do not live in excess. ...

Limit alcohol. Regulate your behavior. Be harmonious in energy and disposition. Do not damage your inner spirit. Do not commit any of the multitude of evils.

Do not criticize or argue about the scriptures and teachings. Do not detest the sages' writings. ... Always act as though you were face to face with the gods.

Be wholehearted and uniform in your deportment and all your actions. Be certain that all your actions between both humans and gods are harmonious and conciliatory. **❞**

From *Taishang dongxuan lingbao chishu yujue miaojing* [*Red Writings and Jade Mysteries*], translated by Jennifer Oldstone-Moore.

Commentary

In the schools of religious Taoism, secret teachings and practices could only be revealed to those who were deemed worthy. A kind of predestination was assumed: the only persons who were permitted to follow the advanced path of the adept were those whose names were written in the celestial registers and who already had "jade bones"—bones made from the incorruptible material that provided a framework for the immortal body that was to be cultivated. However, even with this inheritance, an adept had to live a pure and moral life and to follow esoteric practices in order to become an Immortal. Moral codes often include lists of precepts, vows, and rules. Ethical behavior was an integral part of the overall discipline to which adepts adhered in order to purify their hearts, minds, and bodies.

This excerpt is from one of the texts of the Numinous Jewel school, dating from the late fourth or early fifth century CE. The precepts also act as vows which are taken by adepts who are setting out on their journey to lead the life of the Taoist. The text shows influence from the "Five Precepts" of Buddhism (which prohibit killing, stealing, lying, improper sexual behavior, and intoxicating beverages) and from the Buddhist call to universal salvation and compassion.

CHAPTER SIX

SACRED SPACE

In the Chinese worldview, the cosmos is a sacred place, fundamentally interrelated, holy, and complete. Self-creating and self-sustaining, the cosmos evolves and decays in a ceaseless pattern, and all individual manifestations within it are structured according to this pattern. For this reason, the body is perceived as a sacred microcosm—those who follow the Tao can align themselves with the flow of cosmic power and strive to cultivate and purify the universe within their bodies.

Of particular significance to Taoism are geographical features such as rivers, mountains, and caves. Temples and shrines are often erected on or near these sacred spaces. Taoists consider it beneficial to make pilgrimages to such sites, either in person, or through visualization, in the microcosm of one's body.

LEFT: The spectacular, pine-clad mountainscape of southern Anhui province. In Taoism, mountains are traditionally revered as places of special power, where qi, *or "vital energy," is particularly strong.*

In Taoism, the universe is connected and unitary, for all creation emanates from and is shaped by the Tao, which is before time or creation. From the chaotic but fertile Tao comes *qi*, or "vital matter," in its primordial state. It is divided into *yin qi*, which is heavy and sinks down, and *yang qi*, which is light and ascends. From this basic binary relationship the universe is created, manifest in a variety of groupings and divisions. Of these, pentads, or groupings of five, came to be particularly significant, with the "Five Phases" (*wuxing*) becoming a powerful organizing principle for Chinese and Taoist thinking. The Five Phases (also known as the "Five Elements" or "Agents") articulate *qi* as greater and lesser *yin* (water and metal), greater and lesser *yang* (fire and wood), and a balanced center (earth). These phases are related through patterns that are mutually engendering (wood-fire-earth-metal-water) and mutually destructive (fire-water-earth-wood-metal). Their basic qualities and modes of interaction are used as a highly abstract framework to understand and explain the workings of virtually everything, from the rise and fall of dynasties and the workings of internal organs to the passage of time.

All things, from spirits to rocks, are made of the same material, *qi*. There are some places where *qi* can be found in great quantity and with exceptional quality; it flows through channels and grids in the earth, giving life and energy to all creatures. Mountains are among such places, and have been venerated from ancient times in China, both as deities and as meeting places between the human and the divine. Central to Taoism, they are the source of herbs and minerals for elixirs and medicines, and are reputed to be the homes of Immortals. Both the human body and the ritual altar are conceptualized as mountains in Taoist ritual practices.

The "Five Sacred Peaks" resonate with the symbolism of the Five Phases. These mountains—Tai, Heng, Heng (a different place), Hua, and Song—are important to Chinese religions in general, and have been favored retreats of Taoists and the sites of numerous temples and monasteries. Other important mountains include those identified with specific schools, such as Mount Mao (Shangqing), Mount Longhu (Celestial Masters), and Mount Wutang (home to the Taoist martial arts' school). Some sacred mountains—for example, Mount Kunlun, the home of the Queen Mother of the West—are mythical (there is a range by that name, but it is not the same place).

Mountains form a network of sacred sites with grottoes and blessed realms. Grottoes, literally "cave heavens," were thought to be illuminated by their own light or by light from heaven. They were also considered sources

A Taoist shrine in the Huang mountain range where the Yellow Emperor is said to have ascended to immortality.

of vitalizing energy, places of the gods, and were even seen as sacred microcosms, worlds within themselves. Blessed realms also dotted the landscape. Taoists designated and mapped ten great grotto heavens, thirty-six smaller grotto heavens, and seventy-two blessed realms. These were understood to be connected by subterranean passageways, forming a grid of sacred places and power.

These ideas are related to the ancient art of *feng-shui*, another means of accessing cosmic power. While not strictly Taoist, *feng-shui* (literally, "wind and water") is the art of fixing the most auspicious place for graves, buildings, and even cities, in order to make the most of the *qi* present in the environment and to live harmoniously within the natural order. The *feng-shui* master uses a special compass to take bearings on the site and on visible features of the surrounding landscape—such as mountain peaks, watercourses, paths, and prominent rocks—to determine the auspiciousness of the site.

Channels of energy can be accessed and put to use through *feng-shui*; similarly, the channels of *qi* in the body can be manipulated to advantage through practices such as acupuncture. The parallel between the inner and outer worlds is drawn in elaborate detail. Certain Taoist meditative practices instruct the adept to look inward and observe the "country of the body." This "country" is a sacred microcosm, a faithful duplication of the universe: it has the same structure and features as the cosmos, and is replete with gods, mountains, constellations and heavenly bodies, bridges, lakes and pagodas, and perhaps the "embryo of immortality". It is inhabited by a large population which is administered in the same way as the imperial Chinese state. The prince of the body is found in the heart; his ministers and subordinates manage and govern throughout the body. State, cosmos, and body are all understood to be structured in homologous ways, creating concentric units of sacred space. These units interpenetrate each other— as, for example, in the actions and liturgy of the *jiao* ceremony (see p.267), where the priest simultaneously renews the community and cultivates his "immortal embryo."

The true form of the macrocosm is also presented in the microcosm of sacred drawings, such as talismans and diagrams. These show the internal structure of powerful sources of cosmic energy. By knowing their true form, adepts have control over these sources of power. Diagrams show the true shape of mountains, grottoes, and other geographical features, thus protecting the adept from any dangers that might exist there, such as demons or evil spirits. Talismans, which resemble complex Chinese characters in an archaic style, can portray the sacred places of the body and the cosmos, providing important knowledge to those who would traverse them. Talismans are usually linked to oral formulas that are only given to the initiated to make them efficacious.

Taoist sacred space includes temples and monasteries. Most temples in China are neighborhood temples run by lay people, and are not specifically Taoist. They house images of Taoist deities, such as the Three Pure Ones, as well as other popular spirits, including the Eight Immortals, Guandi, tutelary gods, and figures from the Confucian and Buddhist traditions. Taoist priests may be hired at such temples for ritual purposes. There are also specifically Taoist structures, such as the White Cloud Abbey in Beijing, a monastery of the Complete Truth school. Eastern Peak (Dongyueh) temples, associated with the Orthodox Unity school, have separate chambers that depict the torments and tormenters of Hell as found under Mount Tai, the eastern peak. Lay people present sacrifices at specific chambers in these temples in order to speed the soul of loved ones through judgment and punishment.

Other temples are often situated near natural features, such as holy mountains, that have spiritual significance—many of these have become notable pilgrimage centers. Some temples and abbeys received imperial patronage. During the Tang dynasty (618–907CE), shrines and monasteries were established on numerous sacred peaks and at sites where famous Taoists had "obtained the Way." One monastery, Tower Abbey, was founded on the site where Laozi is said to have revealed the *Tao Te Ching*—it became a dynastic cult center, and was renamed the Abbey of the Holy Ancestor.

Women Pilgrims to Mount Tai

❝ The laywoman said: 'My dear—could there be another
T'ai Shan in the world? From the top you get a perfect
view of all the lands on earth, the dragons' palaces,
ocean treasures, Buddhas' halls, and immortals'
palaces. If such benefits were not to be had, why would
men and women come thousands of miles from their
homes? ... What's more, Our Lady of T'ai Shan controls
life and death, luck and prosperity for people through
all the world. ... The reverent at heart, when they come
before Our Lady, see the goddess's true face in the flesh;
if not reverent at heart, the face they see is only a
gilded face. She is powerful and effective for bringing
good luck and forgiving misdeeds. And on the mountain
there is no end of wonderful sights, like the South-
facing Cave, the Three Heavenly Gates, the Yellow
Flower Island, the Platform of Suicides, the Rock for
Drying Scriptures, the Stele without Inscription, the
Pine of Ch'in, the Cypress of Han, the Golden Slips,
the Jade Writings—all these are where the gods and
immortals make their dwelling. No one with only
average luck could ever get to go there!' **❞**

From *Xingshi yinyuan zhuan* by Xi Zhou Sheng, translated by Glen Dudbridge in Susan Naquin and Chün-fang
Yü, eds., *Pilgrims and Sacred Sites in China*, University of California Press, 1992, p.46.

Commentary

Taoist adepts were avid pilgrims, but they were by no means the only ones who were interested in embarking on sacred journeys. People from all levels of society went on pilgrimages. Emperors demonstrated their sovereignty through their journeys to sacred spots; common people asked for blessings and forgiveness when they reached their destination, or else they traveled to these places in order to see famous sights, as this passage indicates. Of all the sacred peaks, Mount Tai, or T'ai, (Tai Shan) has loomed the largest in Chinese religious history. The god of Mount Tai became an important figure in the celestial bureaucracy, subordinate only to the Jade Emperor. He was in charge of regulating birth, death, and human achievements.

In this story, from the seventeenth or eighteenth century, pilgrims are there not only to sight-see but to ask favors of Our Lady of Tai Shan, the daughter of the god of Mount Tai. Known to the Chinese as Bixia yuan-jun, the Sovereign of the Clouds at Dawn, she became the most popular female Taoist deity in late imperial China. In her compassion and concern for humble people, she resembles Guanyin, the Buddhist goddess of mercy. Mount Tai, its hundreds of shrines and its ascent of 7,000 rock-cut steps remain much visited to this day.

CHAPTER SEVEN

SACRED TIME

Taoists are masters of time as well as space. Their activities reveal their desire to align with the rhythms of the cosmos and with cycles of time that are discernible in the abstract patterns of *yin* and *yang* and the "Five Phases," which explain the workings of time as well as matter. Taoist ritual is based on detailed knowledge of these rhythms, and is formulated either to accelerate time, to bring precious materials (eg., metals) to fruition, or to trace it backward, to return to the moment of creation and to the life-giving original *qi* that will confer immortality.

The patterns of *yin* and *yang* and the Five Phases are also central to pan-Chinese religious festivals. Although not exclusively Taoist, these festivals reflect Taoist beliefs and serve as popular expressions of the tradition's approach to the concepts of time, nature, and destiny.

LEFT:
A Taoist priest officiates at the Hungry Ghosts' festival in Penang, Malaysia. The statues represent ghosts, and it is believed that they come to Earth for one month every year to enjoy good food and entertainment.

In Taoist reckoning, the primordial Tao existed before time, which was not set into motion until after the emergence of primordial *qi*. The pattern of time is thus a part of the unfolding of creation—it is to be identified, learned, and used to one's benefit. This is the basis of most Taoist practice, and is made explicit in "external" and "internal alchemy." In external alchemy (now defunct), adepts controlled time to accelerate the purification of materials that confer immortality. In internal alchemy, the flow of vital essences in the body are reversed in order to reverse the passage and effects of time and return to the state of the newborn, who is full of vital energies. This primal vitality is manifest in the "embryo of immortality" created by such practices. The alchemist, echoing and manipulating the cosmic flow, produces microcosms in time as well as in space. (See also pp.298–299.)

Other practices also correspond to the cosmic movement of time: adepts in Taoist monasteries rise and retire with the sun; and the *jiao* festival of renewal (see p.267) is usually performed around the winter solstice to coincide with the rebirth of *yang* that occurs during this period. The celebrations and observances surrounding the Chinese religious year reflect a similar recognition of the variable characteristics of time—this is evident in the attention that is paid to the cycles of *yin* and *yang* and the "Five Phases" (see p.272). Although not strictly Taoist, they reflect Taoist sensibilities, and Taoist priests may officiate at rituals associated with festivals.

Chinese time is observed according to both the lunar and solar calendars. The lunar calendar is twelve months, with a thirteenth month added every two or three years. In the solar calendar, "nodes," or "breaths," refer to the twenty-four periods of approximately fifteen days into which the year is divided. These divisions correspond to the patterns of the agricultural year. The start of each season in the solar year is determined by the solstices and equinoxes.

Years are then organized into cycles. First, there is the cycle of twelve years, familiar to many from the animals of the Chinese zodiac. This scheme of twelve is then widened into a sixty-year cycle, characterized by two sets of symbols—the "Ten Heavenly Stems" and the "Twelve Earthly Branches." Each animal in the zodiac is associated with one branch. The cycle is completed by associating each stem with one of the "Five Colors" (which correspond to the Five Phases), with two stems per color. The end result is a cycle of sixty, and each animal will be linked with each color once in the cycle. *Jiazi*, the year of the Blue Rat, is the first year of the sixty-year cycle.

Many festivals in the Chinese religious year coincide with significant phases of the moon; others are derived from the agricultural cycle. Annual festivals reflect ancient *yin-yang* and Five-Phase cosmology, corresponding to the phases of the moon, the change of seasons, and movements in the heavens. Holidays frequently fall on days with *yang* symbolism (odd numbers are *yang*) or on the full moon (the fifteenth of each lunar month). These festivals demonstrate a number of significant themes: the importance of the family and the respect shown for forebears; the pursuit of longevity; the desire for blessings; and the propitiation and warding-off of potentially malevolent forces. The festal year includes the worship of the gods and goddesses of the popular religion, particularly in the celebrations to mark their birthdays.

The New Year, or Spring Festival, is the most important holiday in the Chinese calendar. It is a time of beginnings and family reunions. Families sweep out the old with housecleaning, the settling of debts, and the completion of unsettled business. This period is a celebration of the return of *yang* after the winter solstice—*yang* colors (red, gold, and orange) are seen everywhere, particularly in paper decorations and in round foods such as oranges and kumquats (round signifies comple-

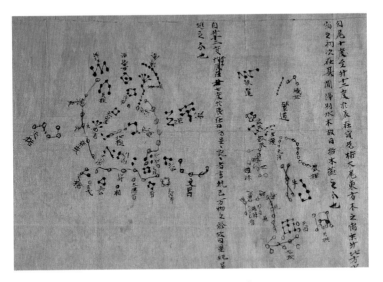

A star map of ca.940CE. For millennia, Chinese astronomer-scribes produced such maps, providing China with the world's most complete records of unusual celestial phenomena.

tion). Ideally, the family comes together on New Year's Eve, and all are careful not to mar the family's fortune for the coming year with cross words or with actions that may be deemed to be unlucky.

New Year festivities end on the fifteenth day of the first month with the Lantern Festival. During the two weeks of celebrations, many popular gods receive offerings. The last day of the holiday is also the birthday of the "Official of Heaven," one of the "Three Officials" (see p.264)—sacrifices to him are presented at dawn on this day. Another major festival is Qingming ("Clear and Bright") which is a time to revive ties with the dead and to celebrate renewal of the family, symbolized by the new life of spring (the festival falls two weeks after the spring equinox).

The Double Fifth festival observes the peak of *yang* at the summer solstice on the fifth day of the fifth lunar month. Any excess, whether of *yin* or *yang*, is considered dangerous (an excess of *yang* is evident in heat and epidemics). Protection is therefore sought at this time by the display of pungent herbs or plants with shapes that resemble sharp weapons. The "Five Poisons" (centipede, snake, scorpion, toad, and lizard) and the "Five Colors" (blue, red, yellow, white, and black) are also believed to offer protection—the former are thought to fend off danger with their toxins and are represented on clothing, food, and amulets; the latter are said to summon forth the power of the "Five Phases."

The Double Fifth also celebrates dragons, water, and a famous poet. During this season, rice seedlings are transplanted into paddies and watered by heavy rains. According to Chinese tradition, this rain is caused by dragons who live in the clouds and who water and bless the Earth with fertility. The "dragon boat" races that are held on the Double Fifth reflect not only this lore but also the legend of Qu Yuan, a poet who served in the government during the Zhou dynasty. When his advice was disregarded, he threw himself into a river in despair. Today's dragon boat races reenact the frantic search for him that took place.

The Feast of the Hungry Ghosts on the fifteenth day of the seventh lunar month focuses on communal protection, which is provided, in part, by the ritual actions of Taoist priests. During this month, the gates of Hell are opened, and its residents are free to wander at will. Those with no descendants to care for them (euphemistically called "the good brethren") are malevolent, unhappy, and potentially dangerous ghosts. The festival is designed to placate such beings with things they may need, such as sustenance and amusements, including music and theater. On Hungry Ghosts' day, a community celebration at an outdoor altar is conducted by both Taoist and Buddhist priests who exhort the ghosts to repent and end their sufferings in the underworld. Ghosts who do not repent are sent back to Hell after the ceremony.

The Chinese celebration of the harvest, the Mid-Autumn festival, falls at full moon in the eighth lunar month, when *yang* has completed its dominance and gives way to *yin* after the autumnal equinox. Chinese tell the story of the rabbit in the moon, who is pounding the ingredients for the elixir of immortality with a pestle, and of Chang E, the woman who drank the elixir intended for her husband and floated up to the moon where she has lived ever since. A festival less frequently observed today is the Double Nine. This number evokes the symbolism of *yang*: nine is the most *yang* of numbers and double *yang* is seen as especially auspicious. It is also the time, just after the autumnal equinox, when *yin* has begun to prevail. Traditionally, the day has been celebrated by drinking chrysanthemum wine and taking mountain hikes, the late autumn blossom symbolizing long life.

The timing of family rites is structurally similar to the timing of festivals and reflects the fluctuation of *yin* and *yang* and the cycles of the Five Phases. In this way, Taoist thinking and practice pervade Chinese life. Taoists may be called upon to determine auspicious days for important events, and to assist in rituals, as need arises. Weddings are a primary means of ensuring the continuation of the family line, a major consideration in Chinese culture. Families must match the bride's and groom's horoscopes to determine their relationship to each other vis-à-vis cosmic time. Before a couple is betrothed, an astrologer will check the "eight characters," the year, month, day, and hour of birth of both parties in order to confirm their compatibility. The almanac remains an important source for selecting the appropriate day. The positioning of the bride's and the groom's families at the various ceremonies of betrothal and marriage reflect *yin* and *yang* relationships, with the bride's family on the west side, and the groom's on the east.

A new mother, having observed various folk traditions during pregnancy to protect the fetus and ensure an easy birth, will "sit the month" after childbirth. This means that she stays at home, where she is nourished by "warm" or *yang* foods and by a soup that provides five medicinal herbs, one for each of the Five Phases.

The rites of passage associated with death use the symbolic language of *yin* and *yang* in the ritual placement of mourners at the funeral: women are placed to the west and men to the east. The same symbolism is also evident in the preparation of the corpse for burial—for example, soon after death, the corpse is oriented with its head toward the south to denote fire (and therefore purification); similarly, the family's grief is expressed by draping the family alter with white coverings, which denotes *yin*, mourning, and death. Periods of crisis and celebration in the family are thus integrated into larger cycles of time and change, easing transition and ensuring the efficacy of rituals.

The Management of Time

❝ Natural cyclically transformed elixir is formed when
flowing mercury, embracing Squire Metal [i.e. lead],
becomes pregnant. Wherever there is cinnabar there
are also lead and silver. In 4,320 years the elixir is
finished … It embraces the *ch'i* [*qi*] of sun and moon,
yin and *yang*, for 4,320 years; thus, upon repletion of
its own *ch'i*, it becomes a cyclically transformed elixir
for immortals of the highest grade and for celestial
beings. When in the world below lead and mercury are
subjected to the alchemical process for purposes of
immortality, [the elixir] is finished in one year. … ❞

From the *Heart-Mirror of Mnemonics and Explanations from Writings on the Elixir* translated by Nathan Sivin in
N. Sivin, "Chinese Alchemy and the Manipulation of Time" in N Sivin, ed., *Science and Technology in East Asia.*
New York: Science History Publications, 1977, p.112.

❝ As for the time of firing the furnace, the fire should be
applied at a midnight which is also the first hour of a
sixty-hour cycle, on the first day of a sixty-day cycle, in
the eleventh month [i.e. the month which contains the
winter solstice]. Begin by firing through door A for 5
days, using 3oz of charcoal… Then open door B and
start the fire, firing for 5 days, using 4 oz of charcoal.
Then open door C and start the fire, firing for 5 days,
using 5oz of charcoal. ❞

From *Arcane Teachings on the Ninefold Cyclically Transfromed Gold Elixir* translated by Nathan Sivin in N.
Sivin, "Chinese Alchemy and the Manipulation of Time" in N Sivin, ed., *Science and Technology in East Asia.*
New York: Science History Publications, 1977, p.115.

Commentary

Control of time is essential in transmuting materials into the "elixir of immortality" (see p.244). The genius of the Taoist alchemist lies in the mastery of the inter-related material, spatial, and temporal aspects of the Tao in the cosmos and the ability to recreate these patterns to nurture one's own body. To hasten the manufacture of potable gold that could be made into an elixir of immortality, alchemists recreated the cosmos in minia-ture in the laboratory, exhibiting their knowledge of the pattern of change through time that occurs in the unfolding of the Tao. (See also pp.298–299.)

In the first extract (opposite, written before 900CE), the alchemist's knowledge of the Tao is used to telescope time in the laboratory. Each day is divided into twelve "hours"—a lunar year of 360 days has 4,320 such hours. One hour in the laboratory was deemed to have the same effect on the metal as one year in the earth.

The second extract, from a manual by the alchemist Chen Shao-wei, ca. 712CE, reveals the care that is taken to mimic the fluctuation of *yin* and *yang* in a calendar year. "Fire phasing" correlated with cosmic cycles, and recre-ated, in miniature, the ebb and flow of heat across the seasons of a year. Thus discernment of temporal patterns was necessary to gaining spiritual and physical benefits.

CHAPTER EIGHT

DEATH AND THE AFTERLIFE

Taoist responses to death vary, but all address the concept of change. Priests help effect the transformation of a dead family member into a benevolent ancestor. Without such a change he or she could become a dangerous ghost.

Some people strive to escape death altogether. Chinese notions of immortality assume the need for a physical body; Taoist practices are therefore directed at refining one's body so as to return it to a condition of undifferentiated potential—like the Tao before creation. In these practices, adepts use cosmic powers and mastery of time and matter to attain deathlessness. Immortals revel in their release from the constraints of human existence. In contrast, a few Taoists marvel at the pattern of creation and destruction, relishing freedom from the fear of death and change more than freedom from death itself.

LEFT:
A Qing dynasty illustration depicting a figure, probably an Immortal, ascending to a celestial palace. From Keepsake from the Cloud Gallery, *or* Yuntai Xianrui *(1750), a text describing the practices of a Tao adept.*

Chinese ideas about the soul and its fate date from ancient times, but were never organized into a single, definitive system. Sources describe two kinds of soul, usually designated as the *hun* and the *po*. The actual number of *hun* and *po* souls residing in a person is disputed. Souls are made of the same vital material, *qi*, as all other things, and thus the boundaries between the living and the dead are relatively fluid. The *hun* soul is made of *yang qi* and represents the spiritual and intellectual aspects; the *po* consists of *yin qi*, which is the bodily, animating principle. At death, the *hun* soul departs from the body and ascends, the *po* soul sinks into the ground. Funerary rituals are performed to settle the *hun* soul into the ancestral tablets that are found on the domestic altar of many Chinese homes; they also ensure that the *po* soul will settle peacefully into the grave.

Beliefs about death and the afterlife draw from the various traditions of Chinese religion, and thus can encompass numerous—and, in some cases, apparently contradictory—notions of one's fate after death. In addition to being settled in the gravesite and in the ancestor tablets, the soul of the deceased is believed to descend into the Chinese underworld, or Hell, to be tried by the infernal judiciary. Important Buddhist concepts were integrated with indigenous Chinese ideas, including the idea of *karma* (an individual's balance of accumulated merits and demerits); the figure of Yama, the king of Hell; and the different punishment levels of Hell, in which sinners suffer to redress their karmic imbalance before being reincarnated on earth.

Like its celestial counterpart, Hell is structured in the same way as the old Chinese imperial bureaucracy and judiciary. On entering it, souls are judged by the Ten Magistrates who preside over the Ten Tribunals of Hell. The books of life and death, in which every person's alloted days are recorded, are managed by this bureaucracy, and Chinese folklore contains many accounts of bureaucractic mistakes that result in a person being wrongly brought to death and judgment until the error is discovered. After judgment, the soul pays for its past crimes by passing through various layers of Hell, where it undergoes torments appropriate to the crimes committed. At last, the soul reaches the final court where, having atoned for shortcomings in the life just past, it is reincarnated in accordance with the merits it has accumulated in its previous existence.

Taoist priests play an important role in death ritual. As officials of the spirit world, Taoists are able to prepare and present the proper documents to the appropriate bureaucrats in the underworld. They are hired by the bereaved to ensure that the soul of a beloved family member spends a minimal amount of time suffering for any misdeeds. The funeral ritual may include the sending of a special document, a writ of pardon, and the drama of the deliverance of the soul from punishment in Hell.

Taoist priests are also important in communicating with the dead and restoring harmony in the family. After the body has been appropriately buried, it is the responsibility of the living to provide the things the dead will need to be comfortable: food, money, and other amenities. For family members, this means daily offerings of incense and periodic offerings of food, drink, and spirit money. Should there be discord or ill fortune in the family, a Taoist priest may be summoned to determine if the family is suffering on account of a discontented ancestor. He—for the individual is invariably male—may then diagnose the appropriate actions to be taken to pacify the unhappy spirit and restore harmony to the family.

Throughout its long history, Taoism has also developed elaborate techniques to escape death altogether. Methods for achieving immortality include both tempering the physical body and purifying one's heart and mind, as there was no radical dichotomy between body and soul. Belief in the possibility of immortality is not exclusively Taoist—however, the schools of Taoism have system-

*A sculpture representing a spirit at East Mountain Temple,
Tainan, Taiwan. Identified with Mount Tai, the temple
recreates in its statuary the places of judgment and punishment.*

atized various techniques. These include meditation, visualization and breathing exercises, gymnastics, sexual practices, dietary control, and concocting special medicines. In ancient times, people sought the elixir or pill of immortality, either in their own laboratories, or from individuals who lived in legendary places at the edges of the known world, such as the Queen Mother of the West (see p.236 and pp.238–239).

A famous Taoist concerned with these practices was Ge Hong (see p.243), whose text *Bao Puzi* has a number of recipes for pills that confer immortality. Especially prized ingredients by alchemists included gold, which does not corrode and is thus associated with immutability, arsenic and lead, and cinnabar, a form of mercury, valued for its red (*yang*) color and because it easily transmutes into various forms (see pp.290–291). Such medicines were very costly. This "external alchemy" correlated the transformations of chemical substances in the laboratory to transformations in the cosmos and the body. The knowledge needed to unlock the secrets of how to change chemical matter was the same knowledge needed to halt the decay and deterioration brought about by old age. Many emperors were eager adepts of external alchemy, and it is thought that, ironically, several may have been poisoned by the medicines.

By the eighth or ninth century, the practice of external alchemy had been interiorized, so that the language of refining and transmuting gold and cinnabar was now used to denote elements and transformations in the crucible of the body (rather than the laboratory). Practitioners of internal alchemy sought the coalescence of purified and perfected bodily essences—such as sexual fluids, saliva, and *qi*—into an "embryo of immortality." Also called the "Red Child," this "holy embryo" was established in the belly of the adept, where, properly nourished through correct practices, it would develop into a perfected body, an immortal, true, real self that would replace the adept's old, corruptible body. Internal alchemy continues to be a defining aspect of Taoist practice to this day.

The assumption underlying all such practices is the correlation of the microcosmic body to the macrocosmic universe. The adept must identify and preserve the "primordial breath" (*yuanqi*) that corresponds to the life-giving, undifferentiated Tao at the beginning of creation. The adept works to retain the vital bodily essences of breath, life force, and spirit, and end the gradual depletion of these essences that leads ultimately to death. Many practices involve reversing, through visualization, the usual flow of bodily fluids, such as sexual fluids, and, in so doing, reverse the effects of time.

In meditation and visualization exercises, the practitioner focuses on the Tao and on powerful gods that reside in Heaven and the body. Breathing techniques aim to produce "embryonic" breathing—breathing that is so slow and shallow that a feather placed on an adept's nose will remain motionless. Purification of the breath and body are enhanced by a special diet, which may include the consumption of foods associated with long life, including certain mushrooms, pine seeds, and pine sap; and the avoidance of foods, especially cereals, that nourish the malevolent and destructive spirits in the body such as the "Three Worms" (see p.265). Sexual techniques aim to control orgasm, which is believed to cause devastating depletion of vital essences, and enable one to benefit from the *yin* or *yang* essence of one's partner. Gymnastic exercises, such as *qigong* and *taiji quan*, both conserve essences and ensure the proper circulation for maximum strength and benefit.

These practices are largely physiological procedure and effect—it is, however, taken for granted that they will be supplemented by a moral lifestyle. Evil and immoral deeds shorten the lifespan as a consequence of reports to celestial gods such as the Three Officials; they may also cause the gods who reside in one's body to depart, hastening or even causing death. In addition to leading a moral life, adepts require a skilled master who can train them in the secret texts and oral instructions that complement the esoteric and opaque written formulae. Those who have the will and ability to complete these rigorous courses join the ranks of the Immortals, living in mountains and grottoes, flying among the stars, and wandering the earth in perfect serenity, nourished by eating the wind and drinking the dew.

Few have the stamina to become Immortals, fewer still embrace death without fear. A distinctive attitude toward death and the afterlife is notable in the earliest texts of Taoism, especially in the compelling stories of Zhuangzi (see pp.242–243). He speculates on the possibility that we may find death preferable to life and claims that our fate is no more than to continue in the process of coagulation and the dissipation of *qi* amid the eternal flux that brought us into being; we can never leave the bosom of the Tao. From this perspective, death and life are but alternating parts of a cycle—they are to be neither sought nor feared. Some of Zhuangzi's most moving and memorable passages celebrate death in this way: marveling at the unique, creative possibilities of transformation during death and life, while "dwelling in the greatest of mansions," the universe which follows the pattern of the Tao.

Secrets of Immortality from *Journey to the West*

❝ You must completely grasp this important secret ...

Spare and cultivate the life forces ...

All is composed of semen, breath and spirit,

Be cautious; make them secure; stop all leakage.

Stop all leakage, preserve them in the body,

Accept my teachings and the Way will flourish. ...

They remove evil desires, lead to purity.

They lead to purity, bright and lustrous,

You can face the Cinnabar Platform and enjoy

the bright moon.

The moon holds the Jade Rabbit; the sun

holds the Raven,

From there also the Tortoise and Snake,

coiled together.

Coiled together, the life forces are strong,

You can plant the golden lotus in the midst of the fire.

Assemble the Five Phases; reverse them to use them,

This work complete, you can be a buddha or an

immortal as you wish. ❞

From *Xiyouji* [*Jouney to the West*] by Wu Chengen. Taipei: Sheng-yang ch'u-pan she, 1988, p.13.
Translated by Jennifer Oldstone-Moore.

Commentary

This passage is from *Journey to the West*, also known as *Monkey*, a highly entertaining novel written in 1592 by Wu Chengen. Still read in China today, it tells the story of a Buddhist monk and his four disciples on a pilgrimage to India. But this popular tale can also be read as an allegory of Taoist immortality, Buddhist enlightenment and Confucian mind-cultivation (all of which have been attained by the end of the novel). Much of the text is loaded with symbolism, taking place in the body of an adept and containing subtle references to Taoist practices throughout. The story shows the way in which the "Three Teachings" of Taoism, Buddhism, and Confucianism are embraced simultaneously.

This poem from the novel relates to the Taoist initiation of Monkey (one of the book's principal characters and the best of the disciples), who has been deemed worthy to receive the secret teachings from a Taoist patriarch. The verse contains many alchemical references: conserving and purifying bodily fluids; symbols such as the snake and tortoise used by Taoists to denote *yin* and *yang*; and the reversal of the "Five Phases" (see pp.272–273) to reverse the effects of time, an indication of the Way which leads ultimately to the transcending of death and the attainment of immortality.

CHAPTER NINE

SOCIETY AND RELIGION

The effect of Taoism on Chinese culture has been profound. Its wide-ranging influence has extended to philosophy, medicine, and government, and has provided an emphasis on the feminine in an otherwise male-oriented culture. The fine arts also often reflect the Taoist ideals of spontaneity, appreciation of nature, and retreat from the world.

Taoist practices have been integrated into society at the very highest levels, influencing emperors, controlling contact with the spirit world, and providing important rituals. Taoism's massive collection of scriptures and its highly trained priesthood distinguish it from the popular tradition, but the close connections that exist between the two are manifested regularly at the community temples, where the effect Taoism has had on ordinary people is revealed.

LEFT:
A worshipper with incense sticks. Incense, more than simply a fragrant offering, is a symbol of the Three Primary Vitalities ("original" breath, essence and spirit), and is believed to draw deities to the altar.

Despite its inherent mysticism, the *Tao Te Ching* is a treatise on government. The ideal ruler portrayed within its pages is so subtle and inconspicuous that his subjects are unaware of being ruled; his statesmanship eradicates distinctions that cause envy and discontent so that people have no superfluous desires. Although this ideal Taoist state has never been put into practice, the role of Taoism in government has nevertheless been manifest in a variety of ways.

At the end of the second century CE, Taoism was implemented as a theocracy mandated by Lord Lao (the divinized Laozi). Confession and absolution by Taoist gods was established by the Celestial Masters in the third century (see pp.224–225). The new state, founded in modern-day Szechwan, was divided into 24 districts which were overseen by a Taoist official and protected by the gods and spiritual beings under his or her command. The Celestial Master government did not last as an autonomous force. However, in ceding civil authority to a political leader, it established a precedent whereby leading Taoist figures became sources of legitimization for kings and emperors who were then sanctioned by Lord Lao. This relationship was especially cultivated in the Period of Disunity, and in the Tang and Song dynasties. State patronage often included the establishment of new temples which not only enhanced Taoism but also bolstered imperial prestige.

From the beginning of organized Taoism, the tradition provided elements of messianic and millenarian expectation—this threatened the status quo and raised government suspicions. Taoist imagery and ideas were used in various rebellions. Among these was a series of revolts connected with the figure Li Hong, who instigated an uprising in the fourth century which was based on a prophecy that he would become king—because of his family name, Li, he was believed to be a manifestation of Laozi, and it was anticipated that he would bring about a utopian age.

Taoism's relationship with the present government of the People's Republic of China is uncertain: only the monastic Taoism of the Complete Perfection school is officially recognized. Other Taoist practices are categorized as "superstitions" and are actively discouraged.

The tradition has also long been associated with the healing arts. The goals and methods of traditional Chinese medicine and Taoism overlap: Chinese medicine is centered on the healthy circulation of *qi*, the balance of *yin* and *yang* in the body, and the use of various substances to nourish the body. These theories also inform the Taoist quest for immortality. Taoist alchemy has been

Taoist orthodox priests take part in a festival in Taiwan. Vestments and texts are passed down from father to son.

described as a protoscience, and attempts by Taoist alchemists to produce the "elixir of immortality" (see p.90) led to other significant discoveries—notably, the invention of gunpowder.

Other Taoist forms of healing reflected the role of the Taoist priest as an authority over spirits. These included faith-healing through the confession of sins and forgiveness from the celestial administrators of life and death; exorcism; and the preparation of talismans for therapeutic medicine. The tradition also developed therapeutic and longevity exercises such as *ch'i-kung* and *t'ai-chi ch'üan*.

Such practices are related to the martial arts, which work to cultivate bodily strength through moral behavior, focused attention, and the conservation and strengthening of *qi*. Two notable Taoist martial arts' schools are the Shaolin and Wutang.

Taoism has had a tremendous effect on the fine arts, including poetry, theatre, painting, and calligraphy. The naturalistic mysticism of Laozi, Zhuangzi, and Huainanzi is evident in Chinese painting. Many famous landscape painters of the Song and Yuan dynasties, such as Fan Kuan, were Taoist-style recluses and eccentrics. His famous landscapes portray Taoist ideas of the relative importance of humans to nature: humans are depicted as minute beings in contrast to the vastness of nature. Calligraphy, the most cherished visual art in China, is closely linked to Taoist ideals of spontenaeity while following the natural pattern: calligraphers must be both perfectly controlled and perfectly spontaneous while exercising their art. Taoist talismans are a special form of calligraphy, demanding elegance as well as a perfect form to be effective.

Chinese poetry often expresses themes such as the desire for retreat from society, the love of nature, wine, and good company. Many poets are famous for their freedom from social convention and for their love of nature. The most famous of these is Li Bo, who exhibits such freedom, and was ordained a Taoist priest at the Tang court. His poems express his love of freedom from the mundane world, and of drinking under the moon— he is said to have drowned while trying to embrace the reflection of the moon in a lake.

Taoist practices continue to be central to the Chinese burial ceremony, which is the culture's most significant life-cycle ritual. The event involves the priest's reenactment of a cosmic drama of rescue and salvation for the souls of the deceased who face the infernal judiciary. Chinese theatre draws extensively on Taoist ritual, and many of its forms have evolved from it. Chinese theatrical works also often reenact stories containing Taoist elements and, prior to their performance, actors who represent certain deities undergo rituals of purification and abstinence which are similar to the ceremonies undertaken by priests before performing their rites.

Despite their frequent rivalry, Taoism provided a means of acculturation for Buddhism to East Asia, which traveled to China from India via the Silk Road at the beginning of the Common Era. Buddhism was first thought to be a foreign version of Taoism, and many Buddhist terms and ideas were translated—incorrectly— using Taoist terminology. This allowed for accommodation of Buddhism to the radically different Chinese context. Translators gradually became more knowledgeable and sophisticated, and Buddhism developed specifically Chinese forms. The most striking of these is the Chan (Zen) school, which has been described as a marriage between Buddhism and Taoism.

Finally, although Taoism did not fundamentally challenge the patriarchal structure of Chinese society, its emphasis on the female deviated from tradition. Taoist cloisters offered women an alternative to family life. Those who might become Taoist nuns included women who were unable to marry because of inauspicious horoscopes, those who were widowed or divorced, and unmarried girls who were permitted by male relatives to follow this vocation. In the Tang dynasty, aristocratic women could be ordained before, after, or between marriages; two princesses were among the ordained. Women were often intermediaries with the divine and also played important roles as libationers in the Celestial Masters government. Female adepts are presumed to have an easier course to follow in internal alchemy and in creating an "embryo of immortality" (see p.299)—their bodies being already prepared for conception and gestation; in some texts, male adepts are given feminine behaviors (such as sitting before urinating) to follow in order to help them attain the Tao.

The Tao and Artistic Creation

❝ It should be possible ... for the human spirit to express
the spirit of the universe through the brushwork without difficulty. For painting is only an art, yet it has the
power of creation of the universe itself. ... When the
artist is ready to start a picture, his mind can plan only
the general type of brushwork and composition. Yet as
the splash of ink descends upon the paper, guided by
the artist's spirit, it comes out in myriad forms entirely
beyond the original plan ... If the artist insists on
doing what he did yesterday, he cannot do it. Why?
Because when an artist insists on something, he is
already obstructing the free flow of the spirit. ... A
scholar painting starts out with nothing in his mind,
but when his spirit begins to move the brush, the
forms of objects present themselves on paper, for it
is the circumstance of a moment, totally unexpected,
and hard to explain in words. In a brief moment the
depths and heights appear, all well expressed by the
brushwork, and the disposition of different objects is
perfect, too, better even than the actual scenery. This
is because the grand idea [of the universe] has been
thereby expressed. **❞**

From *Jiezhou xue huapian* [*The Art of Painting*], by Shen Zongqian, translated by Lin Yutang in
The Chinese Theory of Art. New York: G.P. Putnam's Sons, 1967, p.204.

Commentary

Taoist ideas are integral to the Chinese arts and have had a profound influence on East Asian artistic traditions. The Taoist ideal of creative spontaneity has, in particular, helped to shape theory and practice in various art forms. Creative spontaneity involves the ability to draw upon one's personal resources while responding to a particular moment and circumstance. It is presumed that an artist has cultivated and nurtured their craft—but in creating art, knowledge and skill become experiential and intuitive, the unique possession of the artist and something that cannot be transmitted in words. This also describes the action of the Tao, which draws on limitless and formless content and possibility, and brings forth myriad creation.

Shen Zongqian's words demonstrate a fundamentally Taoist attitude toward the theory of painting, whereby the art form is perceived, in essence, as an act of creation, beginning in the formlessness of the Tao, transforming in time and pattern into creation: what is captured is a universe in miniature, a microcosm. The artist creates this *wu-wei*, not forcing the brush, not thinking discursively, but moving with sensitivity in the moment. In this way, painting becomes a form of meditation, a means of discovering union with Tao, an accomplishment evident in the very best art.

PART FOUR:
CONFUCIANISM

INTRODUCTION

Confucianism—along with the other two formal traditions, Taoism and Buddhism, as well as the pervasive
popular religion—has been one of the most influential
systems of thought in China for centuries and remains an
important aspect of Chinese civilization. It formed the
basis of imperial ideology and was reflected in sacred
rites of the emperor to ensure harmony between human
beings and the cosmos, and in the examinations for the
selection of his administrators. It also underlay social
and family ethics and the rites of ancestor veneration.
The tradition spread with Chinese cultural and political
domination to Korea, Vietnam, and Japan, and to communities of East Asian immigrants worldwide. Just as in
China, it functions in these other cultural contexts as one
part of a complex of religious traditions, all of which
may be seen as complementary rather than exclusive.

The Confucian tradition actually began well before
Confucius (the latinate form of Kong Fuzi, "Master
Kong"), and is known in Chinese as *rujia*, or the "School
of the Ru," *ru* meaning "weak" or "yielding." *Ru* also
referred to the learned aristocracy of the defeated Shang
dynasty (ca. 1766–1050BCE), who nevertheless continued to serve as specialists in *li* (ritual and protocol)—
that is, in determining appropriate behavior and

A 17th-century calligrapher's brush-rest, which represents the world in miniature, comprehensible form, with the five sacred mountains that mark out its center and each compass point.

techniques of government. The willingness of the *ru* to serve their conquerors appears to have been motivated at least in part by their devotion to the *li*. Over time, *ru* came to refer to one trained in the *li* who worked in the government, and was later used more loosely to refer to an educated person. The layers of meanings of this term—including devotion to *li*, motivation by virtue, service to government, and dedication to education—have been key components of what, according to Confucian tradition, constitutes the ideal person.

Confucianism is premised on the idea of a natural hierarchy, which is believed to be the ordering principle of all things and is reflected in ancient Chinese cosmology. This cosmology expresses two fundamental principles: the cosmos is a sacred place; and all aspects of it are interrelated. The central purpose of Chinese religion in general is to uphold this sacredness by maintaining harmony among human beings and between humanity and nature. The focus of Confucianism in particular is on creating harmony in human society. According to the ancient understanding of how the cosmos functions, everything that exists, including Heaven, Earth, human beings, and deities, is made up of the same vital substance, or *qi (ch'i)*. *Qi* is manifested most basically as two complementary forces, *yin* and *yang*. *Yin* denotes that which is dark, moist, inert, turbid, cold, soft, and feminine, and *yang* denotes that which is bright, dry, growing, light, warm, hard, and masculine. All things consist of both *yin* and *yang* in varying proportions.

The *yin-yang* view of the cosmos functions in conjunction with the cycle of the "Five Phases," which furnishes a more detailed structure for understanding how vital forces interact. The phases are represented by "fire," "wood," "metal," "water," and "earth," but rather than being material elements, these are to be understood as metaphysical forces, each exercising a dominating influence at any one time. Everything in the universe—the changes and patterns in nature, the heavenly bodies, time, natural phenomena, and human society—is linked by its participation in cycles of transformation as well as by its varying proportions of *yin* and *yang*.

The action of *yin* and *yang* and the Five Phases are the primal and cosmic patterns that inform human relationships. The teachings of Confucianism are the means by which those human relationships are fulfilled, bringing them into line with cosmic patterns, which will, in a ripple effect, bring harmony to all of society and, ultimately, to the cosmos. In practice, these social patterns are seen most basically in the "Five Relationships" (see p.365–367), especially the relationship between parent and child, which is typified by the Confucian ethic of *xiao*, or filial piety, and in statecraft, which presumed the domination of a benevolent and virtuous ruler over obedient and receptive subjects. Confucian statecraft was the basis of government in East Asia for centuries, disappearing in its official form early in the twentieth century. Although Confucianism is no longer used as state ideology today, it remains a distinctive feature in the life and mores of the region.

CHAPTER ONE

ORIGINS AND HISTORICAL DEVELOPMENT

The Confucian tradition began in Chinese antiquity, many centuries before the birth of Confucius. It was interpreted by classical Confucians and then reformulated in the Han dynasty (206BCE–220CE), creating a powerful imperial ideology. The Neo-Confucian movement that arose during the Song dynasty (960–1279CE) expanded Confucian concerns and established new methods for the attainment of enlightenment.

Due to China's political and cultural dominance in East Asia, Confucianism had a lasting impact in Japan, Vietnam, and Korea—territories well beyond the north Chinese heartland of its origin. Its influence continues to the present day in these cultures, with social harmony and responsibility stressed above individual freedom and rights.

LEFT: Huang Di, the Yellow Emperor, is the semi-mythical fore-father of the Chinese people and propaga-tor of Chinese culture (see pages 322 and 354). It was ancient, heroic figures such as Huang Di who became exemplars of virtuous behavior and kingship.

Confucian ideals and practices were not initiated by the figure Confucius himself, but have their roots many centuries before his existence, in Chinese antiquity in the Yellow River valley, where the legendary Yellow Emperor is said to have established Chinese culture. Myth apart, the hallmarks of Confucianism—ancestor veneration, sacrifice, and a religio-political order—are evident in the earliest Chinese written records, the Shang oracle-bone inscriptions, which were discovered at Anyang in northeast China.

Divination with "oracle bones" was an important practice during the Shang dynasty (ca. 1766–1050BCE) and was adopted by the royal house in order to receive supernatural guidance on a range of concerns, from forecasting the weather and determining the cause of a toothache, to the right time to wage war, the likelihood of success in hunting, and the abundance of the harvest.

Although questions were sometimes put to the supreme being known as Shang Di, the "Lord on High," by far the greatest percentage of oracles was addressed to ancestors, who were believed to be a source of blessing or misfortune, particularly concerning human fertility. At this time only royalty was believed to have ancestors; common people's souls decayed with their bodies. These ancestors could be relied on to have the interests of the family—and therefore the state—as their primary concern. Shang Di was usually considered to be too remote from humanity to consult for most mortal concerns. In making the oracle, a question would be intoned as a heated rod was placed on the shoulder-blade of an ox or sheep or the plastron (underside) of a turtle. A diviner would then interpret the cracks made by the hot rod to reveal the answer to the question. The recorded questions and answers disclose the sense of duty and connection presumed between ancestor and descendant.

In the Zhou dynasty (1050–256BCE), Shang Di was largely replaced by Tian, "Heaven," the source of power and order. Heaven was a non-anthropomorphic force that was able to control and influence events. The Zhou proclaimed that they had received the "Mandate of Heaven," the divinely sanctioned right to rule, because of their virtue in contrast to the depravity of the last Shang rulers. The idea that virtue and beneficent rule are the basis of the state was thus firmly established by this date.

During the Zhou dynasty, various ritual practices, behavioral codes, literary and poetic works, and exemplary deeds of filiality, loyalty, virtue, and good government were distilled into the canonical work, the "Five Classics," which is traditionally attributed to this period (see pp.344–346). By the sixth century BCE, the political

authority of the Zhou rulers had declined, and the ensu-
ing period of disorder saw the formulation of numerous
theories aimed at restoring harmony and peace—these
were collectively known as the "Hundred Schools." It
was in this context that Confucius put forth his ideas
about order in society and the state. Born in 551BCE at
Qufu in modern Shandong province, Confucius (Kong
Qiu, also known as Kongzi, "Master Kong") came from
a poor but respectable family. After serving in the government of the state of Lu, he spent thirteen years traveling the various Chinese states and asking their rulers
to put into practice his ideas about government. He
returned home unsuccessful and disappointed and spent
the rest of his days, until his death in 479BCE, teaching
and, as tradition has it, working on the Five Classics.

Confucius maintained that in order to have a harmonious society and effective government, the primary
relationship of parent and child must be in order. The
obligations of filial piety—the honor, respect, love, and
service owed between parent and child—is a theme
which is paralleled in other relationships in society.
Good government, for example, consists of a similar
process of care and obligation between ruler and subject.
All members of society must be sensitive and practiced
in what is required of them in their various roles.

Attention to rank, obligations, and ritual duties will lead ultimately to the perfection of oneself and the transformation of society.

Confucius' great follower, Mencius (Mengzi, 371– ca. 289BCE), elaborated Confucius' teachings about human virtue and good government, proclaiming the original goodness of human nature and the right of the people to rebel against a wicked ruler.

The third great Confucian thinker of the classical era, Xunzi (active ca. 298–238BCE) offered a very different view of human nature. He claimed that humans were originally evil and became good only through strict laws and harsh punishments, in addition to attention to ritual. Xunzi's views were implemented by the "Legalists"— another of the "Hundred Schools"—who held that laws and punishment, rather than virtuous example and moral suasion, must be the basis of government. The Legalists have been reviled in Chinese history for their role in the brutal reign (221–209BCE) of the first emperor of all China, Qin Shihuangdi—a period characterized by mass book-burnings and intense suspicion of intellectuals.

The Confucian school did not enjoy official patronage for several centuries after the death of Confucius, and was even persecuted under the Qin dynasty (221–207BCE). It was officially adopted in the Han

A scene from the life of Confucius depicting him with his disciples. Ink and watercolor, Qing dynasty (1644–1911).

dynasty (206BCE–220CE), when the emperor recognized that the rituals promoted by the Confucian literati were a source of impressive court ceremonial and a stabilizing force for society. Despite Confucian criticism of Legalism, Han Confucianism was a distinctive blend of Confucian idealism and Legalist pragmatism, a combination which proved effective for virtually two millennia of Chinese imperial rule. The infrastructure of Confucian rule was created at this time: a national university was established, texts lost during the Qin destruction of books were reconstructed, and a system was put into place whereby "men of talent" (ability and good moral character) were identified, trained in Confucian virtues and literature, and brought into government service. This bureaucratic system became the foundation of civil service selections in imperial China, and continued until the twentieth century; this system was eventually adopted in both Vietnam and Korea.

In addition to making Confucianism the basis of the state, the Han Dynasty promoted scholarship and new trends in Confucian thought. Most notable was the work of Dong Zhongshu, who created a philosophical synthesis that included Confucianism, Legalism, and cosmological theories based on the principles of the two complementary forces, *yin* and *yang* (see pp.318–319). Ancient Chinese cosmology posits that everything is made of *qi* (vital matter, life energy or life force). *Qi* is most basically manifest in *yin* and *yang* and all things are made up of various proportions of *yin qi* and *yang qi*. Dong's genius was to combine these cosmological concepts with Confucian political ideals, forming a triad of Heaven, Earth, and humanity. According to this vision, the ruler was perceived as the pivot between the three, ensuring order and harmony for "all under Heaven."

After the fall of the Han dynasty came several centuries of disunity, characterized by the decline of

Confucianism, the growth of Buddhism, and the expanding popularity of Taoism. Confucianism was revitalized in the Song dynasty (960–1279CE) in a movement known as Neo-Confucianism. This movement was characterized by its expansion of Confucian concerns to include metaphysics and new methods for self-cultivation and enlightenment. The most renowned scholar of this period was Zhu Xi (1130–1200CE). He proposed that all things, including human nature, have an ordering principle, *li* (to be distinguished from the homophone *li*, which means "ritual"), that shapes the vital matter, *qi*. Humans must "investigate things" to understand their underlying principles, and cultivate themselves so as to base their actions on the appropriate human behavior. There are clear Buddhist and Taoist influences in the Neo-Confucian advocacy of "quiet sitting" (meditation) as a technique of self-cultivation that leads to transformative experiences of insight.

A later Neo-Confucian who challenged Zhu Xi's teaching was Wang Yangming (Wang Shouren, 1472–1529). Wang advocated "quiet sitting" as a means to self-knowledge and awareness, and the importance of acting upon one's realizations—these insights were summed up in his theory of the unity of knowledge and action. Wang's claim that "knowledge is the beginning of action, and action is the completion of knowledge" implies that knowledge of something, for example of virtue, necessarily includes acting in a like, in this case virtuous, manner; a knowledge of filial piety means acting in a filial manner, and so on.

Vietnam and Korea came under Confucian influence mainly as a consequence of Chinese conquest during the Han dynasty. This early contact established the pattern of Confucian-based government, and although the degree of Chinese control in the following centuries was variable, Confucian learning and ideology remained integral to the government and culture of the Korean and Vietnamese élite. After the collapse of the Tang dynasty in 907CE, Vietnam to a large extent maintained its political independence from China, but nevertheless continued to adopt and adapt Chinese culture, ruling by means of a Confucian-style bureaucracy staffed through civil service exams based on the Chinese Classics. As early as 427CE, a Korean state adopted a Chinese-style government and bureaucracy. Korea also produced what was in many ways the most thoroughly Confucian state ever: the Choson, or Yi, dynasty (1392–1910). In education, bureaucracy, principles of government, and high culture, the Koreans reproduced a model Confucian civilization. The Choson produced an impressive array of scholars of Neo-Confucianism, the most famous of whom was Yi T'ongye (1501–1570), who developed and expanded on Zhu Xi's philosophy.

The situation in Japan differed from that in Korea or Vietnam. As an island state, the Japanese actively chose—as opposed to being forced to import—Confucian ideas. The first great wave of borrowing came in the sixth century CE, and was part of a movement to centralize authority in the Japanese state while adopting Chinese high culture. Prince Shotoku issued the "Seventeen Article Constitution" in 604CE which laid out the basic elements of a Confucian state (see pp.476–477), stressing the importance of central authority and social harmony produced by the specific roles to be played by each person. After this initial era of cultural borrowing, Confucianism became a fundamental, though understated, aspect of Japanese culture.

The high point of Confucian scholarship in Japan was during the Tokugawa period (1600–1868). The Tokugawa rulers saw Confucianism as a means of establishing and perpetuating stability after centuries of civil war. Kaibara Ekken (1630–1714) was the leading figure in the promotion of Japanese Neo-Confucianism, and the man who made Confucian ethics accessible to the average Japanese person.

The Confucian states of China, Vietnam, and Korea disappeared in the nineteenth and twentieth centuries due to imperialist encroachment. Many Chinese reformers and radicals, including Communists, blamed Confucianism as the cause of Chinese weakness in the face of imperialist advancement. Others, however, saw it as the basis of East Asian character and morality, and as essential to the success of modernizing nations.

Despite the disappearance of the Confucian state, Confucian ideals have continued to underpin East Asian civilizations. A new wave of Confucian scholars in the twentieth and twenty-first centuries—including Mou Tsung-san, Carsun Chang, and Tu Weiming—has reinterpreted Confucianism in the light of the modern world. The city-state of Singapore under Lee Kuan Yew and the Republic of China on Taiwan have looked to the ideas of Confucianism as being central to morality and social harmony. Finally, Confucianism has been identified as a vital part of the mixture that has contributed to the booming economies of East Asia in recent decades. It is clear that the Confucian tradition remains fundamental to the assumptions and actions of East Asians and, although diffused through family, society, culture, and political structures, is unmistakably present and formative.

Yao, Shun, and Yu in the *Shu Jing* (*Classic of Documents*) and the *Mencius* (*Mengzi*)

❝ Yu said, 'Oh Sovereign, remember this! ... There are water, fire, metal, wood, earth and grain; these must be regulated. There are the rectification of the people's virtue, attention to tools and conveniences, and ensuring abundance of life's necessities... When these nine services have been put in order, celebrate with song. Admonish the people with gentleness, correct them with authority, exhort them with the Nine Songs, and your reign will not diminish.' **❞**

From the *Shu Jing*, translated by Jennifer Oldstone-Moore

❝ Mengzi said, 'The compass and the square form perfect circles and squares; the sage brings about the perfect person. If one desires to become a ruler, one must carry out completely the role of the ruler; if one desires to become a minister, one must carry out completely the role of the minister. For these two, one need only follow the examples of Yao and Shun. Not to follow the example of Shun serving Yao is to disrespect one's prince; not to follow Yao as the model for governing the people is to harm the people.' **❞**

From the *Mencius* (*Mengzi*), translated by Jennifer Oldstone-Moore

Commentary

Classical Confucianism is generally less concerned with issues such as the creation of the cosmos than with the beginnings of civilization—the origins of which, according to Confucian belief, are to be found in the lives of the legendary "sage kings" of antiquity (see pp.354–355).

Traditional Chinese history begins in the twenty-fourth century BCE with the reign of Yao. Both he and his successor Shun (ca. 2255–ca. 2205 BCE) ruled by ritual and benevolence rather than military might. The loving care that was extended to the people by them is an early and powerful expression of the idea of a ruler who is essentially a father to his subjects. Statecraft, as described (opposite) to Shun by his exemplary minister Yu, is concerned with the people's material and moral welfare—both of which were persistent themes in East Asian theories of kingship.

Yao, Shun, and Yu were held up by later generations as model rulers and ministers, as evidenced in the passage from the *Mencius*. Their actions and judgments were analyzed to provide solutions to contemporary problems. In the nineteenth century, faced with serious challenges from the West, Chinese Confucian scholars drew upon the examples of Yao and Shun in formulating their arguments for change.

CHAPTER TWO

ASPECTS OF THE DIVINE

Confucian concepts of the divine take two main forms. On the one hand, concerns focus on ordering principles—on cosmic forces and concepts of ultimate reality, such as Heaven and the Great Ultimate—which are subjects of contemplation rather than worship. On the other hand, there is a wide range of deities and spiritual beings, which are venerated and placated at shrines and temples.

In Confucianism, the worlds of the living and of the deities and spirits are closely linked. Ancestors are deceased family members; ghosts are dangerous beings who are placated through offerings. Humans who live exemplary lives may become gods and be appointed to the celestial hierarchy after death. Gods are, in turn, petitioned by humans, whose offerings sustain and nourish them.

LEFT: A scholar listens intently to running water. Landscape paintings had moral, ethical, and cosmological significance: they reflected the eternal principle (li) that orders all creation and the disposition of a single object.

Confucian concepts of the divine focus on an accessible spirit world and awesome but remote cosmic forces. These ancient beliefs are evident in the first Chinese records, the Shang oracle bones (see pp.322–323). Shang rulers sacrificed to their ancestors and also venerated a supreme being, Shang Di, the "Lord on High." With his subsequent displacement by Tian, or "Heaven," the "Mandate of Heaven" (see p.323) became central to the Confucian theory of government. This belief revealed Heaven as an entity with a will, concerned about and responsive to the welfare of the people. Confucius himself clearly understood Heaven as being both a natural and a moral order and believed that one must strive to know Heaven's will.

Perceiving the nature of cosmic order became an important aspect of Confucianism from the tenth century onward. Neo-Confucians developed a cosmology based on *li*, an ordering principle that shapes *qi*, the vital matter that makes up all things (see pp.316–318). Although there is apparent diversity in creation, all things are united by the Great Ultimate, *Taiji* (*T'ai-chi*), the ordering principle of the cosmos. Through contemplation and investigation, humans can experience unity with the holy cosmos. The Neo-Confucian method of self-cultivation included intensive scholarship, a reverent attitude and disciplined mind, and "quiet-sitting"—meditation for purifying and focusing the mind which can produce a profoundly transformative experience. These ideas and practices became part of Confucian orthodoxy throughout East Asia.

Of more immediate concern to most people, however, was the multitude of spirits who could harm or help humans. The spirit world includes ancestors and gods, who receive offerings and reciprocate by means of favors and blessings, and ghosts, who are the unhappy, unpropitiated dead. "Heaven" is the dwelling place of the gods and is envisioned as a vast bureaucracy. The officials of the celestial realm wear the same regalia as those in the imperial bureaucracy; they are approached and petitioned in the same way as human officials—because they are just as susceptible to bribes and favors. In short, the worlds of the living and the dead not only mirror but interpenetrate each other.

At the top of this bureaucracy is the Jade Emperor, the spiritual counterpart of the terrestrial emperor. He is the supreme judge and sovereign of Heaven, the overseer of the administrative hierarchy. Appropriately, the Jade Emperor is a distant figure and it is possible to communicate with him only through intermediaries, just as an average person could not directly petition the emperor.

The ceiling of the Temple of Heaven, Beijing. The square base and the round, vaulted ceiling symbolize Earth and Heaven. Here, the emperor would perform annual sacrificial rituals to call upon Heaven to guarantee the order of his realm.

The lowest official in the celestial bureaucracy is one's local tutelary god, Tudi Gong, the "God of the Earth." Every neighborhood or village has its own Tudi Gong, who is likened to a village policeman or magistrate. It is his job to keep the peace, to quell local ghosts who cause trouble, and to be aware of what goes on in the area. Villagers might report events such as births, deaths, and marriages, both to Tudi Gong and to the local (mortal) police station. Tudi Gong passes on any relevant happenings to his superior in the celestial hierarchy.

One of the primary ideals of Confucianism is to promote virtuous officials in the bureaucracy. This ideal also applies to the spirit world, and can be seen in the story of Mazu, a fisherman's daughter who became Empress of Heaven. Mazu lived a short but exemplary life, and exhibited extraordinary spiritual powers. After she died at age twenty-eight, her spirit was venerated by the local population, and boats began to carry an image of her for protection. After two centuries of popular veneration, local Confucian literati noticed the popularity of her cult and tales of her generosity and service to the people. They recommended that she be promoted, and by imperial command she rose through the ranks of the celestial hierarchy until she was designated Empress of Heaven (Tian Hou), and became a consort of the Jade Emperor. Today, Mazu continues to be one of the most popular deities in southern China and Taiwan. Her story illustrates the connection between the élite and popular traditions, and Confucianism's effectiveness in influencing political and social structures.

The *Western Inscription* by Zhang Zai (1020–1077)

" Heaven is my father and Earth is my mother, and even such a small creature as I finds an intimate place in their midst. Therefore that which fills the universe I regard as my body and that which directs the universe I consider as my nature. All people are my brothers and sisters, and all things are my companions. The great ruler (the emperor) is the eldest son of my parents (Heaven and Earth), and the great ministers are his stewards. Respect the aged—this is the way to treat them as elders should be treated. Show deep love toward the orphaned and the weak—this is the way to treat them as the young should be treated. ... Do nothing shameful in the recesses of your own house and thus bring no dishonor to [Heaven and Earth]. Preserve your mind and nourish your nature and thus (serve them) with untiring effort. ...Wealth, honor, blessing, and benefits are meant for the enrichment of my life, while poverty, humble station, and sorrow are meant to help me to fulfillment. In life I follow and serve (Heaven and Earth). In death I will be at peace. "

From *A Source Book in Chinese Philosophy*, by Wing-tsit Chan. Princeton University Press: Princeton, 1963, pp.497–98. Note: (Parentheses) are in the translator's original; [square brackets] are author's addition.

Commentary

In the *Western Inscription*, the Neo-Confucian scholar Zhang Zai succinctly and poetically describes the fundamentally interrelated nature of the cosmos and evokes the holiness and completeness of the created order. The influential text (which the author inscribed on the western wall of his study) reflects the idea that there is a principle—*li*—that underlies all creation. This principle is manifest in the orderly pattern of nature, which in an eternal cycle unfolds in creation and eventually returns to its undifferentiated state.

The underlying principle to which Zhang Zai refers is the Great Ultimate, or *Taiji*, the basis for all growth and change. *Taiji* is manifest as *qi*, vital matter, which differentiates into the *yin* and *yang* polarities, and then into the "Five Phases" (see pp.318–319) and myriad creation. All things, spiritual and physical, are made of *qi*, and thus all things are related: the universe is one. The text uses the evocative Confucian language of family relationships to articulate the relationship between all things in a cosmos in which there is no creator standing apart from creation. The sage strives to perceive the unity of the universe, comprehend its pattern, and harmonize with it.

CHAPTER THREE

SACRED TEXTS

In many religions, sacred texts are considered to be "divinely revealed"—the Confucian canon, however, is almost exclusively attributed to human beings. It includes the works of founding figures such as Confucius and Mencius, and covers subjects ranging from the origins of civilization and good government to the history and protocol of early dynasties.

The dominance of the Confucian canon in early East Asian civilizations was equal to that of the Bible in the West. In China, its texts were the source for moral and intellectual development, and they were the means by which the Chinese élite culture was transmitted to other East Asian civilizations. Although the canon no longer has the prominence it once did, the ideals that it promotes still have tremendous power in East Asian culture.

LEFT: An early 18th-century Chinese painting depicting the examination of county magistrates. Entry into this important stratum of the government bureaucracy was through open civil service tests, which would have required considerable knowledge of the Confucian Classics.

At the heart of the Confucian tradition are its scriptures, especially the "Five Classics" and the "Four Books." The Five Classics were revered in ancient China and, by the time of the Han dynasty, constituted the core of Confucian learning in Vietnam and Korea as well as in China. They were memorized by every aspiring student, formed the basis of civil service examinations, and were quoted not only by scholars and philosophers but also by bureaucrats. In Japan, the Five Classics were an important part of the borrowed heritage of China. In Korea and Vietnam, due to early Chinese political control, they formed the basis of élite culture.

Confucius saw himself as a mediator of the wisdom of the "sage kings" of antiquity (see pp.354–355). For him, this wisdom was accessible primarily through the study of the Classics: the *Classic of Changes* (*Yijing*, also *I Ching*), the *Classic of Documents* (*Shu Jing*), the *Classic of Poetry* (*Shi Jing*), the *Record of Rites* (*Li Ji*), and the *Spring and Autumn Annals* (*Chunqiu*). A sixth text, the *Classic of Music* (*Yue Jing*), was lost before the third century BCE.

Each of the Classics captures an important component of wisdom, promotes harmony and order, and provides the means to self-cultivation and becoming fully human. The *Classic of Changes* captures the tremendous importance of the ancient practice and theory of divination; it also underscores the intimate connection between the human and natural realm, and the availability of guidance from the cosmos for those who are sensitive to it. Attributed to the mythic emperor and culture-bearer Fu Xi, the *Classic of Changes*' system of divination is based on sixty-four hexagrams representing various combinations of *yin* and *yang* (see pp.318–319). These hexagrams are taken to represent all possible situations and developments in the constantly changing universe. Confucius is traditionally credited with writing the "Ten Wings," commentaries and expositions which help to decipher the abstruse judgments of the text.

The *Classic of Documents* is a record of historical events, some traditionally dated to China's remote past (third millennium BCE), providing lessons in moral behavior and good government. The *Spring and Autumn Annals* records events in the Zhou dynasty and has also been read for moral judgments and guidance for rulers. Both texts articulate the Confucian emphasis on looking to the past for direction and guidance.

The *Classic of Poetry* is a collection of 305 poems ranging from courtly airs to folk songs. One tradition has it that the Zhou kings collected the poems to assess the mood and concerns of the people—knowledge vital to a ruler who wishes to keep the Mandate of Heaven (see p.323). Many of the poems are read as allegorical commentaries on government. The *Record of Rites* is a collection of material that incorporates mundane household instructions for the young, protocol for royalty, and philosophy. It articulates the template for the transformative *li*—ritual, etiquette, and propriety—which is the basis of Confucian self-cultivation (see pp.364–365).

Traditionally, Confucius is credited with writing the *Spring and Autumn Annals* as well as the "Ten Wings," and with editing the four other classic texts. Modern scholarship holds that these texts were compiled throughout the Zhou dynasty, and the received texts are the result of recension in the Han following the Qin dynasty's practice of book burning (see p.325).

The Five Classics were augmented by other texts through the centuries, with a total of thirteen identified by the ninth century CE. Song philosopher Zhu Xi brought together the "Four Books," asserting that they summed up the teachings of Confucius. They became the core texts of Confucian teaching in China from 1313 to 1905, with Zhu's commentary considered orthodoxy. The Four Books consist of the *Analects* (*Lunyu*) of Confucius, the *Mencius* (*Mengzi*), the *Great Learning* (*Daxue*) and the *Doctrine of the Mean* (*Zhongyong*).

The *Analects*, which formed part of the canon from

the Han dynasty onward, is a record of Confucius' own prescriptions for an ideal society recorded by his students. In it, he demonstrates how the rites (*li*) of early Chinese rulers provide a template for appropriate human interaction and methods of achieving virtuous government and a harmonious society. The *Mencius*, the works of Confucius' eponymous follower, expands on Confucius' teachings in the *Analects*. In this text, Mencius developed a theory of human beings as fundamentally good and educable—it is a theory that has had tremendous influence in the Confucian world. Another innovation of the *Mencius* is its assertion that subjects have the right to overthrow a corrupt or tyrannical ruler.

The *Great Learning* and the *Doctrine of the Mean* were originally written as chapters in the *Record of Rites*, and were selected by Zhu Xi for their philosophical and metaphysical import. The *Great Learning* teaches that the first step in bringing the world into harmony is the cultivation of the individual. Self-cultivation has a ripple effect that will spread eventually to the family, locality, region, world, and cosmos. The *Doctrine of the Mean* asserts that cosmos and humanity form a unity through sincere effort.

All of the texts in the Confucian canon are written in the terse, refined language of classical, "adorned,"

"Friendship with the
upright, the devoted and
the learned is profitable."

"Think of justice at the
sight of profit, and sacrifice
when faced with danger."

"If you do not consider
the future, you will be in
trouble when it comes near."

"If you find you make a
mistake, then you must not
be afraid of correcting it."

"Harmony is the most valuable."

"Rule by moral force."

A selection of maxims from Confucius' work, the Analects,
which has been described as the most influential text ever.

Chinese—their complexity gave rise to a tradition of commentary aimed at elucidation and interpretation. Study of the canon required years of focused effort. Chinese children began learning to write Chinese characters as young as four years old and were aided by texts that presented Confucian teachings in the form of jingles for easy memorization. Once capable, students would learn their texts by rote, only later studying commentaries to assist in understanding. For scholars in Japan, Korea, and Vietnam, mastering the Classics and other books of the canon also involved mastering a foreign language.

The lessons contained within the classic texts were disseminated in a number of ways for those who were unable to read them. In China, community schools were established and simplified manuals were written to teach the essence of the canon to the unlettered. During the Qing dynasty, the *Sacred Edict*, which contained basic teachings of Confucian morality and virtue, was read and explained to the populace by imperial decree. Morality tracts that contained Confucian lessons were popular, and texts featuring exemplars of filial piety were widely read in both China and Korea. Some accomplished scholars, notably Zhu Xi in China and Kaibara Ekken in Japan, wrote texts and manuals expressly for the use and edification of the common person.

"North Wind" from the *Classic of Poetry*

❝ The north wind is so cold;

The snow falls so thick.

Be tender; love me

Take my hand and we will go together.

You're so timid and so slow—

We must hurry, hurry! ❞

❝ The north wind is so strong;

The snow whirls so fast.

Be tender; love me

Take my hand and we will return together.

You're so timid and so slow—

We must hurry, hurry! ❞

❝ Nothing so red as the fox,

Nothing blacker than the crow;

Be tender; love me

Take my hand and we will ride in the carriage together.

You're so timid and so slow—

We must hurry, hurry! ❞

From the *Shi Jing*, translated by Jennifer Oldstone-Moore

Commentary

The *Classic of Poetry* (from which this poem is taken; see pp.345–346) has been pivotal in Chinese literature and culture. It has been used to gauge the mood of the people, and thus to guide the government; as a repository of hymns for official functions; and as part of the required canon for the civil service. The poems in the collection are said to date from the twelfth to the seventh century BCE and range from courtly airs to folk songs. Their subject matter also varies greatly and includes love, war, agriculture, sacrifice, and dynastic legends.

"North Wind" is from a series of folk songs in the volume that speaks of the joys and concerns of common people—many of the pieces being love songs. However, Confucian literature always has a moral gloss and this poem has traditionally been interpreted not so much as a love poem as an indictment of a cruel government, a warning against tyrannical rule, and an advocacy of righteous and beneficent leadership. According to this reading, the first two stanzas are metaphorical references to oppressive conditions; the fox and the crow who appear in the final stanza are intended as omens of evil. In stressing rule by virtue, Confucians warn that subjects will flee a tyrant and flock to the country of a just ruler—illustrated here by the speaker's insistence on a hurried departure.

備箕畴富
長　王百子久
芳
憑誰士生

CHAPTER FOUR

SACRED PERSONS

In the Confucian tradition, various historic, leg-endary, semilegendary, and mythical figures are recognized for their saintly or heroic acts. These exemplars brought culture, social institutions, and good government to China to establish its golden age of antiquity. It is to them that Confucius looked when shaping the tradition he received, and the lives of many of them are related in the "Five Classics" (see pp.344–346).

Other illustrious individuals lived well after the golden age. They ranged from outstanding scholars who dutifully transmitted the ideals that Confucius had espoused, to ordinary peo-ple who exhibited exceptional behavior. Finally, some worthies so distinguished themselves in the mortal realm that they continued to exert influence in the lives of ordinary people from the celestial realm.

LEFT: A 17th–18th-century wood-block print of King Wen, the "civilizing king" who was one of the founders of the Zhou dynasty. Here he is depicted watching children at play among lotus flowers.

In China there is a rich mythology of heroes and culture bearers (semi-mythical figures believed to have brought humanity the basics of civilization). The most noted of these are Fu Xi, Shen Nong, and Huang Di. Fu Xi is credited with domesticating animals and inventing nets for catching animals and fish. He established the art of divination by devising the hexagram system of the Eight Trigrams used in the *Classic of Changes* (see pp.344–345) and, with his consort Nuwa, invented marriage and the family. Shen Nong, the Divine Farmer, invented the plow and hoe and taught humanity the skills of agriculture. He discovered the rudiments of medicine and pharmacology by determining the therapeutic qualities of all plants. Huang Di, the Yellow Emperor (see illustration, p.320), invented warfare and defeated "barbarians" to secure what became the heart of the Chinese state.

Chinese tradition considers the period following the culture bearers as the golden age of antiquity, the time of the "sage kings," especially Shun, Yao and Yu who exemplify the dedication, intelligence, and virtue appropriate to a ruler. Shun and Yao were praised by Confucius as examples of perfect rulers. Yao determined that none of his sons—ten in number—were worthy to rule, and therefore searched for the most virtuous man in the kingdom to succeed him. His criterion of virtue was filial piety, which was demonstrated by Shun, who continued to serve his father and stepbrother without complaint, despite their attempts to harm and even murder him. Shun became king and later also bypassed his sons, handing the succession to Yu, the founder of the legendary Xia dynasty (2205–1766BCE).

The story of Yu exemplifies the Chinese view of the ideal state, which is characterized by beneficent government and just rulers who strive to bring about order and harmony between nature and humanity. Yu's worthiness was demonstrated in his ceaseless physical labor to protect the people from flooding, China's most frequent form of natural disaster. His dedication to this task was so great that for ten years he did not visit his own home, even when he passed by so closely that he could hear the cries of his young children.

A complement to the ideal ruler and much praised by Confucius, the duke of Zhou (died 1094BCE) has long served as a model of the exemplary public servant who did his duty to uphold order and his dynasty, but without seeking the throne for himself. The duke was the brother of King Wu, founder of the Zhou dynasty, and showed his sensitivity to familial and social obligations by being an exemplary younger brother, devoted son, and loyal minister. After Wu died, the duke acted as regent for Wu's young son for seven years, never attempting to usurp the throne, in spite of accusations—subsequently disproved—to the contrary. This heroic role model proved so enduring that "duke of Zhou" was a popular nickname for the respected Communist premier Zhou Enlai (1898–1976). Yao, Shun, Yu and the duke of Zhou served as models of rulers and ministers in East Asia for centuries.

The great sage, Confucius, is also revered in the tradition, and with him his illustrious followers. In China, temples venerating Confucius were first established in the Han dynasty, and the temple at Qufu, Confucius's home town, became a national shrine. The first Confucian temple was built in Qufu in 478BCE, although no official sacrifice was made to the sage himself until 195BCE, when the Han emperor Gaodi (r. 206–195) offered the "Great Sacrifice" (*daji*), including the offering of an ox, at the tomb of Confucius. Confucian temples, which by the late empire were found in every province of China, held memorial services for Confucius in the second and eighth months of the Chinese lunar year. The Confucian temples honored Confucius and his most esteemed followers, some contemporaries of Confucius, and other later figures such as Mencius and Zhu Xi. The temples contained the memorial tablets of a

China's Emperor Kangxi (1662–1723) was a patron of Neo-Confucian learning and his practical system of dykes rivaled the work of the sage king Yu, the "Flood-tamer."

number of illustrious Confucians, carefully arranged according to rank and seniority. Confucius himself continued to be honored by state sponsored and mandated sacrifices throughout Chinese history. However, his status as a human and not a god was resolutely maintained, despite the not unusual practice of apotheosizing human heroes into the celestial bureaucracy. Today, his birthday is celebrated in a solemn and ancient ceremony at the Memorial Hall in Qufu and also at the Confucian temple in Taipei, where he is remembered as the First Teacher.

Confucian ideals were also the basis for recognizing contemporary worthies. In every dynasty there were heroes and heroines who embodied such ideals as the filial child, the chaste and devoted wife, and the virtuous and selfless public servant. In Korea and China their stories are recounted in texts such as the *Classic of Filial Piety*, the *Biographies of Heroic Women*, and the *Record of Filial Behavior*. Such stories include that of Laizi, who pretended to be a child even when he was more than seventy, so that his aged parents would not feel old; others tell of girls who committed suicide at the death of their fiancés in order to be loyal to their betrothed, and of the secondary wife who ran into a burning house to rescue the children of her husband's primary wife, leaving her own to perish.

Confucian ideals are also evident in the pantheon of Chinese popular religion. Even today, the pantheon is structured to parallel the Chinese imperial Confucian government—a celestial bureaucracy which complements the earthly bureaucracy below. Members of the hierarchy may be identified as being Taoist, Buddhist, or some other designation, but all are subject to the same expectations of an official in the bureaucracy, patterned on stereotypes of Confucian bureaucrats. Confucian statecraft holds that those who exhibit virtue such as filiality, loyalty, righteousness, and selflessness should be promoted. Likewise, deities in the imperial pantheon could be promoted, often by (terrestrial) imperial decree, through the ranks of the celestial hierarchy. Perhaps the most famous example of this is the widely popular Guandi, a military hero of the Han era (206BCE–220CE). Throughout the centuries, he was promoted by imperial decree through the ranks of the celestial hierarchy, and continues today to be the patron god of many trades and professions. The apotheosis of Guandi and other figures in the Chinese pantheon demonstrates the pervasive influence of Confucian ideas and structures in the popular imagination, and the syncretic nature of the popular religion, which incorporates Confucian ideals seamlessly with those of other traditions.

Selections from the *Analects* of Confucius

❝ 2:4 Confucius said, 'At fifteen it was my desire to learn. At thirty I was established. At forty I had no more doubts. At fifty I knew Heaven's will. At sixty I could obey what I heard. At seventy I could follow my heart's desire and not transgress what is right.' **❞**

❝ 5:25 Zilu said, 'I would like to hear your ideals.' Confucius said, 'My ideals are to bring solace to the old, to be faithful to friends, and to cherish the young.' **❞**

❝ 7:7 Confucius said, 'Upon receiving as little as a few pieces of dried meat for tuition, I have not yet refused to teach a person.' **❞**

❝ 7:18 The Duke of She asked Zilu about Confucius and Zilu did not answer. Confucius said, 'Why didn't you say that I am a person who studies with such eagerness that he forgets his food, is so happy that he forgets his cares, and does not notice the coming of old age?' **❞**

❝ 7:19 Confucius said, 'I am not one who was born with knowledge; I am one who loves antiquity and diligently seeks knowledge there.' **❞**

From the *Analects* (*Lunyu*) of Confucius, translated by Jennifer Oldstone-Moore

Commentary

Confucius, or Kong Qiu (known in China as Kongzi or Master Kong), was born in 552BCE in the state of Lu, which is in modern-day Shandong province. It is thought that he was descended from nobility, perhaps even the Shang royal family; however, his own family was humble and he was orphaned as a child. He died in 479BCE, age 73. His most significant contribution was as an educator rather than as a government official, and he is still celebrated as the first and greatest teacher in much of East Asia.

The most reliable source of information about Confucius is the *Analects* (*Lunyu*), the recorded conversations between him and his disciples. In this text, he is revealed as one who loved learning and culture, observed the details of ritual with sincere earnestness rather than pompous formalism, and was committed and attentive to others, especially his disciples (Zilu, mentioned in the extract opposite, was one of his favorite students). Although most of his teachings focused on the human realm, it is clear that he perceived his civilizing mission as coming from Heaven, which protected and inspired him. Confucius has perhaps been the single most important figure in East Asian culture—his teachings remain influential in the present day

CHAPTER FIVE

ETHICAL PRINCIPLES

Confucian ethics, which have served as the basis of East Asian society for at least 2,000 years, are directed toward the creation of a harmonious society and a virtuous, benevolent state. It is believed that these ideals can be achieved through the practice of *li* (ritual and protocol) and *ren* (humaneness).

Confucianism demands that all people be treated with humanity, but within a well-articulated hierarchy. Filial piety is a central Confucian virtue, as is behaving according to one's rank. The most important relationships are those between parent and child, husband and wife, elder brother and younger brother, friend and friend, ruler and subject. An ordered, harmonious society is dependent on self-education and on each person playing his or her part appropriately and with good intent.

LEFT: A 19th-century print of a Chinese wedding ceremony shows the bride and groom kneeling before a tablet honoring "Heaven, Earth, parents, and teachers." The husband-and-wife family unit was central to the transmission of Confucian values in society.

Confucians hold that actions are transformative—to become an ethical person, one must be self-cultivated through the study and practice of appropriate behavior. At the heart of Confucian ethics is the *li*, the "guiding principle of all things great and small" (*Analects* 1:12), which is held to be the behavior of the sages of antiquity as recorded in the classic texts. *Li* has a range of meanings: ritual, propriety, etiquette, and ceremony; it denotes ideal behavior, and moral and righteous action, and is the means by which one works to "cut, carve, file and polish," in order to become a superior person and cultivate ethical behavior.

Other forms of cultivation also contribute to ethical development. Refinement in the arts, or *wen*, follows the example of the sages who created poetry, music, and ritual. According to Confucius, those who study literature extensively and who are restrained by the *li*, are truly superior, and will not violate the "Confucian Way." Thus, Confucians strive to master the fine arts—such refinement is the mark not only of aesthetic taste, but also of moral training.

The *li* provides a template for appropriate action which, once internalized, is expressed in human interaction. The actions of the self-cultivated person are *ren*, the ethical term referred to most frequently by Confucius in the *Analects*. *Ren* is defined as goodness, humane-ness, love, benevolence, human-heartedness, and humanity. The word is rendered with two component parts that denote "person" and "two," indicating the relationship between two people. Together *li* and *ren* form the basis of ethical behavior which is balanced between self-cultivation and learning and the effortless extension of learning into human interaction.

Action in accordance with *ren* is manifest in attitude and external expression in two other virtues—reciproc-ity (*shu*) and sincerity (*zhong*). Reciprocity forms the basis of the Confucian golden rule—"What you do not want done to you, do not do to others" (*Analects* 15:23). Rather than assuming that others will like what one likes, one must consider actions from the other person's point of view. The ethic of *zhong* provides a basis for the action of reciprocity—sincerity is a feeling, an internal orientation, that manifests itself in proper action.

All interaction must be based in *ren*, but specific actions are delineated within a clearly defined hierarchy (hierarchy is considered to be natural and essential to the creation of harmony). Key roles and corresponding virtues are outlined in the "Five Relationships," namely, those between parent and child, elder brother and younger brother, husband and wife, friend and friend, and ruler and subject. Each relationship has its specific roles and responsibilities: a parent owes a child education, care, and moral formation; a child owes a parent obedience, respect, and care in old age and after death. The parent/child relationship establishes the basic pattern for other relationships—thus, the virtue of filiality (*xiao*) is the basis for social structure. A husband and wife are to care for each other, with the husband protecting and providing, and the wife being obedient and maintaining the household. The elder brother has responsibility for younger siblings who owe him deference (birth order is very clearly delineated in East Asian kinship terms). The relationship between ruler and subject parallels that of parent and child, for the ruler is to provide care and guidance, and the subject is to be obedient as well as loyal. Friends are to be loyal—this is the only relationship that has the potential of being between people of equal rank, but even here, a hierarchy of age is often reflected.

Although obedience and deference are demanded from subordinates within this structure of relationships, a good son, worthy wife, and loyal minister have a duty to remonstrate unethical behavior. All five relationships (as well as others, such as those between teacher and student, and employer and employee) have serious mutual responsibilities, and both familial and non-familial bonds are presumed to last a lifetime. Ethical action includes the "rectification of names," which means knowing one's roles in the web of relationships that create community, and behaving accordingly so as to insure social harmony.

Confucian ethics are particularly important in the realm of government. The ruler as sovereign and father-figure is to be an active exemplar of virtue. "The ruler is to be like the wind; the people like the grass that bends in whatever direction the wind blows (*Analects* 12:19). Self-cultivation, a cultured education, and a life lived according to *li* were deemed essential for the aspiring government official. Such figures were urged to exhibit their firm principles by chastising the emperor himself if his rule was not virtuous and withdrawing from service rather than aiding a despot: "Show yourself when the Way prevails in the empire; when it does not, then hide" (*Analects* 8:13). After the Mongols invaded China and founded the Yuan dynasty in 1279, many courtiers chose "virtuous retirement" in preference to serving the "barbarian" foreign ruler.

Confidence in the universality of Confucian ethics was challenged in the nineteenth and twentieth centuries as a consequence of the influence of Western ideas and technology. Many hoped that Confucianism would continue to provide the ethical basis of East Asian life; others saw it as the root of East Asian weakness and called for a complete dismantling of the systems and ideas of which Confucianism was a central part. Some hoped that its values could be combined with Western technology, or, as it was stated in China, "Chinese studies for substance; Western studies for function."

This hope has been repeatedly reformulated and revisited throughout East Asia in the last 100 years. The new Chinese republic drafted a constitution in 1913 that advocated Confucianism as the basis of moral cultivation and education; Chiang Kai-shek attempted to impress Confucian values on the populace of the Republic of China through various programs and proclamations; today, groups in Taiwan and Korea advocate Confucian teachings and a return to "traditional values." The city-state of Singapore is especially notable for its systematic program of Confucian ethics in the schools, which was promoted by the government in the 1980s. The cardinal principles of this program show the Confucian emphasis on harmony and working to the good of the group. They teach the importance of considering community over self, affirm the family as the basic unit of society, and emphasize the necessity for tolerance and

A 16th-century ceramic box lid depicts a district magistrate trying a case. As the local representatives of the imperial government, magistrates were steeped in Confucian learning.

harmony in a religiously and ethnically diverse society. These programs have been instigated and supported by top officials in Singapore to strengthen Asian cultural heritage and to protect the region from the venality and excess of Western culture, demonstrating both continuity and change in classical Confucian ethics.

Daxue (the *Great Learning*)

" . . . Things have their roots and their branches ... their conclusions and beginnings. When one knows what comes first and what comes last, one will come near the Way. Those of old who wished to manifest clear virtue to all the world first governed their states; those who wished to govern their states first set their families in order; those who wished to set their families in order first cultivated their persons; those who wished to cultivate their persons first rectified their own hearts and minds; those who wished to rectify their own hearts and minds first made their thoughts sincere; those who wished to make their thoughts sincere first extended their knowledge. Extension of knowledge rests in the investigation of things.

When things are investigated, knowledge is extended; when knowledge is extended, thoughts are made sincere; when thoughts are made sincere, the heart and mind are rectified; when the heart and mind are rectified, one's person is cultivated; when one's person is cultivated, the family is set in order; when the family is set in order, the state is governed; when the state is governed, there is peace in all the world. "

From the *Daxue*, translated by Jennifer Oldstone-Moore.

Commentary

The *Great Learning*, or *Daxue*, which also means "adult education," was originally a chapter in the *Record of Rites* (one of the "Five Classics"). It was among the texts selected by the Neo-Confucian philosopher Zhu Xi in his compilation of the "Four Books" (see pp.344–347), and was one of the first texts learned by all students. With its focus on self-cultivation, education, and bringing order to the world, the *Great Learning* sums up the Confucian program for balancing development of the self with responsibility to others. It is a work that has had a profound influence on Confucian ethics, practice, and philosophy.

The Confucian program for transformation is accomplished in eight stages that have been described as a blueprint for putting the ethical principle of *ren* (humaneness, see pp.364–365) into practice. Transformation through *ren* begins with the self and leads ultimately to the pacification of "All under Heaven." Vital to this process is the ability to discern "roots and ... branches," "conclusions and beginnings," and the "first and ... last." Perceiving the relative importance of things—such as knowing one's specific obligations, which range from courtesy to a stranger to obedience to parents—is understood to be at the heart of this endeavour.

CHAPTER SIX

SACRED SPACE

In Confucianism there is frequently no clear distinction between the sacred and the profane—the sacred may be encountered in nature and in the world at large, as well as in temples, shrines, and the home. Space that is specifically designated as sacred is primarily ritual space, and ranges from simple sites where small offerings are made, to grand imperial spaces where complex rites are conducted.

Since the end of the traditional Confucian state, many temples have decayed or declined in use. However, some have been restored and maintained and, in 1988, amid lavish celebrations, a new Confucian temple was opened in Andong county in Korea—ceremonies were performed to install the ritual tablets of eighteen Chinese disciples and eighteen Korean scholars of Confucianism.

LEFT: *The Jade Bridge at the Temple of Confucius in Qufu, in Shandong province. First built in 478BCE, and much expanded since, the complex has hundreds of buildings, including Confucius' tomb in the Kong family cemetery.*

Confucian temples are monuments to human beings rather than to gods and serve to honor Confucius and his disciples, as well as worthy scholars through the ages. The human orientation of the temples is further emphasized by the general lack of images and statues—instead, Confucius' name, as well as the names of his disciples and illustrious followers, are inscribed on tablets which act as the focus of veneration.

Members of the state bureaucracy traditionally honored Confucius in twice-yearly sacrifices on the equinoxes. The most important offering was on Confucius' birthday, which is still celebrated at Confucian temples. The event generally falls on September 28 and is celebrated as "Teacher's Day" in Taiwan. Participants dress in the garb of ancient China, perform dance and music, and offer sacrifices to the great sage.

Confucian temple architecture echoes the architecture of the emperor's palace—notably, the north–south axis on which the important halls are located. The temples are built on a square base, and internally they are symmetrical, with each wall a mirror-image of the one opposite, conveying the order associated with Confucian thought. Temples were public spaces—results of civil service examinations were posted in them and they were also used for training in music and ritual.

The first Confucian temple was built in Qufu in Shandong province in 478BCE, the year after Confucius' death. Official sacrifices to Confucius began in 195BCE, when the Han emperor offered a Grand Sacrifice at Qufu; the Han later adopted Confucianism as the basis of the state cult. Adjacent to the temple is the Kong family mansion, the home of the direct descendants of Confucius from the first century BCE, when the Han government granted the family a fiefdom and title. Later dynasties also supported the temple and the family with grants of land and imperial funds. The Confucian temple and the family mansion have defined and, through the extent of their landholdings, dominated Qufu. Beginning in the Ming dynasty, the district magistrate's office was located within the mansion compound; the only other residence also to serve as a government office was the imperial palace.

Other places of import for the Confucian tradition are schools and academies. These were centers for moral formation, places that provided the means and context to experience the ultimate as prescribed by Zhu Xi's "investigation of things", constituted communities for Confucian scholars, and were the locus for many rituals honoring the Great Sage. Schools supported by the state were established in Korea, China, and Vietnam. In China, although the wealthiest had the easiest access to

An annual ritual in honor of Confucius being conducted at the Munmyo shrine in Seoul, the heart of Korean Confucianism.

education, most dynasties sought to make education available to exceptional students regardless of background or ability to pay. Schools were staffed by men who had received a classical Confucian education or had passed but not taken up a government appointment. In premodern East Asia, numerous academies in China and Korea were places of advanced learning where scholars and their disciples gathered to discuss Confucian thought, and to compile, preserve, and, in the last several centuries, publish texts. Scholars attached to an academy might be assigned a room and a stipend. Some academies still exist today: Korea's Seongkyunkwan University, which was the center of Confucian studies in Seoul, continues to perform rites for Confucians twice yearly, and still, theoretically, controls the local Confucian schools, of which there are more than 200.

South of the emperor's palace in Beijing is a large sacred complex that was one of the holiest sites of imperial China: the Temple of Heaven. Here, the emperor would perform rituals such as the annual sacrifices on the winter solstice when *yin* energy was at its peak and *yang*, bringing growth, warmth, and light, was just beginning to reemerge. As the Son of Heaven, the sole intermediary between Heaven (Tian) and the empire (Tian Xia, "All under Heaven"), he alone could perform such sacrifices. Through his sacrifices, the emperor of China played his part to guarantee cosmic order.

The Temple of Heaven was sacred ground—commoners were not allowed even to watch the silent procession of the emperor and his entourage from the imperial palace to the temple. On the winter solstice, the emperor offered incense, jade, silk, and wine. He sacrificed a red bullock, symbolizing *yang*, and prostrated himself nine times (nine is considered the most *yang* of numbers) before the altar to Heaven.

For most people, however, the family altar and the ancestral shrine are the most significant places of sacred activity. The home itself is the basic unit of Confucian practice—it is here that important relationships are played out, and where individuals receive the training that will shape them into virtuous members of the family and society. The altar—where gods and spirits as well as family ancestors may reside—is usually in the main living space of the house. Manuals outlining procedures for ritual carefully delineate correct placement of spirit tablets, which house ancestors. The tablets include the names of individual ancestors and birth and death dates, and often the number of sons. When three to five generations have passed, tablets are taken to the ancestral shrine where they receive regular sacrifices which are conducted by the extended family.

Confucianism affirms the sacrality of the universe. Human destiny, which is realized through fulfilment of one's social roles, is as much a part of cosmic order as any aspect of nature. Human virtues are evident in the patterns of creation, such as the regularity of the nodes on bamboo, which is associated with human constancy. Certain features of the landscape—for example, rivers, caves, and mountains—are believed to possess spiritual power. In China, Mount Tai, the most important of five sacred mountains, was seen as a provider of fertility, a preventer of natural disasters, and a symbol of stability. It was worshipped as part of the folk tradition in spring and fall to ensure a successful planting and an abundant harvest. It was also the site of the rare *feng* and *shan* sacrifices. These rituals, addressed to Heaven and Earth, were performed by emperors to mark the founding of a new dynasty or the achievements of the emperor who requested favor for the dynasty from Heaven and Earth.

According to Confucian thought, the links between Heaven and humankind, and the responsiveness of Heaven to human affairs, were manifest in nature. The emperor's mandate to govern and his fulfilment of ritual duties and continued virtuous rule were evident in the regular and predictable motion of heavenly bodies, the successful growth of crops, and the continuation of order in the empire. If Heaven was not satisfied with the emperor, the harmony and regular rhythms of the natural and human worlds would be disrupted. Portents of chaos, such as floods, earthquakes, famine, drought, and uprisings, indicated Heaven's displeasure—and if they continued, they could ultimately legitimate the replacement of the dynasty.

The National Academy

❝ At daybreak each morning, with the beating of a
drum, the headmaster along with the instructors of the
academy assemble the students in the courtyard ... the
students enter the hall where lectures and discussions on
the Classics take place. They study, deliberate, counsel,
and assist one another to reach a full understanding of
the relationships between ruler and minister, father and
son, husband and wife, elder brother and younger
brother, and friend and friend. For days and months,
together they work and rest as one body to train themselves ... It is from these students that the future loyal
ministers and the future filial sons are produced in
prolific number to serve the state and their families. [...]
Some people object that since the sage's teachings are
many, there is no reason why this hall alone should be
called the Hall of Illustrating the Cardinal Principles.
To them I say: The relationships between ruler and
minister, father and son, husband and wife, elder
brother and younger brother, and friend and friend are
rooted in the heavenly principle, and hence they are
unchanging and everlasting. How can there be any
teaching more important than this? ❞

From *Sinjŭng Tongguk yŏji sŭngnam*, translated by Yongho Ch'oe, cited in *Sourcebook of Korean
Civilization*, Vol. 1, edited by Peter H. Lee. Columbia University Press: New York, 1993, pp.523–24

Commentary

Two persistent characteristics of the Confucian tradition, both of which are evident in the source quoted here, are its sense of the sacredness of everyday existence and the penetration of its ethical teachings into all aspects of East Asian culture and society. The intellectual emphasis of the teaching of Korea's sixteenth-century National Academy was the same as that of the Confucian "sage kings" of antiquity (see pp.354–355)—that is, the "Five Relationships" were considered to be the basis of all moral and intellectual development. Teachers were required to be stern taskmasters and disciplinarians, for it was believed that the fate of society and the state was in their hands.

The Neo-Confucian scholar Zhu Xi (1130–1200CE) held that since all human beings share the same nature, all should receive appropriate education. To that end, there was a proliferation of schools and academies, both privately and government-funded, ranging from national universities to humble regional schools. During the Choson, or Yi, period (1392–1910), Korea had an exemplary educational system—to such an extent that court officials would offer "royal lectures" to the ruler, reflecting the Confucian ideal that it is an enlightened and cultured monarch who can best serve the people.

CHAPTER SEVEN

SACRED TIME

There is great regional variety in East Asian observances of sacred time. The Confucian emphasis on family and society is a common theme linking the diverse celebrations of China, Korea, Japan, and Vietnam, which can simultaneously express various ideals, including those of Buddhism, Taoism, Shinto, and local religious practices. Confucianism has always been influential in shaping the region's celebrations, and historically, the Chinese calendar has included the observances of the state cult which were formally linked with the Confucian tradition.

In the Confucian world, success and good fortune are contingent upon a person's ability to align his or her actions with cosmic forces—discerning and responding to temporal patterns are therefore essential to auspicious behavior and the timely fulfillment of obligations.

LEFT:
Offerings of incense are made in honor of the dead at the Qingming festival, which follows two weeks after the spring equinox. The festival focuses on uniting family members and renewing ties with the dead.

In China, time is reckoned using a complex system combining solar and lunar calendars. Underlying this system is the ancient *yin-yang* cosmology (see pp.318–319), manifest in the waxing (*yang*) and waning (*yin*) phases of the moon and the seasonal round of growth and decay in the agricultural year. The lunar calendar consists of twelve months, with intercalary months added every two or three years. The solar year is divided into twenty-four periods of approximately fifteen days, called "nodes," or "breaths." The "breaths" reflect the patterns of climatic and celestial change through the year: eight are named after the equinoxes, solstices, and starts of seasons; others evoke agriculturally and meteorologically significant phenomena and have names such as "Insects Awaken" (early March); "Limit of Heat" (late August); and "Frost Descends" (late October).

The years are organized into a twelve-year cycle represented by the animals of the Chinese zodiac. This in turn is part of a sixty-year cycle which employs the zodiac animals, the "Five Colors" (blue, red, yellow, white, and black), and two sets of symbols, the "Ten Heavenly Stems" and "Twelve Earthly Branches." Each animal is associated with one Branch, and each color correlates to two Stems. Thus, 2000 was the year of the White Dragon; 2012 will be the year of the Black

Dragon. The first year of the sixty-year cycle is *jiazi*, the year of the Blue Rat (most recently, 1984).

Within the year, there are a number of widely observed celebrations. It would be inaccurate to designate these as strictly Confucian; rather, Confucian ideals —such as the desire for children, family togetherness, and harmony—permeate the actions and sentiments of the festivals. These themes are combined with objectives identified with other religious traditions, such as the pursuit of longevity, salvation from Hell, and protection from malevolent forces.

The most important holiday of the Chinese calendar, and one celebrated throughout East Asia, is the Lunar New Year or Spring Festival, celebrated to mark the return of the creative forces of *yang* after the peak of *yin* at the winter solstice. The festival begins on the first day of the first lunar month, usually between January 21st and February 19th. All family members return home, debts are paid, and quarrels settled. Seasonal foods are prepared, and the house is thoroughly cleansed of the old year's dirt and "inauspicious breaths," and decorated with the lucky color red and auspicious words and symbols. On New Year's Eve, the entire family gathers for a feast. The table is set to include dead family members, who are present in spirit. Having sealed the door against evil spirits, the family talks and plays games through the night, carefully avoiding unlucky or negative topics and words. The seal of the door is broken at the moment of the New Year to welcome the first

During an annual visit to the tomb of Fu Xi, China's great ancestral figure, villagers offer a prayer at a hexagram, the original of which he was said to have discovered in antiquity.

breath of spring. For the first two days of the year no one is to work, and there are prohibitions on sweeping or using blades for fear of "brushing away" or "cutting off" the good luck of the New Year. The final night of the two-week festival is the Lantern Festival, the first full moon of the New Year. Crowds gather amid beautiful displays of lanterns to watch stiltwalkers, lion dancers, and people in traditional costumes.

The Clear and Bright festival (Qingming) follows two weeks after the spring equinox. Ideally, the entire family gathers at Qingming to tend the family gravesite and share a picnic. The offerings include the deceased's favorite foods, and "saluting the tomb rice" and "longevity noodles" which symbolize blessings conferred by the ancestors and the hopes of the family. These offerings are presented with eating utensils and condiments, as one would serve food to any family member. Once the ancestors have consumed the "spiritual essence" of the food, the living family members consume the remainder. Qingming is a means of demonstrating family unity to outsiders while at the same time ritually remembering the dead and reinforcing family bonds.

Other widely celebrated holidays are the Double Fifth, Hungry Ghost, and Mid-Autumn festivals. The Double Fifth falls on the fifth day of the fifth lunar month, close to the summer solstice, when *yang* forces are at their annual peak. Traditionally the season of epidemics, this is a time to avert danger to the family through the use of prophylactic herbs and grasses which are hung on front doors, and the symbolism of the "Five Poisons" (centipede, snake, scorpion, toad, and lizard), which repel danger with their power. This is also the season of heavy rains and transplanting rice seedlings into paddies. Traditionally, the water was linked to dragons who bless the Earth with fertility.

The famous "dragon boat" races that take place on the Double Fifth reflect this lore as well as the legend of Zhou dynasty poet and dedicated minister Qu Yuan. After giving unpopular advice he was sent into exile, where he composed his most famous poem, *Li Sao* ("Encountering Sorrow"). Brokenhearted, he threw himself into the Miluo river in present-day Hunan province. People raced out in boats but failed to save him; they threw rice into the water so that the fish would eat the grain instead of Qu Yuan's body. Tradition has it that dragon boat races reenact the frantic search for Qu Yuan. The rice thrown to the fish is represented today by *zongzi*, sticky rice dumplings wrapped in bamboo leaves.

Like Qingming, the spirits of the deceased are central to the Hungry Ghost Festival, which falls on the fifteenth day of the seventh month. This festival is markedly different from Qingming, however, in that those propitiated are the dispossessed dead rather than beloved family members. Popular lore has it that the gates of Hell are opened during the seventh month; ghosts must be propitiated with offerings of food to avert danger and they are exhorted in formal Buddhist and Taoist ceremonies to turn from their evil ways. Comparing the food offerings given to ancestors and ghosts is instructive: ghosts are fed "at the back door" and given coarse foods that require little preparation. Ancestors, on the other hand, are offered carefully prepared dishes. They are honored members of the family who are tended at their burial sites and in the home.

The Mid-Autumn festival falls at full moon, the fifteenth day of the eighth lunar month. A harvest festival and a time for family gathering, it also celebrates the moon and the quest for immortality. In Chinese myth, the moon is home to a rabbit that pounds special herbs to make the elixir of immortality, and to the moon goddess, Chang E. A table is set up outdoors and laden with "moon cakes" and round, moon-shaped fruit such as oranges and melons. Families gather to watch the harvest moon and they recite stories and poems on lunar themes.

Chinese religious celebrations focus on family and community rather than the individual. Other than death, when a person becomes an ancestor, the most significant Chinese rite of passage is marriage, which assures the continuation of the family through the promise of descendants. Traditionally, a marriage became official when the couple bowed before the ancestral tablets of the groom, introducing the bride to her husband's forebears. Such practices maintain the link between the living and the dead, represent proper filial behavior, and ensure the blessings of the ancestors on the family. There were also coming of age ceremonies for boys and girls, but these were not of primary importance, and over time they came to be celebrated just before marriage rather than at a particular age. The sixtieth birthday is significant, however, for it symbolizes the completion of the cycle of years.

The observances that could most appropriately be deemed "Confucian" were those of the state cult which were performed by the emperor and his designated representatives, the scholar-officials. These solemn rituals had their roots in Chinese antiquity and showed the confluence of the ideals of filial behavior and virtuous, Heaven-mandated government. In the imperial capital, the emperor made offerings to the great celestial and earthly forces. Worship of Heaven and Earth at the winter and summer solstices respectively was particularly significant. The emperor was the pivot between Heaven, Earth, and humanity and his timely sacrifices ensured that cosmos and humanity remained in proper balance. As the symbolic son of Heaven and Earth, the emperor would kneel and prostrate himself to these powers as an act of filiality and on behalf of all the people of the state. At Qingming the emperor ensured the proper relation to imperial forebears and exemplars through his sacrifice to his own ancestors, to those of all past emperors, and to the culture heroes of antiquity. Finally, he sanctioned the semi-annual sacrifices made to Confucius on his behalf.

The emperor alone had the privilege and responsibility of worshipping these great cosmic forces—for anyone else to do so was considered an act of rebellion. Setting the calendar was also an imperial prerogative. Rites and festivals in the empire were carried out in accordance with an annual almanac of predicted celestial events issued by the official Bureau of Astronomy, a department of the Ministry of Rites. Imperial foreknowledge in such matters indicated harmony between the emperor and Heaven; any unexpected cosmic event could be interpreted as a sign of imminent loss of the sovereign's mandate to rule.

A Prayer to the Ruler on High, Shang Di

❝ 'Of old in the beginning, there was the great chaos, without form and dark. The five elements had not begun to revolve, nor the sun and the moon to shine. In the midst thereof there existed neither form nor sound. Thou, O spiritual Sovereign, camest forth in Thy presidency, and first didst divide the grosser parts from the purer. Thou madest heaven; Thou madest earth; Thou madest man. All things with their reproducing power, got their being....

'Thou hast vouchsafed, O Te [Shang Di], to hear us, for Thou regardest us as a Father. I, Thy child, dull and unenlightened, am unable to show forth my dutiful feelings. I thank Thee, that Thou has accepted the intimation. Honourable is Thy great name. With reverence we spread out these gems and silks, and, as swallows rejoicing in the spring, praise Thine abundant love. . . The meat has been boiled in the large caldrons, and the fragrant provisions have been prepared. Enjoy the offering, O Te, then shall all the people have happiness. I, Thy servant, receiving Thy favours, am blessed indeed.' **❞**

From *The Notions of the Chinese Concerning Gods and Spirits* by James Legge (his excerpt translation). Hong Kong, 1852), p. 28.

Commentary

According to the *yin-yang* cosmology of East Asia, time was cyclical rather than linear; the annual rites of the winter solstice at the Altar of Heaven ensured the continuation of proper temporal patterns. These were acts of the highest reverence, and the exalted nature of the high god Shang Di required that the emperor undergo extensive rites of purification. After extensive preparations, the elaborate rituals began before daylight on the winter solstice, with a large retinue, rich offerings, and humble prostrations.

Correct timing was crucial to these rites of renewal. Various departments of the Ministry of Rites painstakingly prepared a ritual calendar of sacred and lucky days (almanacs with this information are still used throughout East Asia to determine the appropriate times for various activities). The calendar was then issued to government offices and local magistrates, in order to guarantee timely performance of ritual duties. For the emperor's part, at the Altar of Heaven on the winter solstice, time and space would intersect in his person and actions, ensuring that the cosmic ebb and flow of *yin* and *yang* would continue smoothly and that the *yang* force of spring would return.

CHAPTER EIGHT

DEATH AND THE AFTERLIFE

East Asian attitudes toward death and the afterlife reflect ideas drawn from all the major regional traditions. Confucianism is not directly concerned with belief in an afterlife, although the Confucian virtue of filial piety is crucial to understanding the life of the dead and the responsibility of the living toward them. Several celebrated sayings by Confucius show his reluctance to speculate on the spirit world and his preference to focus on the responsibility of humans in this life.

However, in popular practice and belief, Confucian rites are part of a long history of communication with the spirit world. Here, ritual involves care for revered ancestors and the placation of ghosts—such rituals for the dead link the idealism and humanitarianism of the élite and the beliefs of the common people.

LEFT: A late 17th- or early 18th-century ancestor portrait. The Chinese have long believed that ancestors watch over and protect the living. Confucius emphasized the practice of ancestor worship, teaching that it could play an important role in insuring the continuity of the family.

Although it is difficult to speak of Confucian ideas of the afterlife independently of the other traditions that constitute East Asian religions, there are many ways in which Confucian beliefs have contributed to shaping the attitudes and practices of East Asians relating to death and the afterlife.

The rites of ancestor veneration, which are a significant reflection of attitudes toward death and the afterlife, have been a defining feature of East Asian civilizations for millennia. Concerns about the dead and communication with them date at least to the Chinese Shang dynasty (ca. 1766–1050BCE). The Shang presumed a close relationship between the living and the dead—ritual was highly significant in that it bridged the gap between the two realms. These rituals and sacrifices were codified in the Zhou dynasty (1050–256BCE), and were part of the *li* revered by Confucius.

Early Confucians outlined the obligations and appropriate behavior of children toward deceased forebears rather than described the fate of the dead or the nature of the afterlife. Confucius wished to create a righteous society, and saw rites for the dead as expressions of filial piety which revealed the depth and sincerity of love for forebears. Such rites would be performed by all people, regardless of rank and, like all *li*, had a transformative effect—they were thus of tremendous importance as it was believed that they were instrumental in creating a harmonious and ordered society.

Early Confucians assumed the existence of an afterlife, but the few comments made by Confucius on the subject indicate a reluctance to discuss such matters. He spoke of respecting spiritual beings while at the same time keeping one's focus firmly on the human realm and on performing duties on behalf of humankind; he criticized as mere flatterers those who would make sacrifices to other people's ancestors. In one famous *Analects'* passage, he asked, "If we are not able to serve humanity, how can we serve spiritual beings?... If we do not understand life, how can we know about death?" (11:11). Such aloofness characterized the attitude of the élite toward a host of practices and beliefs that were part of the popular tradition—they focused instead on a legacy of virtuous example, service in government, and the study of scholarly works passed down through the ages.

But for the literati and the common people alike, rituals were of the utmost importance. The most basic are the daily rites at the family altar, which is in many ways the locus of family unity, encompassing all generations, alive and dead. The altar houses the spirit tablets in which ancestral spirits are believed to reside. The tablets typically record the names, birth and death dates, and number of sons of each ancestor. The ancestors are addressed and treated as close family members and are informed of family news such as births, deaths, engagements, travel and business plans. Ideally, it is the forebears of the senior male who are represented on the altar, but under certain circumstances other tablets may be present. For example, in a family with no sons, a daughter may put her natal family's tablets on the family altar of her husband.

The tablets go back three to five generations. The ancestors are offered incense twice daily (those who offer it vary between cultures). On death-day anniversaries and special holidays, such as New Year and the Mid-Autumn festival, the ancestors may also be offered food, drink, spirit money ("money" bought for the purpose of ancestral sacrifice), and paper clothes. During the funerary ritual, the dead are provided with spirit money as well as useful items rendered in paper, such as cars, servants, houses, and domestic furnishings. When offered food and drink, ancestors are believed to consume the "essence" and leave the coarse material part for the family to enjoy. The paper goods and spirit money are burned so that they ascend to the ancestors in smoke. In return, ancestors grant blessings of fertility, good

Smoke from incense and offerings before the tomb of Fu Xi, the "Ancestor of the Human Race," in Zhoukou.

luck, and harmony to their descendants—such rituals not only ensure blessings for the living, but also proclaim the unity and strength of the family.

As each generation passes away, the oldest tablets are removed from the altar and placed in an ancestral hall used by several households of the same extended family. Here, devotion takes place to the ancestors as a group; attitudes are more formal and indicative of gratitude to the host of forebears rather than the emotional bond and close relationship toward the more recently departed. Manuals that codified correct procedure and the details of the setup of the family altar and the ancestral hall were made available to the general population.

Ideas about the exact nature of the soul enshrined in the spirit tablets are vague and the material boundaries between the living and the dead are fluid. Those who reside in this world and the next are composed of the same vital material (*qi*) in its *yin* and *yang* forms (see pp.318–319). There is no formal agreement on the number of souls a person has, but since ancient times in China it is believed that everyone has at least two—a *hun* soul, made up of *yang qi*, and a *po* soul, made up of *yin qi*. At death, the *hun*, which represents the spiritual and intellectual aspect of the soul, departs from the body and ascends, due to its *yang* nature; it ultimately comes to reside in the ancestral tablets. The *po* soul, as *yin* energy, sinks into the ground. It remains with the body so long as it has been buried with the proper rites and is propitiated by tomb offerings.

Ancestors are propitiated family spirits. Those who are not properly cared for after death—through neglect or a lack of descendants—and those who die prematurely or by violence, become ghosts; they are likened to bandits and vagrants of the spirit world and are considered to be dangerous, malevolent forces that need to be placated. An ancestor may become a troublesome spirit if the burial is not performed correctly, or if the death was irregular, or if the spirit is not propitiated, preventing the *hun* soul from rising to reside in the ancestral tablets and the *po* soul from descending into the grave. The spirit of the deceased will haunt the living as a ghost until appropriate measures have been taken.

Other concerns over death and the afterlife in the popular tradition reflect the syncretistic tendency of East Asian religions, encompassing numerous—and, in some cases, apparently contradictory—notions of the fate of the soul after death. Thus, although the *po* soul of the deceased is at the gravesite, it is also believed to descend into the underworld, or Hell, where it will be judged and tried for its sins by the infernal judiciary before being punished and, eventually, reincarnated. Despite the fact that the concept of Hell existed in pre-Buddhist China, notions of the fate of the soul after death are heavily influenced by such Buddhist beliefs as: *karma* (an individual's balance of accumulated merits and demerits); the king of Hell; and the different punishment levels of Hell, in which sinners suffer to redress their karmic imbalance before being reincarnated

On entering Hell, souls are judged by the Ten Magistrates, depicted in the costumes of the old Chinese imperial judiciary, who preside over the Ten Tribunals of Hell, each of which tries different crimes. Families can speed the passage of their loved ones in Hell through offerings and good works, such as the chanting of Buddhist *sutra*s. Both Heaven and Hell are envisioned as bureaucracies, with officials who are the celestial counterparts of Confucian literati-officials of the earthly realm in attire, role, and behavior. Buddhist cosmology was combined with Confucian filial piety in stories such as that of Mulian. A monk with no children, Mulian would have been considered unfilial by Confucians. However, he proved his superior filial piety by rescuing his mother from the torments of the lowest level of Hell, which was accessible to him because of his advanced achievements in Buddhist meditation.

The use of shamans and spirit mediums is another example of how Confucian values are combined with other practices in the management of the relationship with the dead. Unhappy ancestors may be the cause of problems in families troubled by illness or bad luck. In such cases, shamans or mediums are employed to communicate the grievances of the dead, typically through utterances or spirit writing. Although calling upon these persons was discouraged by the élite, their widespread use throughout East Asia shows a popular means by which family harmony can be restored and familial duty to the dead can be rectified.

Rites for the dead continue today, although they are discouraged by the Communist Party, which promotes atheism—observance in Communist countries thus depends on the prevailing political atmosphere. Christians have challenged Confucian rites since the Jesuit missions in the sixteenth century, questioning whether ancestor veneration is merely memorial or whether it is spirit-worship. Current Catholic ruling allows the rituals so long as they are for remembrance; Protestant interpretations vary. But regardless of ruling, a large percentage of Christian East Asians continues these practices, which are central to their identity and tradition. In Japan, rites are conducted at the family's Buddhist altar, but the rationale for the practices reflects Confucian sensibilities. Rites for the dead are widely observed in South Korea, and many homes will have manuals on proper practices of ancestral rituals. Observance of these rituals is costly and time-consuming—in 1980 the Korean government promulgated the "Guideline for Family Rituals" to curb the expense of honoring ancestors. Although the law is in effect, practices continue relatively unchanged, for ancestral rites are a primary way of expressing filial piety and family unity.

Family Rituals by Zhu Xi

❝ When a man of virtue builds a house his first task
is always to set up an offering hall to the east of the
main room of his house. For this hall four altars to
hold the spirit tablets of the ancestors are made;
collateral relatives who died without descendants may
have associated offerings made to them there according
to their generational seniority. Sacrificial fields should
be established and sacrificial utensils prepared. Once
the hall is completed, early each morning the master
enters the outer gate to pay a visit. All comings and
goings are reported there. On New Year's Day, the
solstices and each new and full moon, visits are made.
On the customary festivals, seasonal foods are offered,
and when an event occurs, reports are made. Should
there be flood, fire, robbers, or bandits, the offering
hall is the first thing to be saved. The spirit tablets,
inherited manuscripts, and then the sacrificial utensils
should be moved; only afterward may the family's
valuables be taken. As one generation succeeds another,
the spirit tablets are reinscribed and moved to their
new places. **❞**

From *Chu Hsi's Family Rituals*, translated by Patricia Buckley Ebrey. Princeton University Press: Princeton, 1991, p.5.

Commentary

Classic books of ritual practice such as the *Record of Rites* were valued in the Confucian tradition because they represented the wisdom of the ancients, and because they were guides to orthodox ritual behavior. However, there were practical difficulties involved in following their prescriptions due to the fact that they were derived from Chinese antiquity. Aware that such rites were too complicated and expensive for most people, and anxious to avoid divergent rites, the twelfth-century scholar Zhu Xi prepared the practical handbook *Family Rituals* as a resource for discouraging irregular practices and ensuring that essential rituals were performed properly.

Family Rituals outlines the four major family rituals: weddings, coming-of-age ceremonies, funerals, and ancestor veneration. Nearly half of the text discusses death ceremonies, including burial procedures and the complex rituals that were conducted to transform the dead into ancestors. Versions of Zhu Xi's text were tremendously popular and influential throughout East Asia, perhaps reflecting the existence of a widespread desire among the public for a ritual manual. The guidelines that were established in *Family Rituals* still form the basis of ancestor veneration in Korea today.

CHAPTER NINE

SOCIETY AND RELIGION

Confucianism has played a prominent role in shaping the social norms and expectations of East Asian society. Although integration with indigenous traditions and historical and geographical factors have given rise to variations in its influence, the tradition has nevertheless been an ordering principle of the family, the state, and social structure.

The patterns of influence of Confucianism have changed dramatically in the last 150 years. Social upheaval and encounters with the West have undoubtedly thrown into question its viability in the modern world. To some, the end of explicitly Confucian states has meant the death of Confucianism. But others believe there is evidence that the tradition is too strong to be broken altogether, despite the sometimes severe strains placed upon it.

LEFT: The three towering figures in East Asia's religious and philosophical traditions are brought together in this 18th-century Chinese painting. Confucius (right) holds the infant Buddha, while the Taoist sage Laozi looks on.

Confucianism has shaped East Asian social expectations and norms to such an extent that many cultural attitudes drawn from Confucian precepts are designated as being simply part of the cultural and national identity, rather than from a specific religious tradition. East Asian religions are a blend of many different traditions, and of these, Confucianism has remained the dominant influence in the realms of socialization, social structure, and ideals and practice of government.

In keeping with the Confucian ethic of filial piety, the primary relationship in East Asian society is that between parent and child. Traditionally, children owed their parents absolute loyalty and obedience. Chinese law reflected this relationship: for example, a father was within his rights to kill a disobedient child, and a son could be executed for striking his father. Children were expected to care for parents in their old age, to produce descendants who would continue the family line, and to perform ancestral rites.

Confucianism also provided the rationale for an authoritarian and hierarchical social structure in which males were highly privileged. In Confucian thought, each member of the family and of society had a specific role. In the Chinese view of the universe, women were considered embodiments of *yin* energy, and therefore passive and nurturing, in contrast to the dynamic *yang* of males (see pp.318–319). According to this scheme, they were subordinate to men and were expected to live in obedience to their fathers when girls, to their husbands when married, and to their sons when widowed. A married woman was supposed to show filial devotion to her husband's parents, with whom the couple often lived.

Confucianism's impact on society was especially significant in the realm of government. In China, emperors were understood to rule with the "Mandate of Heaven" (see p.323)—Heaven's sanction was endowed upon a virtuous and able leader who could benefit the people and pacify all under Heaven. Emperors were given the title "Son of Heaven," and through their ritual actions expressed their filiality and obedience to ancestors, and Heaven and Earth. The emperor was assisted by cultured, educated bureaucrats steeped in Confucian ethics. This system assumed that a centralized bureaucracy was the ordained manner of rule.

Confucius is revered as the first teacher, and his followers throughout the centuries have made education a high priority. In China, even the poorest people strove to educate their sons in the hope that at least one would pass the civil service examinations, bringing prestige and influence to their family.

Beijing Opera, one of the highest expressions of Chinese culture, includes lessons about Confucian ethics in its stories.

After serving as the theoretical basis for government and morality for two millennia, Confucianism came under attack as stiflingly traditional and as the underlying cause of China's political and military weakness. But since the beginning of the twentieth century, Confucian attitudes and orientations have come to accommodate modernity. This is apparent in Taiwan, Hong Kong, Singapore, and many overseas communities where Confucianism is often actively promoted. It is still evident in mainland China where Communism has imposed its own pressures, often in the form of severe persecution. However, although successive Communist leaders have vilified Confucianism, official rhetoric about working for the good of the state, party, or collective, and submitting to its authority, is not different in kind from the traditional Confucian emphasis on the group over the individual. In recent years, official pressure from the Communist Party has lessened and Confucianism is even promoted, mainly for its historical interest and value to tourism.

The strong emphasis on family unity and the relationship between child and parent continues in mainland China, although it has lessened in degree. It came under severe strain during the Cultural Revolution (1966–76), when Mao Zedong encouraged children and juniors to denounce the ways of their elders and seniors as "feudal" and counter-revolutionary. This experience, so profoundly opposed to the tradition of filial piety, undoubtedly left deep psychological scars. Even in the officially egalitarian People's Republic, there is still a marked preference for sons over daughters—the Communist policy of allowing couples only one child to counter overpopulation has given rise to a range of methods to ensure that the child is male.

South Koreans have had a different history. The Choson dynasty, which ended in 1910, saw perhaps the most distinctly Confucian state in history. The Confucian heritage in South Korea is still evident in patterns of daily life. The tremendous economic growth of the region has been fueled in part by the language of loyalty and obligations, where workers and citizens are called to sacrifice for the good of the company or the state. Families have a remarkably low divorce rate, and still prize the male family line and the need for male heirs. Practice of ancestral rites is widespread. An overwhelming percentage of the population, even among those who identify themselves as Christian, practices Confucian rituals and ceremonies, primarily in the form of ancestor veneration. There also continues to be a range of Confucian associations—from local Confucian temples to Seongkyunkwan University in Seoul. Groups such as *yurim*, or Confucian Forest, study and locally promote Confucian learning.

Vietnamese rulers, even when independent of Chinese control, followed the Confucian model of government and social order, including issuing imperial edicts of Confucian virtue for the populace and honoring filial sons and chaste wives. The Vietnamese retained distinctive aspects of their southeast Asian culture as well, sometimes to the disapproval of Chinese observers. In the nineteenth and twentieth centuries, with colonization by the French and the rise of Communism, Confucianism was no longer the foundation of state ideology, but continued to be the basis for social interaction. Since the Vietnam War and massive emigration, there has been disjuncture between the experience of generations—the expectations of the older generation are not always fulfilled by the younger.

The Japanese pattern is more diffuse than that of either Korea or Vietnam. The Japanese imported Confucianism with other aspects of Chinese culture in the sixth century. For them, Confucianism provided support to a centralized state and social hierarchy. However, once the basic elements were established, for many centuries Confucianism became a backdrop rather than a conscious pattern of life. Confucian studies were revived in the seventeenth century and again in the nineteenth century as a means of justifying the political and social hierarchy. Most notably, Confucianism was combined with aspects of Shinto in the period leading up to and during World War II to conflate loyalty to the emperor with filial piety to parents. Since the war, Confucian ideas have again become a part of the background to being Japanese, visible in the workplace, at school, and in gender roles and family structure.

Instructions for the Inner Quarters by Empress Xu

❝ Being upright and modest, reserved and quiet, correct and dignified, sincere and honest: these constitute the moral nature of a woman. Being filial and respectful, humane and perspicacious, loving and warm, meek and gentle: these represent the complete development of the moral nature. The moral nature being innate in our endowment, it becomes transformed and fulfilled through practice. It is not something that comes from the outside but is actually rooted in our very selves. . . .

The accumulation of small faults will mount up to great harm to one's virtue. Therefore a great house will topple over if the foundation is not solid. One's moral nature will have deficiencies if the self is not restrained.

Beautiful jade with no flaws can be made into a precious jewel. An upright woman of pure character can be made the wife of a great family. If you constantly examine your actions to see if they are correct, you can be a model mother. If you are hard-working and frugal without a trace of jealousy, you are fit to be an exemplar for the women's quarters. ❞

From *Neixun*, or "Instructions for the Inner Quarters," cited in *Sources of Chinese Tradition*, Vol. 1, compiled by William Theodore de Bary and Irene Bloom. Columbia University Press: New York, 1999, pp. 834–35.

Commentary

In Confucian society, women were thought to be *yin*, like the earth, and thus to be passive and yielding. They nevertheless played a crucial role in the family: they were responsible for the early education and nurturing of children, and for remonstrating with husbands who erred. Many illustrious figures credited female family members for having contributed to their achievements. One famous example was Mencius' mother, who moved three times with her son to ensure that he grew up in surroundings that would nurture moral and intellectual growth.

Many manuals for the "inner quarters" were written by highly educated and accomplished women. These books gave guidance on following the "wifely Way": sacrificing to ancestors, caring for parents-in-law, and bearing children. This extract from the *Instructions for the Inner Quarters* (written in the Ming dynasty by Empress Xu, and well received in Korea and Japan as well as China) affirms the Confucian teachings of the "Great Learning," which asserts that one's own character must be developed in order to, ultimately, bring order to the world. It therefore describes not only a woman's domestic duties, but also the means for her self-cultivation, an achievement which contributes to the general good.

PART FIVE:

SHINTO

INTRODUCTION

The inhabitants of Japan simultaneously espouse two major faiths, Shinto and Buddhism, which have co-existed and influenced one another for the past fifteen hundred years. Shinto is indigenous to Japan and, although stripped of the privileged status it enjoyed from 1868 until the end of the Second World War in 1945, the religion still permeates almost every aspect of Japanese life.

The reverence shown by the Japanese toward nature stems from Shinto's most ancient and fundamental belief that spirit-beings govern the natural world. These spirits, or deities, are known as *kami* (see pp.436–437)—the religion itself is called the "Way of the Gods (or Spirits)," which is expressed both by the native phrase *Kami no Michi* and the synonymous term Shinto, a Japanese articulation of the Chinese *shen* ("spirit") and *dao* ("way"). Both phrases are written with the Chinese characters for *shen* and *dao*. Shinto has been the more usual expression since the resurgence of the religion in the eighteenth and nineteenth centuries—an irony, since the promoters of the revival tended to be anti-Chinese.

Shinto, unlike Buddhism or Christianity, has no known founder. It was not until the late prehistoric Yayoi culture (ca. 300BCE–300CE) that features emerged that are reminiscent of some of the religion's central aspects (for example, the *kami*). Archaic Shinto seems to have evolved by the beginning of the final phase of Japanese prehistory, the Kofun, or "Tumulus," era (ca. 300–550CE). This belief system was intensely local, focusing on the spiritual power inherent in nearby topographical features and on the divine ancestors of clans and lineages. As the Yamato ("Sun") clan gained influence over the others, its divine ancestor, the sun goddess Amaterasu (see pp.440–442), rose to prominence. This laid the foundations for the emperor cult, which was relegated to a symbolic role during the reign of the shoguns (in the twelfth to nineteenth centuries), but returned to dominate Shinto in modern times.

In the mid-sixth century CE, Buddhism was brought to Japan from China via Korea. Confucianism and Daoism also made their appearance in Japan in this period. All three religions, but particularly Buddhism, had a distinct influence on Shinto—the line between Buddhism and Shintoism can sometimes be hazy: for example, many Buddhist deities came to be worshipped as Shinto *kami*. But despite the impact of Chinese belief and philosophy, Japan always remained distinct from its neighbor across the sea. The nation's deep-rooted tendency to adapt and transform what it borrows from other cultures manifested itself, and many Buddhist sects that took root or emerged in Japan soon became, and have remained, uniquely Japanese.

In 1868, after more than 250 years of rule by the Tokugawa shogunate, the Meiji restoration returned power to the emperor (enthroned in 1867), and in 1871

Worshippers bow before a Shinto shrine at Karatsu on Kyushu island during the annual Kunchi festival, held in November.

Shinto was established as the state religion. Along with the newly instituted imperial army and navy, "State Shinto" became a principal mechanism for fostering Japanese nationalism and loyalty to the emperor. The word "Shinto" dates from this period—before this time, the religion was simply the worship of the *kami*.

"State Shinto" came to an abrupt end with the conclusion of the Second World War in 1945. The emperor renounced all claims to divinity, and Japan's post-war constitution of 1947 specifically prohibited the state from having any involvement in religious affairs. As a result of these changes, Shinto reverted to what it had been for most of its long history: a loosely organized collection of local *jinja* ("shrines") dedicated to an almost infinite number of *kami* who, for the most part, were unique to their local communities.

In more recent years, Japan has witnessed the establishment of the so-called "New Religions" (see pp.512–515), and the reemergence of Christianity, which reached Japan in the sixteenth century but was subsequently suppressed. The growth of these faiths was stimulated respectively by the social chaos of the last three decades (1838–67) of the Tokugawa shogunate and by the rapid economic development that followed the Second World War. But in each case, the end result has been quintessentially Japanese, a relatively seamless blend of foreign and indigenous ideas, customs, rites, and beliefs.

Syncretism (the fusion of disparate beliefs and practices into a single system) has long been a feature of religious life in Japan, together with what in the West might be considered a high degree of "ambiguity tolerance." With some important exceptions, most Japanese people would probably consider themselves to be both Shintoists and Buddhists and would perceive no contradiction in practicing two faiths with such radically different roots. Broadly speaking, Shinto focuses on matters relating to this world, on procreation, the promotion of fertility, on spiritual purity, and physical well-being. Buddhism, on the other hand, although it does not reject the real world, has always placed greater emphasis on salvation and the possibility of an afterlife—hence it is often associated with human concerns over mortality and most Japanese prefer its funeral practices.

Any assessment of the role played by religion in ancient or modern Japan must take into account certain fundamental aspects of Japanese culture. Most important is the subordination of the individual to the group, epitomized in the Japanese expression, "the nail that sticks up will be hammered down." Many scholars believe that this ethos has its roots in the close cooperation and collective decision-making necessitated by wet-rice cultivation, which until recently was Japan's prime source of sustenance. The rice paddy, introduced to Japan in the late first millennium BCE, is labor-intensive: before mechanization, each rice plant had to be individually inserted into the ground. Even in modern times, household members subordinate their personal inclinations to work together for the good of the crop—and, by extension, for mutual survival. At a broader level, it is a village affair, in which a cluster of households assist one another in planting, weeding, and harvesting.

Such social cooperation and the absence of marked individualism have characterized Shinto from the outset. Over the centuries, the religion has always made a virtue of subordination to the well-being of the larger social unit, whether that unit be a household, a rice-growing village, a feudal domain, or the body of "salarymen" employed by a modern multinational corporation.

Despite the shadow of Japanese militarism and imperialism that fell across Shinto in the early post-war period, the religion continues to thrive and to command the affection, if not absolute loyalty, of the majority of the Japanese people. Indeed, in a great many respects, to be Japanese is to be Shinto, no matter what other religions one espouses.

ORIGINS AND HISTORICAL DEVELOPMENT

Shinto is deeply embedded in Japanese culture. For at least two thousand years—and perhaps far longer—it has commanded the devotion of the Japanese people, despite the introduction into the country of Buddhism, Confucianism, Daoism, and, more recently, Christianity. The evolution of Shinto can be traced from early archeological evidence (ca. 300BCE–300CE), through the Shinto revival in the eighteenth century and the period of "State Shinto" (1871–1945), to its current status in a country that is now a major economic power. In addition to noting how Buddhism and Shinto have complemented one another over the centuries, it is important to recognize the manner in which Shinto has absorbed elements of foreign religions while, at the same time, remaining distinctly Japanese.

LEFT: A pine tree atop a rock at Kiri-Kiri, Iwate. Such places of beauty have the powerful essence of natural kami *(spirits), which are central to Shinto belief.*

The origins of Shinto lie deep in the ancient past. It is open to question whether the prehistoric Jomon culture (ca. 11,000–300BCE) possessed a faith centered on the reverence of *kami* ("spirit," "deity," "divine being," or "god/goddess"; see pp.435–445), at least in anything like the form known today. These preliterate, semino-madic foragers and fisherfolk produced *dogu*, stylized female figurines with exaggerated hips and breasts. The precise nature of the beliefs surrounding *dogu* is unknown, although they probably reflect the existence of a fertility cult. *Dogu* were often placed in or near graves after being deliberately broken, perhaps ritually "killed," in order to release the spiritual "essence" of the *dogu*. But whether this "essence" was conceived in terms of anything resembling a prototypical Shinto *kami* remains entirely a matter of speculation.

However, strikingly Shintoistic iconographic evidence begins to appear with the arrival of the more complex Yayoi culture (ca. 300BCE–300CE). Among the grave goods associated with the Yayoi—rice cultivators whose homeland probably lay somewhere in southeastern Asia or southern China—are small ceramic images of grain storehouses that are remarkably similar to the architecture of the shrine at Ise, a form that has remained unaltered for at least twelve hundred years, although it is periodically rebuilt (see pp.474–475). Female fertility images also occur, as well as stone clubs that appear to have phallic symbolism. The introduction of rice-paddy agriculture seems to have brought with it rituals connected with sowing and harvesting that were probably fundamentally similar to rice-related Shinto rituals that persist to the present in rural Japan.

Closely associated with the Yayoi fertility cult are jewels called *magatama*, ceremonial mirrors, and sacred swords, all of which play a significant role in Shinto mythology (see p.441) and form part of the imperial regalia to this day. Many scholars suspect that the majority of the *ujigami*—the tutelary deities associated with the most ancient recorded Japanese *uji* ("clans")—date from this period. The most important *ujigami* was (and is) Amaterasu, the sun goddess (see pp.440–442)

Many scholars believe, that in the fourth century CE, Japan was conquered by horse-riding nomads from Central Asia—almost certainly a ruling élite rather than an invading population—and a new form of chieftain's tomb appeared: the *kofun*, or tumulus. Votive figurines of horses and warriors, known as *hanniwa*, were often placed around the periphery of these massive, keyhole-shaped mounds to accompany the deceased warlord on his journey to the afterworld.

A hanniwa *tomb figurine of a warrior—perhaps engaged in an act of devotion to a deity or lord—found at Yamato-mura in Ibaraki prefecture, eastern Honshu.*

By the early sixth century CE, the Yamato emperor exercised authority over most of the country to the south and west of the Kanto plain. It was to this embryonic state that the first substantial contingent of Buddhist missionaries traveled, in 552CE according to tradition, although scholars think 538CE more likely.

Many Yamato courtiers enthusiastically embraced Buddhism—albeit for the most part in a highly Shintoistic way, worshipping statues of the Buddha as manifestations of a powerful *kami*—while others resented its intrusion. However, in 592CE, the regent Prince Shotoku (Shotoku-Taishi) declared Buddhism the official religion of the imperial court. But most Japanese remained untouched by it until the early Heian era (794–1185CE). Buddhists did not attempt to undermine or supplant

Shinto, but simply founded their temples next to Shinto shrines and proclaimed that there was no fundamental conflict between the two faiths. Toward the end of the Heian era, this sense of inclusiveness led to the development of Ryobu Shinto, or "Double Shinto," in which Shinto *kami* and Buddhist *bosatsu* (*bodhisattva*s—an "enlightenment being" or *buddha*-to-be) were formally combined into single divine entities. This theological fusion was often visually represented by images of *kami* in human form "dreaming" of their *bosatsu* counterparts.

The last years of the Heian era were marked by a civil war that culminated in the appointment of Minamoto no Yoritomo to the new imperial office of shogun, or "generalissimo." Four centuries of almost constant internal strife followed. The most significant religious development of this period was the introduction of Christianity in 1549, but its initial gains were reversed following the assassination in 1582 of its early patron, the powerful *daimyo*, or warlord, Oda Nobunaga. Under the Tokugawa shogunate (1603–1867), Buddhism was in the ascendant, Chinese Neoconfucianism was also espoused, and Daoism came to occupy an important role.

However, in the late eighteenth century, the efforts of Motoori Norinaga (1730–1800) and other Shinto scholars led to a renewed interest in the *Kojiki*, the

Nihonshoki, and other ancient Shinto texts (see pp.449–457). A century later, this Shinto revival, which strongly emphasized the imperial cult, was a major factor in the collapse of the, by then, economically moribund shogunate and the restoration in 1868 of imperial power under Emperor Meiji. In the years immediately following the Meiji restoration, Shinto became the official religion of Japan (known as "State Shinto") and Buddhism went into a brief eclipse.

In the 1870s, Christian missionaries returned to a newly tolerant Japan, but few Japanese saw any merit in switching from Shinto, a faith closely associated with the imperial regime and hence also with the growing prosperity that was the result of the government's policy of Western-style industrialization. Today only around 600,000 Japanese profess the Christian faith (approximately half of them Roman Catholics).

In the late 1880s, the imperial government put an end to the backlash against Buddhism, and the Buddhist establishment made a rapid comeback. Shinto remained the state religion until 1945, but the historic balance between the two faiths was restored and persists to this day. "State Shinto" was disestablished after the end of the Second World War, and since then no faith has enjoyed official status.

Shinto, though, pervades Japanese life in many unexpected ways. For example, the national sport is sumo wrestling, which derives from an ancient Shinto ritual honoring the *kami*. The canopy over the ring is reminiscent of a Shinto shrine, the referee is dressed in garb similar to that of a Shinto priest, and the throwing of salt (thought to have magical properties) before a bout is believed to purify the ring. It is associations such as these that make the faith part of the social fabric.

An important phenomenon in the recent history of religion in Japan is the growth of the Shinko Shukyo ("New Religions"; see p.512), a term used to cover the new sects that began to arise in the early nineteenth century amid the social chaos that marked the collapse of shogun feudalism. For the most part, these sects were blends of Shinto and Buddhism, but since the Meiji restoration some have adopted elements of Christianity and other faiths. Many ceremonies and festivals are a blend of Shinto and Buddhism: for example, during Tokyo's annual Sanja festival, the *mikoshi* ("portable shrine") is carried through the grounds of the Asakusa temple and shrine. The Shinto shrine itself, which is adjacent to the Buddhist temple, is dedicated to three deified humans who had retrieved the Buddha image from the Sumida River and enshrined it.

A History of the Kingdom of Wei, ca. 297CE

66 The people of Wa [Japan] dwell in the middle of
the ocean on the mountainous islands southeast of
[the prefecture of] Tai-fang. They formerly comprised
more than one hundred communities. During the Han
dynasty, [Wa] envoys appeared at the court; today,
thirty of their communities maintain intercourse with
us through envoys and scribes....

The land of Wa is warm and mild. In winter as in
summer the people live on raw vegetables and go about
barefooted. They have [or live in] houses; father and
mother, elder and younger, sleep separately. They smear
their bodies with pink and scarlet, just as the Chinese
use powder. They serve food on bamboo and wooden
trays, helping themselves with their fingers. When a
person dies, they prepare a single coffin, without an
outer one. They cover the graves with earth to make a
mound. When death occurs, mourning is observed for
more than ten days, during which period they do not
eat meat. The head mourners wail and lament, while
friends sing, dance, and drink liquor. When the funeral
is over, all members of the family go into the water to
cleanse themselves in a bath of purification. 99

Tsunoda and Goodrich cited in *Sources of Japanese Tradition*, edited by Tsunoda, Rusaku., et al. Columbia
University Press: New York, 1958, pp.6–7.

Commentary

Although there is some evidence of contact with China before ca. 250–60CE—in the form of inscriptions containing Chinese characters—the *Wei Chih* is the earliest account of Japan in a Chinese chronicle. It forms part of the history of the Kingdom of Wei (220–65CE), a successor state to the Han dynasty, which collapsed in 220CE. An embassy, composed primarily of merchants, visited what the Chinese called the "Kingdom of Wa" some time in the middle of the third century and returned with a detailed account of life in this "barbarian" neighbor that lay to the east of the Middle Kingdom. It was included, together with accounts of other barbarian realms on the fringe of China, when the official chronicle of the Kingdom of Wei was compiled ca. 297CE. The Chinese were intrigued by the fact that Wa had recently had a female ruler (Empress Pimiko) and that there were no horses there.

It also gives us our earliest glimpse of Shinto, especially as regards funeral practices. The construction of earthen mounds is reflected in the archeological record, while the account of the ten-day mourning period provides an insight into an important aspect of early Shinto that has all but disappeared since the advent of Buddhism in the sixth century CE (see p.428).

CHAPTER TWO

ASPECTS OF THE DIVINE

Shinto belief and practice revolve around the worship of supernatural beings known as *kami* who oversee all aspects of nature and human life. Such divine beings are believed to animate every object in the universe—from prominent geographical sites, such as Mount Fuji, to the souls of deceased children. The Shinto pantheon is said to contain an infinite number of *kami*—many of these are deities that have been incorporated from Buddhism and Daoism.

The oldest Japanese texts, the *Kojiki* and the *Nihonshoki* (see pp.449–451), tell how the world was created by the celestial deities Izanagi and Izanami. After what amounted to a false start, the primal pair gave birth to a host of *kami*, including the sovereign sun goddess Amaterasu, whose descendant, Jimmu Tenno, became the first emperor.

LEFT: Susano—the god of storms and brother of Amaterasu, the sun goddess—is one of Shinto's principal kami. *He is depicted in this late 19th-century hanging scroll slaying the eight-headed dragon Yamato no Orochi.*

The Shinto faith, like many of the world's major belief systems, conceives of a superior, or "divine," realm which informs and guides human existence. This realm is populated by a host of beings known as *kami*. Some aspects of the Shinto pantheon resemble the pantheons of other ancient religions, in the simple sense that gods and goddesses are venerated. However, other features of the Shinto divine are reminiscent of what in other belief systems are heroic rather than divine figures: a great many *kami* are far more "human" than the gods and goddesses of other religions and, in some cases, take human form.

The Japanese word *kami* is often translated as "deity," but in fact it designates an extremely wide range of spirit-beings together with a host of mysterious and supernatural forces and "essences." In the *Kojiki* (see p.450), it is said that there are eight million *kami* (in Japanese mythology, eight is a sacred number that means simply "many", and thus expresses infinite). These include countless vaguely defined tutelary divinities of clans, villages, and neighborhoods (*ujigami*); "spirits of place"—the essences of prominent geographical features, including mountains, rivers, and waterfalls; and other natural phenomena, such as the *kamikaze* ("divine wind"), the typhoon that saved Japan from a seaborne Mongol invasion in the thirteenth century.

Many *kami* live in the sky and come down to Earth periodically to visit sacred places and shrines. They are considered so sacred that worshippers must purify themselves before entering shrine precincts or taking part in festivals (see pp.493–496) that are held in their honor.

Some *kami* are benign imported Buddhist and Daoist deities; others are demonic, vengeful spirits who are responsible for a wide variety of mortal troubles. In Japanese tradition, most evil spirits or *oni* ("demons") are invisible, although some are claimed to be giants, of various colors, with horns and sometimes three eyes. Others, however, are thought to be animal spirits who have the capacity to possess a person—in such cases, they must be exorcised by a priest. Among the most feared is the fox spirit—possession by this being can bring about all sorts of calamities, including illness and death. In parts of rural Japan, especially in the north, where old customs and beliefs often linger, the *yamabushi* ("mountain warriors"; see p.487, are considered particularly adept at exorcising such spirits and thereby restoring the victim to good health.

Another variety of evil spirit is the *obake*, or ghost. These entities are also believed to be capable of causing considerable harm, but they can be driven off with appropriately respectful rituals (see pp.504–505).

Worshippers parade with a mikoshi *("portable shrine")*
in front of the spectacular waterfall in Akita, northwestern
Honshu, which is thought to be favored by the local kami.

The Shinto tradition does not believe that there is an
absolute dichotomy of good and evil. Rather, all phenomena, both animate and inanimate, are thought to
possess both "rough" and "gentle," or negative and positive, characteristics and it is possible for a given entity
to manifest either of these characteristics depending on
the circumstances. Thus, in spite of their malevolence,

oni are somewhat ambivalent characters. For example, the malicious fox spirit is also closely associated with Inari, the rice god, who is an extremely popular and charitable *kami* (see p.442). Similarly, the grotesque bird-man figures called *tengu* can also be the benevolent guardians of *kami*, and for this reason they are often impersonated at Shinto festivals. Another example of this ambivalence is Susano, who, after his banishment from heaven, became a positive figure, slaying a dragon and saving a maiden in distress (see p.441). In all cases, the misfortunes inflicted by *oni* are seen as the result of a temporary disruption of the natural order of things, and not the manifestation of an inherent evil force.

Ancestral spirits form another important category of *kami*. In Shinto, a person's soul is believed to become a *kami* after the death of its mortal "host," and the *kami* of a family's ancestors are revered at household shrines. Some ancestral *kami*, such as the spirits of Emperor Meiji (reigned 1867–1912) and other rulers, may become the focus of more widespread cults. For example, Meiji's shrine is the most important Shinto shrine in Tokyo. The *kami* of all Japan's war dead since 1872 are worshipped at Tokyo's controversial Yasukuni shrine (see pp.511–512).

The most widely known *kami* are the anthropomorphic gods and goddesses who emerged during what ancient texts call the "Age of the Gods." Accounts of this primeval era—when deities were active on Earth before establishing the rule of their mortal descendants, the emperors, and then withdrawing to the heavenly domain—are given in the epics the *Kojiki* (712CE) and the *Nihonshoki* (720CE), together with the stories of the great gods and goddesses of Shinto (see pp.449–455).

The greatest of these divine offspring of Izanagi and Izanami was the venerated sun goddess, Amaterasu (the "Person Who Makes the Heavens Shine"), chief of the pantheon and the most important Shinto divinity. After she had established her sovereignty, following an argument with her brother Susano (see pp.454–455), she established the imperial line through her descendant Jimmu Tenno, who became Japan's first emperor.

The *kami* in the "Age of the Gods" are the *amatsukami* ("heavenly *kami*") and the *kunitsukami* ("earthly *kami*"). Amaterasu is one of the former, while the popular Okuninushi, the guardian god of Japan and its emperors, is one of the latter. The story of the establishment of the rule of Jimmu Tenno and the Japanese imperial line is an important part of Shinto belief and is closely associated with the Yamato region of Honshu, the main island and the area where Shinto's most important shrine is located: that of Amaterasu at Ise (see p.474).

After Susano's descent to the "Reed Plain" (Earth), he saved a beautiful maiden from a hideous dragon, found a fabulous sword in one of its eight tails, and gave it to his sister, Amaterasu, as a peace offering. He married the maiden, built a palace near Izumo, and fathered a dynasty of powerful deities who came to rule the Earth. The greatest of them was Okuninushi, the "Great Lord of the Country." Alarmed at Okuninushi's power, Amaterasu sent her grandson Honinigi to the mortal world to reestablish her sovereignty over the Earth.

Honinigi bore three talismans of sovereignty—a sacred mirror, which had been used to trick Amaterasu into returning after an argument with Susano (see p.454); a magical sword, later called Kusanagi, which Susano had discovered in the dragon's tail; and a wondrous fertility jewel called a *magatama*, which Susano had used to produce offspring in the contest with his sister (see p.454).

According to tradition, Honinigi landed at Mount Takachio, in Kyushu, and struck a deal with Okuninushi. In return for the latter's loyalty, Honinigi promised that his grandmother would recognize Okuninushi as the perpetual protector of the imperial family, which was later founded by Honinigi's great-grandson, the aforementioned Jimmu Tenno. Okuninushi is enshrined at Izumo-*taisha*, the second most important Shinto shrine in Japan (after Ise), and since the days of Jimmu Tenno the earthly descendants of Amaterasu have ruled Japan as emperors.

Another prominent *kami* is Inari, the rice god, who is widely venerated as the deity who ensures an abundant rice harvest and, by extension, general prosperity throughout the land—thus he is especially important to shopkeepers, merchants, and artisans. Inari's messenger and guardian is the fox, and images of this wily animal are prominent at all the god's shrines (see p.478).

There are also the so-called *Shichifukujin* ("Seven Lucky Gods"), each of whom personifies a desirable characteristic or condition. The most popular of the septet are Daikokuten and Ebisu, who are often enshrined together and are sometimes said to be father and son. Both personify wealth and material abundance. Daikokuten, typically depicted with a large sack slung over his left shoulder, is a tutelary god of the kitchen and is particularly revered by cooks and restaurateurs. He is frequently assimilated to Okuninushi (see p.441), who is also known as Daikokusama. Ebisu carries a fishing rod in one hand and a sea bream under his other arm. The other five are Benten (god of skill in music and other arts), Fukurokuju (god of popularity), Hotei (god of contentment and magnanimity), Jurojin (god of longevity), and, finally, Bishamonten (god of benevolent authority).

In Japanese Buddhism a similarly broad array of sacred beings, known as *butsu* and *bosatsu* ("enlightened being") are venerated. Three of these divine beings loom especially large—Amida, Kannon, and Jizo. Amida presides over the "Pure Land," or Western Paradise; Kannon is the protector of children, dead souls, and women in childbirth; it is also the *bosatsu* to whom worshippers turn for mercy and forgiveness; and the *bosatsu* Jizo is also concerned with children, particularly with the souls of those who have died (including, in recent times, aborted fetuses). Jizo is the protector of all who suffer pain. Kannon and Jizo are also worshipped as *kami* by vast numbers of Japanese. In fact, in popular worship, the distinction between Shinto *kami* and Buddhist *bosatsu* and *butsu* is very blurred. At times in the past, Shinto priests have used the phrase "*kami*-nature" in a fashion analogous to the Buddhist term "*buddha*-nature," which is a reference to our true nature or essence.

Both *kami* and *bosatsu* are seen as essentially complementary, and a number of divinities are important to both faiths, such as Hachiman, an important warrior-god largely derived from the semilegendary emperor

Ojin (ca. 300CE). Hachiman is widely worshipped throughout Japan at both Buddhist temples and Shinto shrines. Most notably, he is the tutelary deity of the Todaiji temple in Nara (which also houses the largest statue of the Buddha in Japan) and of the Hachiman shrine in Kamakura.

Hachiman shrines are favorite venues for the ritual called *omiyamairi* in which infants—primarily boys in the case of Hachiman—are taken to shrines for the first time and purified (see p.497). At the same time, Hachiman's image is to be found in a great many Buddhist temples, where he is venerated as a *bosatsu*.

Hachiman is not the only deity with historical or quasihistorical roots. Possibly the best example of all is Sugawara no Michizane, otherwise known as Tenjin, or "Heaven Person." A brilliant administrator and scholar, Sugawara (845–903CE) was at the peak of his career as a member of the Heian court when several jealous colleagues conspired against him. Falsely accused of misconduct in office, Sugawara was banished from his native city and spent the rest of his life as a restless political exile on the island of Kyushu, where he eventually died an unhappy death. After his demise, Heian, the imperial capital (modern-day Kyoto), was devastated by fires and pestilence. The imperial authorities were convinced that this was divine retribution for their treatment of Sugawara no Michizane and they sought to appease his angry spirit and placate his ghost by building a major shrine to the dead scholar as a *kami* under the name Tenjin—the magnificent Kitano Temmangu shrine, which remains one of the most important Shinto shrines in modern Kyoto.

According to the story, conditions in Heian immediately improved. Thereafter, Tenjin became an important member of the Shinto pantheon, venerated throughout Japan as the patron of learning and scholarship—his cult spread the length and breadth of the country. Tenjin shrines are visited regularly by students (and their parents), who want to invoke the *kami*'s assistance prior to the taking of important examinations, and by scholars who are seeking divine help in their research.

New additions are frequently made to the roster of major *kami*. For example, the spirit of Emperor Meiji, during whose reign (1867–1912) Japan moved from being a backward East Asian country to the status of a world power, is venerated in the largest shrine in Tokyo, the Meiji-*jingu*; and the spirit of Ieyasu, the first Tokugawa shogun (died 1616), is magnificently enshrined at Nikko. This ability to grow and change with the times is part of the essential genius of Shinto.

Japan: The Land of the Gods

❝ People all over the world refer to Japan as the Land
of the Gods and call us the descendants of the gods.
Indeed, it is exactly as they say: our country, as a
special mark of favor from the heavenly gods, was
begotten by them, and there is thus so immense a
difference between Japan and all the other countries
of the world as to defy comparison. Ours is a splendid
and blessed country, the Land of the Gods beyond any
doubt, and we, down to the most humble man and
woman, are the descendants of the gods. Nevertheless,
there are unhappily many people who do not understand why Japan is the Land of the Gods and we their
descendants....

Is this not a lamentable state of affairs? Japanese
differ completely from and are superior to the peoples
of China, India, Russia, Holland, Siam, Cambodia,
and all other countries of the world, and for us to have
called our country the Land of the Gods was not mere
vainglory. It was the gods who formed all the lands
of the world at the Creation, and these gods were
without exception born in Japan. Japan is thus the
homeland of the gods, and that is why we call it the
Land of the Gods. ❞

From *Kodo Taii* in *Hirata Atsutane Zenshu I*, pp.22–3, cited in *Sources of Japanese Tradition*, edited
by Tsunoda, Rusaku., et al. Columbia University Press: New York, 1958, p.544.

Commentary

Hirata Atsutane (1776–1843) was a disciple of the great Shinto scholar Motoori Norinaga (see pp. 461–462) who carried on the latter's ground-breaking research and textual criticism. In the passage cited he explains why Japan is the "Land of the Gods." Despite Japan's deliberate political isolation from the rest of the world during the Tokugawa shogunate (1603–1867), memories of the so-called "Christian century" (ca. 1550–1650) lingered on, and Western ideas continued to trickle into Japan via the Dutch presence in Nagasaki.

Drawing on his knowledge of both Chinese and Western religious ideas, Hirata concluded that it was Shinto and its pantheon of divine figures that set Japan apart from other nations. In his opinion, the Japanese people were ultimately descended from the *kami* who populate the *Kojiki* and the *Nihonshoki* (also called the *Nihongi)* and they were therefore superior to other races. Indeed, as he saw it, unlike other countries with which he was familiar, Japan was the homeland of the gods and therefore especially blessed. Like those of his mentor Motoori, Hirata's writings fueled the later stages of the Shinto Revival (1770s–1870s) and helped to lay the foundation for the emergence of "State Shinto" in the wake of the Meiji restoration in 1868.

CHAPTER THREE

SACRED TEXTS

The most important written sources for Shinto are the *Kojiki* and *Nihonshoki*, which were composed, respectively, in 712CE by the Heian courtier Ono Yasumaro and in 720CE by a committee of scholars, who sought to rectify what they believed to be Ono's excessive emphasis on the imperial, or Yamato, clan.

Unlike the Western "scriptures"—divinely revealed (or dictated) messages—these works are genealogically based chronicles that record both the divine and human generations that have unfolded since the "Age of the Gods" (see p.440) and the creation of the world. Both texts undoubtedly owe a debt to the ancient Chinese tradition (the *Nihonshoki* is written in classical Chinese) which had such a dramatic impact on Japanese culture and belief in the eighth century CE.

LEFT:
A Shinto priest intones prayers as part of the annual Saigusa Matsuri (Lily Festival) at the Isagawa shrine in Nara.

The *Kojiki* ("Record of Ancient Matters"), the oldest sur-
viving text in Japanese, was compiled and edited in
712CE by the scholar-courtier Ono Yasumaro from a
number of earlier sources. These sources, some written
(and since lost) and others oral, were for the most part
genealogies of the several powerful *uji* ("clans"), that
dominated Japanese political life in the Nara period
(710–94CE), the most important being the imperial
Yamato clan. Each genealogy traced the descent of the *uji*
in question back to a particular *kami* ("spirit"; see p.436).

At this period, Japan was actively borrowing almost
every conceivable cultural trait from China. Inspired by
the Chinese genre of "imperial chronicle," which served
to legitimize the ruling dynasty, the Japanese court commissioned Ono to compile a coherent Japanese chronicle that would establish for all time the supremacy of the
Yamato clan. The early part of Ono's text contains the
primary account of Shinto cosmology and theogony:
the creation of the islands of Japan by the primordial
deities Izanagi and Izanami; the birth of the sun goddess
Amaterasu; the extension of her authority to the "Reed
Plain" (Earth); and the appearance of her descendant
Jimmu Tenno, the first emperor (see pp.440–442).

The leading Japanese clans were apparently dissatis-
fied with the *Kojiki* even before Ono had completed it,

largely because it emphasized the history of the imperial clan at the expense of their own. The court acted on the dissatisfaction the clans expressed by commissioning the *Nihonshoki* ("Chronicles of Japan"), also known as the *Nihongi*, from a committee of courtiers.

Ono had produced a relatively straightforward narrative, but the authors of the *Nihonshoki* felt compelled to retell each important mythological event from a variety of perspectives, reflecting the versions sacred to the several major clans. The result was a jumble of compromises, redundancies, and even contradictions. Nonetheless, the *Nihonshoki*, compiled in 720CE, is a treasure trove of tales that shed a great deal of light on the range and diversity of ancient Shinto mythology and its *kami*.

Unlike the *Kojiki*, the *Nihonshoki* is written in classical Chinese, although it includes poetic sections in archaic Japanese. Wherever possible, the authors presented the myths from a Chinese perspective, and the text contains a great many Chinese mythological themes and references—a good example is the Pan Gu story, a Chinese creation myth that recurs in almost identical form at several points in the *Nihonshoki*.

Both the *Kojiki* and the *Nihonshoki* state that in the beginning, when the world was a fluid, turbulent,

formless chaos, there arose seven successive generations of invisible *kami*. In the eighth generation, the heavenly divinity Izanagi (the "August Male") and his sister the goddess Izanami (the "August Female") came into being and, standing on the "Floating Bridge of Heaven" (probably to be interpreted as a rainbow), they dipped a jeweled spear into the jelly-like mass and created an island, Onogoro. This was the first land. Izanagi and Izanami descended to the island. At this point they became aware of their gender difference and had sexual intercourse. But Izanami's first offspring was a "leech-

Omamori are sacred talismans used to contain prayers and invocations that ensure the wearer's general good fortune.

child" (that is, a monster), and the couple sought help from the older *kami*. Izanami then gave birth to an array of *kami* and also islands—the Japanese archipelago. But the birth of her last child, the fire god, caused her such severe burns that she died and went to Yomi, the land of the dead (see pp.506–507).

Izanagi ventured into Yomi in an attempt to retrieve his beloved wife, but, like the Greek Orpheus in his attempt to rescue his beloved Eurydice from Hades, Izanagi disregarded her plea not to look upon her. He saw that Izanami had become a rotting, hideous demon, and fled in horror, pursued by Izanami and the so-called "Hags of Yomi." His effort was unsuccessful, and he barely escaped with his life.

To purify himself of Yomi's pollution, Izanagi bathed in the sacred Hi River. As he washed, the sun goddess

Amaterasu was born from his left eye, the moon god Tsukiyomi from his right eye, and the storm god Susano (also known as the "Raging Male") from his nose. Izanagi then retired to the northwest part of Kyushu island, where today there are a handful of shrines dedicated to him and Izanami. Before retiring, Izanagi handed power to his offspring: Amaterasu (the "Person Who Makes the Heavens Shine") was to be supreme deity, Tsukiyomi became lord of the night (the moon god), and Susano was given dominion of the sea.

However, Susano was jealous of his sister and challenged her authority. After claiming victory in a divinatory contest, wherein he and his divine sister vied to see who could produce the greater number of offspring (Susano produced more, but Amaterasu's brood included a greater number of males), Susano rampaged through heaven, causing chaos. Amaterasu's response was to shut herself away in the "Heavenly Cave of Darkness," which made matters worse by depriving the world of sunlight and causing the crops to wither. Using a reflective mirror to entice her, the gods eventually tricked Amaterasu into reappearing and, as she did so, the sunlight returned. Susano was then banished from heaven—descending to Earth in Izumo near the headwaters of the Hi River—and the sun goddess's sovereignty was confirmed. Her descendant Jimmu Tenno became the first emperor, and with the establishment of the imperial line, the "Age of the Gods" came to an end.

The *Kojiki* and *Nihonshoki* are by no means the only sources of Shinto beliefs. Other writings include the *Manyoshu* ("Collection of 10,000 Leaves," ca. 760CE), a vast anthology of poetry that embraces poems on religious, mythological, and secular themes. This is considered the single greatest piece of literature dating from the Nara period and is best known, not for its thousands of examples of classic Japanese verse known as *tanka*s, but for the very long poems called *choka* which provide a means of dealing with important subjects, such as the imperial family.

In addition, there are the *Fudoki*—provincial chronicles commissioned in 713CE that include legends of local *kami*—and the literature on the laws of Shinto contained in a large body of books, some fifty in total, known as the *Engishiki*. This collection dates from the late tenth century CE—it is named for the Engi era (901–22CE)—and includes a vast anthology of *norito* (Shinto ritual prayers and liturgies for use in public ceremonies), as well as instructions on how to apply the *jingi-ryo*—rules that must be adhered to when conducting Shinto and shrine ceremonies.

Japan's Creation in the *Kojiki* and the *Nihonshoki*

❝ At this time the heavenly deities, all with one
command, said to the two deities Izanagi-nö-mikötö
and Izanami-nö-mikötö: 'Complete and solidify this
drifting land!'

Giving them the Heavenly Jeweled Spear, they
entrusted the mission to them.

Thereupon, the two deities stood on the Heavenly
Floating Bridge and, lowering the jeweled spear,
stirred with it. They stirred the brine with a churning-
churning sound; and when they lifted up [the spear]
again, the brine dripping down from the tip of the
spear piled up and became an island. This was the
island Onögörö. [*Kojiki*] **❞**

❝ Izanagi no Mikoto and Izanami no Mikoto stood
on the floating bridge of Heaven, and held counsel
together, saying: 'Is there not a country beneath?'
Thereupon they thrust down the jewel-spear of
Heaven, and groping about therewith found the
ocean. The brine dripped from the point of the spear
coagulated and became an island which received the
name of Ono-goro-jima. [*Nihonshoki*] **❞**

From *Kojiki*, translated by Donald L. Philippi. Princeton University Press: Princeton, 1969, p.49 and *Nihongi, Chronicles of Japan from the Earliest Times to A.D. 697. Vol 1*, translated by W.G. Aston. Kegan Paul, Trench, Trübner & Co. Limited: London, 1896, pp.10–12.

Commentary

The narratives contained in the *Kojiki* and *Nihonshoki*, especially in the early sections thereof, are the closest approximation in Shinto of "scriptural" texts. Izanagi and Izanami (see p.452) have been called the "Japanese Adam and Eve," and their role in Japan's mythology is essentially similar to that of the Old Testament pair—although in a number of important respects it is much more extensive, because they not only procreate divine beings but also bring into existence a long list of islands and other inanimate phenomena.

The passages opposite—the same episode as it is described in the *Kojiki* and then the *Nihonshoki*—relate to the couple's creation of the primordial Japanese island, Onogoro (see p.452). Like a great many other creation stories, these versions assume that the primeval state of things is one of flux and that form needs to be given where none exists (a similar example of this is the ancient Greek concept of *chaos*, a "void" out of which order was brought forth). Thus, the Japanese divine pair is charged by the heavenly divinities with congealing this amorphous, gel-like substance into a solid mass. This they do with a "jeweled spear"—symbolic, perhaps, of the male reproductive organ. Thus is the ordered, Japanese "cosmos" created from primeval chaos.

CHAPTER FOUR

SACRED PERSONS

Every major religion recognizes the special significance of one or more individuals to its tradition, whether they be embodiments of the godhead, founder figures, scholars, teachers, saints, mystics, or guides. Although Shinto has no known founder, there are several individuals whose lives and ideas are deeply embedded in the tradition—figures such as Ono Yasumaro, who compiled the *Kokiji*; Motoori Norinaga, the great eighteenth-century Shinto scholar; Miki Nakayama, the founder of Tenrikyo; as well as the many Buddhists, including Honen and Nichiren, whose influence on the faith has been profound. Equally significant is the figure of the emperor who, after 1868, was established as the incarnation of Japanese nationhood and was believed to be a direct descendant of Shinto's principal deity, Amaterasu.

LEFT: *Jimmu Tenno, Japan's legendary first emperor and descendant of the sun goddess Amaterasu. He is depicted in this 19th-century print delivering his people to their new homeland with the help of his divine crow.*

In the last two thousand years, great contributions have been made to Japan's religious development by a wide range of individuals—from priests and monks to bureaucrats, princes, and emperors. Among these were the mainstream Buddhist, Honen (1133–1212) and the quarrelsome, charismatic, fanatical, and ultra-patriotic Buddhist, Nichiren (1222–82), who cut against the Japanese grain and whose teachings remained relatively insignificant until the twentieth century, when an organization called the Soka Gakkai (the "Value-Creating Society") launched a campaign to revive them. Since the Second World War, Soka Gakkai and Nichiren-shoshu (a sect based on Nichiren's teachings) have gained millions of supporters, but remain controversial among mainstream Shintoists and Buddhists.

Of the many Shinto and Buddhist thinkers and scholars who have appeared in Japan in the centuries since, none—including the great eighteenth-century Shinto scholar Motoori Norinaga—rivals the stature of the galaxy of seminal figures who emerged in the lifetimes of Honen and Nichiren. Between them, they established the religious framework that still governs Japanese Buddhism and that has also had a profound impact on the evolution of Shinto, as the two faiths have sought to find common ground.

Those who have featured prominently in the history of Shinto include scholars who have striven tirelessly to preserve the ancient stories of the *kami* faith. Prominent among them are Ono Yasumaro, compiler of the *Kojiki*, and, a millennium later, Motoori Norinaga (1730–1800C, who was probably the greatest of all Shinto scholars. Motoori was largely responsible for bringing about the Shinto revival known as Kokugaku ("National Learning Movement") from the late 1700s. He studied medicine before devoting himself to the study of Japanese mythological classics, especially the *Kojiki* and the *Nihonshoki* (see pp.450–455). He was inspired by the Shingon Buddhist monk Keichu (1640–1701) and, more immediately, by Kamo no Mabuchi (1697–1769). Both had sought to define Japanese national identity with reference to the ancient Shinto texts.

After his medical studies, Motoori spent his life interpreting the *kami* faith and attracted a wide following. His masterpiece, the monumental, forty-four-volume *Kojiki den* ("Interpretation of the *Kojiki*," 1798) is both an exhaustive exegesis of the *Kojiki* and a vast compendium of knowledge about ancient Japan. Motoori came to believe that Chinese influence—including Buddhism—had long obscured the essential Japanese character. Neither Motoori nor his two intellectual predecessors explicitly renounced Buddhism, but their attitude toward it was generally negative. Motoori attacked Buddhists and Confucian scholars for seeking to "know the unknowable."

Anti-Chinese sentiment and the importance of the Shinto *kami*—two themes that Motoori promoted tirelessly—were significant elements in Kokugaku and had a profound influence on the men who engineered the Meiji restoration in 1868. By the end of the Meiji era in 1912, thirteen Shinto-based sects were recognized by the Japanese government (see p.514). One of these was the Tenrikyo ("Heavenly Truth") sect. It was founded in 1838 by a farmer's wife named Miki Nakayama (1798–1887), who lived near the ancient capital, Nara. One night, while caring for her sick son, she went into a trance and was possessed by a *kami* who identified himself as Tentaishogun, the "Great Heavenly Generalissimo." In a series of possessions, Tentaishogun revealed that he and his nine subordinate entities were the only true *kami*, and that they had chosen Miki to spread their message. This message was eventually set down in a 1,711-verse poem called the *Ofudesaki* (literally, "The Tip of the Divine Writing Brush"). Completed in 1883, after fifteen years of work, the poem contains the revelations that Miki received concerning the nature of heaven, the *kami* who dwell there, and the role of humankind in the divine scheme of things—a role which is analogous to that played by a child with regard to his or her parents. Thus, the prime manifestation of the godhead in the Tenrikyo faith is called the Oyakami, "God the Parent."

In time, Tenrikyo developed into a major Shinto sect and is one of the most successful of Japan's "New Religions" (see pp.512–515). Although its concern with the afterlife reflects some features of the Buddhist "Pure Land" theology, its core doctrine stems directly from the fundamental Shinto concept of *kami*, and the idea that the universe and all that it contains are animated by a hierarchy of deities (see pp.436–437).

For much of Japanese history, the nominal head of the country has been just that—a ruler in name only, conducting rites for the nation as a sort of high priest of Shintoism but exercising little, if any, real power. The advent of "State Shinto" in 1872 was intimately linked with the cult of the emperor and beneath the whole elaborate structure of emperor-worship lay an infrastructure of myth that had its roots in the *Kojiki* (see p.450).

Under the Meiji reforms, the emperor continued to have little to do with the day-to-day business of government, but he became the focus of an intense cult as

*A 19th-century triptych showing the sun goddess Amaterasu,
whose return to the world is greeted with joy by the other gods.*

the living incarnation of Japanese nationhood. After
1868, the divinity of the emperor—previously accepted
in an abstract way—became a central tenet of state ideology. Children were taught in school that he was a
direct descendant of Amaterasu, the sun goddess; they
learned, too, that the nation's history began in 660BCE
with the legendary emperor Jimmu Tenno, the great-
great-great-grandson of this principal deity.

While most patriotic Japanese were happy to accept
this version of events, extreme nationalists went further,
claiming that the divine descent made the Japanese

distinct from all other peoples—they were the "children of the gods." In the 1930s, such claims were to be used to justify imperialism on the grounds that foreign nationals were intrinsically inferior (see p.34). Indeed, it was not until the imposition by the occupying powers of the post-war constitution in 1947 that the emperor renounced his divinity—reigning henceforth not as a god but a constitutional monarch, or, more specifically, as the "symbol" rather than the "head" of state—and Japan firmly separated religion and the state.

Since the war, the importance of the emperor as the repository of peaceful desires has been stressed. An article of the Constitution of the Association of Shinto Shrines in 1956 stressed: "In accordance with the emperor's will, let us be harmonious and peaceful, and pray for the nation's development as well as the world's co-prosperity."

To this day, the imperial rituals, including enthronement, marriage, the symbolic planting of rice in the imperial palace paddy, and the emperor's annual visit to the Meiji shrine to pay homage to his ancestor, are all Shinto based. Although the post-war constitution stipulates that they are the private religious practices of the family, it is clear that many Japanese still regard them as having significance for the well-being of the nation.

The Supremacy of the Sun Goddess

" That the Sun Goddess is the sun in heaven is clear
from the records of the *Kojiki* and the *Nihongi*
[*Nihonshoki*]. If it is so beyond any doubt, is not
the person who raises an objection the one who is
obstinate? This Sun Goddess casts her light to the very
extremities of the universe, but in the beginning it was
in our Imperial Land that she made her appearance,
and as the sovereign of the Imperial Line, that is, of the
Imperial Land, she has reigned supreme over the Four
Seas until now. When this Goddess hid herself in a
cave in heaven, closing its doors, darkness fell over the
countries of the world. You ask why darkness did not
reign everywhere before her birth, a question a child
might well ask. It seems childish indeed when a
question which might spring from the doubts of a
child is asked with such insistence by you. But this
very point proves that the ancient happenings of the
Divine Age are the facts and not fabrications. Some
say that the records are the fabrication of later sovereigns, but who would fabricate such shallow sounding,
incredible things? This is a point you should reflect
upon seriously. "

Cited in *Sources of Japanese Tradition*, edited by Tsunoda, Rusaku., et al. Columbia University Press: New York, 1958, p.524.

Commentary

In the extract opposite, Motoori Norinaga—perhaps the most important Shinto theologian, who, almost single-handedly, brought about the Shinto revival in the late eighteenth-century—is responding to an objection that Amaterasu cannot be the sun, because the sun was present before the goddess's birth. In so doing, Motoori is attacking the Confucianist assumption that there is inevitably a rationalist solution to every problem. He counters by pointing out that the goddess "casts her light to the very extremities of the universe," and that when she withdrew into a cave (known as Ama-no-Iwato, or the "Heavenly Cave of Darkness," and said to have been in the vicinity of Ise) in response to Susano's rampage through heaven (see p.454), the world was plunged into a terrifying and life-threatening darkness.

Motoori goes on to assert that there must have been light before Amaterasu was born, but that once she was present she came to embody the sun as the prime source of light and its life-giving energy. Confucian rationalism, he concludes, is not sufficient to explain the "real" events that occurred during the "Age of the Gods." Indeed, Motoori argues that because no one would fabricate such an account, therefore the events must be true.

CHAPTER FIVE

ETHICAL PRINCIPLES

One of the most important ancient ethical codes informing Japanese belief and behavior is the prioritization of group solidarity over individual identity. Although to some extent inherited from Chinese culture, this code is powerfully reinforced by Shinto's long-standing emphasis upon the veneration of ancestral spirits, and family, and clan, solidarity.

Of equal significance is the tradition's concentration upon personal and ritual purity, and reverence for nature—all of which are basic tenets of the faith. Such principles have profoundly influenced Japanese behavior, from prehistoric times onward, and have played important roles in the modern Japanese environmental movement—those people caring for local Shinto shrines have often been at the forefront of efforts to clean up the countryside.

LEFT: A young boy petitioner respectfully lights a candle at a shrine to Inari. Characteristic torii ("sacred gateways") can be seen in the background.

It is sometimes claimed that the Japanese rely solely on their Buddhist heritage for ethical guidance. However, this does not stand up to scrutiny. At the core of Shinto theology lies the idea that *wa* ("benign harmony") is inherent in nature and human relationships, and that anything that disrupts this state is bad. This helps to explain the widespread and deeply rooted Japanese belief that the individual is less important than the group, be it family, school, or workplace. Rules governing human behavior are considered necessary for the maintenance of *wa*, without which both society and the natural world would disintegrate into chaos. This ancient Chinese concept has guided both Japanese Shinto and Buddhist behavior for more than fifteen hundred years.

Confucian and Daoist ideas imported from China also claimed that chaos would follow if social nonconformity was tolerated, but these concepts served principally to reinforce the existing Shinto ethic, which sprang from the clan-based society of prehistoric and ancient Japan. This ethic revolves around two fundamental and intimately related concepts: the need to maintain the *tatemae* ("face") that a person presents to the outside world; and the *ie* ("extended household"), which includes all the ancestral spirits (see pp.502–503). The idea that Japanese ethics are based on shame rather than guilt has been exaggerated, but it is nonetheless true that conformity is enforced to a large degree by the loss of *tatemae* that an individual—and consequently his or her *ie*, school, employer, or other social group—would suffer as a result of violating part of the social code. Depending on the seriousness of the loss of face, a person may atone by bowing deeply, by a ceremonial act of gift-giving, or by committing suicide. Even today, suicide is often blamed on a person's inability to cope with the shame of, say, failing an examination.

If a whole group is stigmatized, a collective act of atonement is made. For example, when Japan's famous Shinkansen "Bullet Train" is late, every employee from the engineer to the conductor, hostesses, and ticket sellers feels responsible and will apologize profusely to delayed passengers. Once atonement is made, the shame ceases and the burden it imposes is lifted.

The Shinto ethic reached its apogee during the "State Shinto" era (1872–1945), when obedience to the emperor became the noblest form of behavior—up to and including sacrificing one's life for his benefit. It is very much a "this-worldly" phenomenon, with little or no emphasis placed on reward or punishment in the afterlife (see pp.502–505). However, the state of the soul after death is very much the concern of Japan's Buddhist traditions. From the outset, Mahayana Buddhism has had a well-defined concept of inherent human wickedness, and the Buddhist's ultimate goal is to achieve salvation in the form of *nirvana*, or release from the cycle of birth, death, and rebirth. This cycle is fueled by the accumulation of merit and demerit, a concept known as *karma*. In the Buddhist view, demerit springs from

Purification rituals at Japanese shrines and temples involve cleaning the hands and mouth with fresh water.

desire, and the loss of desire is thus the key to salvation. In Japan, this deep-rooted Buddhist insistence on suppressing personal desire complements the Shinto ethical tradition that demands subordination to the group in such a way that *wa* is nourished and maintained.

Anything that contributes to *wa* is, by definition, good; those things—behavior, emotions, desire, and so on—that disrupt it are perceived as being fundamentally evil. This belief also applies to humankind's relationship with nature and underscores the pervasive Shinto concern with maintaining a balance between the human and natural realms. Indeed, those individuals associated with local Shinto shrines have often taken the lead in campaigns to clean up rivers and lakes.

The Shinto obsession with *wa* is also reflected in a variety of Japanese customs that, at first glance, might not seem religious, such as removing one's shoes before entering a house and taking a daily bath (known as *ofuro*). Both customs are, essentially, expressions not only of purification—the interior of a home is, after all, a "sacred space" compared to the outside world—but also of the maintenance of a harmonious balance in the world.

Renewal and purification are, then, persistent themes of Shinto practice and belief. Every shrine has a

trough containing pure water for the ritual ablutions—
rinsing of the hands and mouth—required before one
approaches the image of the *kami*. The worshipper
scoops out some water with a bamboo dipper, pours it
over his or her hands, and lightly rinses the mouth,
thereby purifying the body both inside and out, and
making it fit to enter the presence of the gods. The
human body is thus cleansed and its internal balance is
restored through acts of ritual purification such as these,
which are known as *oharai*. A similar ritual is undertaken by *miko* girls ("shrine virgins") when they perform
a dance known as a *kagura*, which is a celebration of the
renewal of life.

Other important purification and renewal practices
include the annual replacement of miniature family
shrines and the periodic rebuilding of major shrines in
order to invest them with life and vigor. All the buildings in Shinto's most sacred and revered shrine complex,
Ise (see p.481)—near the coast southeast of Nara in Mie
prefecture—have, since the eighth century CE, been
replaced every twenty years by replicas that are exact
copies down to the last wooden peg (the most recent
rebuilding occurred in 1993). The symbolism here is
extremely important: with each rebuilding both the sun
goddess, Amaterasu (the divine ancestor of the imperial

house, see p.440), and the harvest goddess, Toyouke, acquire renewed vigor, and this also ensures the continuing vitality of both the imperial line and the rice crop, without either of which it would be impossible for the nation to survive.

At the end of the twenty-year cycle, the new shrine buildings are erected on a site alongside the old ones. For a brief period, the visitor might be forgiven for experiencing a sense of double vision, because the complex and its copy stand side-by-side until the sacred images have been ritually transferred to the new shrine by the distinctively clad Ise priests. Only then are the old structures dismantled and the ground cleared, to be carefully maintained until the rebuilding cycle comes around again.

The dismantled buildings continue to be imbued with the powerful sacred essence of the goddesses and are not destroyed. Instead, pieces are distributed to shrines throughout Japan and incorporated into their walls, thereby spiritually reinvigorating the entire Shinto universe. The new structures are built by carpenters who typically come from families who have participated in this activity for generations. Thus, the Ise shrines are steeped in ancient tradition, but at the same time always appear new and fresh.

Articles VII and XVII from Shotoku's Constitution

" VII. Let every man have his own charge, and let not the spheres of duty be confused. When wise men are entrusted with office, the sound of praise arises. If unprincipled men hold office, disasters and tumults are multiplied. In this world, few are born with knowledge: wisdom is the product of earnest meditation. In all things, whether great or small, find the right man, and they will surely be well managed: on all occasions, be they urgent or the reverse, meet but with a wise man, and they will of themselves be amenable. In this way will the State be lasting and the Temples of the Earth and of Grain will be free from danger. Therefore did the wise sovereigns of antiquity seek the man to fill the office, and not the office for the sake of the man. **"**

" XVII. Decisions on important matters should not be made by one person alone. They should be discussed with many. But small matters are of less consequence. It is unnecessary to consult a number of people. It is only in the case of the discussion of weighty affairs, when there is a suspicion that they may miscarry, that one should arrange matters in concert with others, so as to arrive at the right conclusion. **"**

Cited in *Sources of Japanese Tradition*, edited by Tsunoda, Rusaku., et al. Columbia University Press: New York, 1958, p.50–53.

Commentary

Shotoku-Taishi's "Seventeen-Article Constitution" (604CE) is arguably the most important single document in Japanese history, because it established the foundation for all subsequent articulations of Japanese ethical and moral principles. Although it is grounded in the Confucian ideology that the prince had so assiduously studied, the constitution also expresses a uniquely Japanese concern with the establishment and maintenance of *wa* ("benign harmony").

Article VII stresses the importance of seeking wise men to hold office, and of fostering a hierarchical order in which the "spheres of duty" are clearly delimited. Article XVII stresses the necessity of collective decision-making, especially when it comes to "weighty affairs." This is a principle that still guides Japanese decision-making, and was applied in the decision on the part of the *sodaikai* ("shrine elders' association") to allow young women to carry the *mikoshi* in the Tokyo neighborhood of Nishi-Waseda (see p.494 and p.511). Indeed, it has been said that the constitution introduced by Shotoku-Taishi could easily serve as the charter for a modern Japanese corporation.

CHAPTER SIX

SACRED SPACE

Although, according to Shinto, all of Japan may be considered a "sacred space," the focal point of worship is the *jinja*, or shrine, where one or more *kami* are enshrined. Distinguishable from Buddhist temples, or *otera*, by the presence of sacred gateways known as *torii*, these *jinja*s range in size and importance from tiny enclaves on the roofs of modern high-rise buildings in big cities to the Naiku and Geku—the "Inner" and "Outer" shrines at Ise—and the massive Meiji-*jingu* in Tokyo, which is dedicated to the spirit of Emperor Meiji (reigned 1867–1912).

In addition to these hallowed precincts, where worshippers celebrate and practice their faith, the Shinto tradition considers some features of the natural landscape, such as Mount Fuji, or Fuji-*san* (revered as a deity in its own right), to be equally sacred.

LEFT: Fox figures guard the shrine of the rice god, Inari, at Fushimi, near Kyoto—it is the largest of more than 40,000 shrines in Japan dedicated to the god. The fox is both Inari's guardian and messenger.

Shinto has always been a highly personal and local religion, except during the period in which it became established as the state cult (see p.430). Its *jinja*, or shrines, dedicated to countlesss *kami* ("spirits"; see pp.436–437), are scattered throughout Japan, and, because these beings are believed to animate features of the environment, many natural places are also considered sacred in the Shinto faith.

The typical Shinto *jinja* is a complex of several buildings, and, with the exception of the tiny shrines sometimes found on the roofs of domestic structures, they are almost always located in natural settings, even if this is only a few trees shading an urban open space.

Because Shinto is such an ancient tradition, its shrines reflect the evolution of Japanese history and technology. The earliest *jinja* were simple outdoor altars, often carved from local rock, upon which offerings could be laid. As time went on, these sacred open-air precincts—frequently constructed around a revered natural object such as a tree or stone—were enclosed and the new structures came to resemble the ceramic storehouses of the Yayoi culture (see pp.426–427). Many of the enclosed shrines were used for the veneration of rice deities and were modeled on thatched rice storehouses. The two most ancient Shinto shrines are also the most sacred—those of Ise and Izumo. Dedicated to the patron god of the Izumo region, Okuninushi (see pp.441–442), the "Great Lord of the Country," the *jinja* at Izumo is built of wood and thatch and, like Ise, has been rebuilt frequently to an identical design.

The Grand Shrines at Ise (see pp.474–475) stand next to the Isuzu River. The complex is dedicated to two major divinities and has been the destination of Japanese pilgrims for over a millennium. The site's most ancient shrine—and Shinto's holiest place—is the Naiku ("Inner Shrine"), dedicated to the sun goddess Amaterasu. The site also includes the Geku ("Outer Shrine") of the goddess of the harvest, Toyouke. Amaterasu holds the sacred mirror, a prime symbol of the sun goddess and one of three imperial talismans, which were supposedly brought to Earth by Amaterasu's grandson Honinigi (see p.441). The Japanese emperor traditionally makes an annual pilgrimage to the Naiku to report the year's events to his divine ancestor as well as to pray for a good year's rice crop.

Ise is distinguished from all other Shinto shrines by the fact that it is completely torn down and then rebuilt every twenty years (see pp.474–475). This custom, which began in the eighth century CE, serves, by extension, to renew the enshrined divinities.

During the Nara period (710–94CE), many Shinto shrines were transformed due to the influence of Buddhism. Not only did Shinto theology adapt to the alien faith, but also its shrine architecture began to incorporate elements of Chinese design, such as upturned gables, elaborate ornamentation, and bright vermilion paint instead of natural wood—such aspects marked a significant departure from the simplicity of Ise.

An important early example of the new Chinese style is the Kasuga-*jinja* in Nara. From this time on, the Shinto *jinja* and Buddhist *otera* came to look very similar. However, just as the presence of a *pagoda* is a common means of identifying an *otera*, the *jinja* is instantly recognizable by its ceremonial *torii*, or sacred gateway, which is usually festooned with *gohei*—paired strips of paper, each torn in four places to symbolize the presence of *kami*.

In its simplest form, as at Ise, the *torii* consists of a pair of posts topped by two crossbars, one of which extends beyond the uprights. The *torii* serves to mark the boundary between the impure, outer, secular world and the sacred confines of the shrine. In passing through it, a visitor to the shrine symbolically undergoes a ritual purification of the pollution accumulated in the outer world. Japan's most famous *torii* is in the sea off

An 18th-century woodblock print depicting Ise, the most sacred shrine complex in Japan, attended by visitors. The emperor presides over annual rituals at Ise, and only the imperial family and Shinto priests can enter the sacred precincts of the Naiku ("Inner Shrine").

the island of Miyajima and marks the entrance to the shrine of Itsukushima (see illustration, p.416). Visitors must pass through the gateway by boat before entering the shrine.

Beyond the *torii*, the *jinja*—whether it be a vast complex, such as the Meiji-*jingu* in Tokyo and the Heian shrine in Kyoto, or a tiny rooftop shrine—will follow a fundamentally standard layout. Typically it is composed of two principal elements: the *honden* ("sanctuary"), which holds the image of the *kami* to which the shrine is dedicated and is rarely, if ever, visited by laypeople, and the *haiden* ("oratory"). There will also be one or more storehouses, an outer building before which worshippers pray and make offerings, and a stone trough containing pure water for the ritual ablutions required before one ventures near the image of the *kami* (see p.474).

Once purified, the worshipper approaches the *haiden*, makes a small monetary offering, and either rings a bell attached to a long rope or claps twice (or both) to attract the attention of the *kami*. He or she then bows, pressing the hands together in an attitude of prayer, and silently asks a favor of the *kami*. When the request has been made, the worshipper claps to signal the end of the prayer. If the favor is granted, the petitioner is expected to return to thank the *kami*.

Larger shrines typically have a public meeting hall, a stage for ritual performances, one or more storehouses, in which *mikoshi* ("portable shrines") are kept between festivals, and stalls where *miko* ("shrine virgins") sell good-luck charms and personal fortunes. If the buyer approves of the fortune, they will tie it to a tree in the grounds so that the local god may take note of it.

The Shinto shrine serves as the focus of a great many rituals and associated activities (see pp.473–475). Personal requests are the most ubiquitous form of religious observance in Shinto, but the most important time is when the local *kami* is feted by the community.

All Shinto shrines are managed by groups of lay people who pay the *guji* and *kannushi*—the head priest and the other priests—and generally oversee the affairs of the shrine. Some major shrines, such as Tokyo's Meiji-*jingu*, have dozens of priests, whereas smaller neighborhood *jinja* often have no full-time *guji* and the tasks of one are generally performed by a *sodai*, a lay member of the *sodaikai* ("shrine elders' association").

Every traditional Japanese family home has a miniature shrine, or *kamidana* (literally, a "god-shelf"). This contains a small replica of a *honden* with the names of family ancestors who are honored as *kami*. An elderly member of the household, often the grandmother, tends the *kamidana* by placing on it each morning small cups of *saké*, or rice wine, and dishes containing a few grains of rice and vegetables. Priests distribute similar offerings at shrines, because all *kami* must be nourished if they are to perform at peak efficiency.

As far as the natural landscape is concerned, a reverence for mountains and a fascination with their sanctity has long been a marked feature of Shinto. The most famous of all Japanese sacred mountains is Mount Fuji, or Fuji-*san*, which is traditionally considered an important *kami* in its own right. It has long been a place of mass pilgrimage, and each year thousands of devotees climb it to worship at the small shrine at the summit—an act that is, in effect, a performance of worship. In the nineteenth century, when travel was more difficult, a "Fuji cult" developed that involved erecting small replicas of the mountain at local Shinto *jinja* in many parts of Japan. Those unable to climb the real mountain would walk up the replica in a symbolic act of pilgrimage.

It may be no coincidence that as Shinto shrines adopted more Chinese architectural characteristics in the Nara period, and thus came to resemble Buddhist temples in appearance (see p.482), the process of syncretism between the two faiths proceeded accordingly. Indeed, almost every major Buddhist *otera* includes at least one small Shinto *jinja*. A curious result of this process was the movement known as Shugendo ("Way of the Mountain"), which took shape in the Heian period (794–1185CE). Spread by mystics known as *yamabushi* (literally, "mountain warriors"), it involved a fusion of Buddhist *bosatsu* ("enlightened beings") and Shinto *kami* (see p.436), especially the *kami* believed to live on mountains. Shugendo survives to this day in parts of northern Japan and is practiced in sacred buildings that are at once *otera* and *jinja*.

In addition to mountains, countless other natural features are also held to be sacred. Indeed, almost every distinctive rock outcrop, river, hill, and waterfall is likely to have some association with a local temple, shrine, or both. Examples include the magnificent Nachi waterfall in Wakayama prefecture and a spectacular waterfall in Akita, Honshu, both of which, like Fuji-*san*, are widely conceived to be powerful *kami*—deities in their own right—and therefore offer propitious places for worshippers to parade with a *mikoshi* (see illustration, p.438). Whole regions are also considered sacred because of their association with particular Shinto deities. For example, the Yamato region is revered as the homeland of the imperial dynasty which, according to Shinto myth, is of divine descent (see p.450).

The Holy Place of Amaterasu

66 3rd month, 10th day. Amaterasu no Oho-kami
[Amaterasu] was taken from [the princess] Toyo-suki-
iri-hime no Mikoto, and entrusted to [the princess]
Yamato-hime no Mikoto. Now Yamato-hime no
Mikoto sought for a place where she might enshrine
the Great Goddess. So she proceeded to Sasahata in
Uda. Then turning back from thence, she entered the
land of Ohomi, and went round eastwards to Mino,
whence she arrived in the province of Ise.

Now Amaterasu no Oho-kami instructed Yamato-
hime no Mikoto, saying: 'The province of Ise, of the
divine wind, is the land whither repair the waves from
the eternal world, the successive waves. It is a secluded
and pleasant land. In this land I wish to dwell.'
In compliance, therefore, with the instruction of
the Great Goddess, a shrine was erected to her in the
province of Ise. Accordingly an Abstinence Palace was
built at Kaha-kami in Isuzu. This was called the palace
of Iso. It was there that Amaterasu no Oho-kami first
descended from Heaven. 99

From *Nihongi, Chronicles of Japan from the Earliest Times to A.D. 697. Vol 1*, translated by W.G. Aston. Kegan Paul, Trench, Trübner & Co. Limited: London, 1896, p.176.

Commentary

Ise, the site of the Grand Shrine of the sun goddess Amaterasu (to give her name in its simplified English form), is the most sacred location in the Shinto religion. As this passage from the *Nihonshoki* indicates, the goddess was originally in the care of a princess named Toyo-suki-iri-hime. But according to the chronicle, around the beginning of the Common Era she was entrusted to a royal princess called Yamato-hime and enshrined in what is now the Naiku ("Inner Shrine") at Ise, near the coast southeast of Nara in Mie prefecture, Honshu. Indeed, the *Nihonshoki* asserts that Amaterasu herself selected the location, because it was where she first descended to Earth.

Yamato-hime became the first High Priestess of Ise, a role that was eventually absorbed by male priests, although early accounts of figures such as Yamato-hime have been drawn upon to justify an expanded role for women in modern Shinto. The High Priestess's residence was called the "Abstinence Palace," because custom dictated that she must remain unmarried while she served Amaterasu. It was not until the eighth century CE that the practice of rebuilding the Ise shrines at twenty-year intervals was established. The next rebuilding will take place in 2013.

CHAPTER SEVEN

SACRED TIME

The Shinto calendar has a great abundance of local festivals and rituals. Some of these, such as Obon, the annual festival honoring the souls of the dead, and Shogatsu Matsuri, the three-day New Year's festival, overlap with Buddhist rituals, while others are purely Shinto-based.

These practices provide a channel through which human beings are able to communicate with the divine realm and, in the process, maintain both their own and their community's well-being. Examples of local Shinto rituals include petitioning the *kami* to grant good health, prosperity, and success; tending the family *kami-dana* ("household shrine"); and participating in a *matsuri* ("festival"), in which a *mikoshi* ("portable shrine") is carried through a village or neighborhood, thereby sanctifying both the carriers and the community as a whole.

LEFT: An enormous lacquered fish is hauled through the streets of Karatsu on Kyushu island during the city's annual Kunchi matsuri. Giant colorful floats of various creatures are a feature of this 300-year-old festival.

The three-day Japanese New Year festival, Shogatsu Matsuri, has been celebrated from January 1 to January 3 since Japan abandoned the Chinese lunar calendar in favor of the Gregorian on January 1, 1873. In the days immediately preceding the New Year, houses are cleaned thoroughly in order to begin the year unpolluted. During the festival, family meals include a special soup (*ozoni*) and pounded rice cakes (*mochi*); and gifts are given to superiors as tokens of appreciation.

But the most important activity of Shogatsu Matsuri is a visit to a shrine or temple to make an offering and pray for prosperity and good health in the coming months. In some sects, miniature household shrines and the tablets bearing the names of family ancestors are ritually burned and replaced with new ones.

One of the most widely conducted of all Japanese festivals is Obon, the Buddhist celebration of the annual return of the dead to their ancestral homes in mid-August (the date is still determined by the lunar calendar). Many people visit their hometowns at this time to clean family gravestones. They also say prayers for the dead, especially the newly departed, and join in *bon-odori*, a traditional Shinto dance to honor the deceased.

At other times of the year, regular ancestor rites take place in the home. From the Shinto standpoint, the souls of the dead take on the status of a low level of deity; from the Buddhist perspective, they are seen as souls seeking salvation. But both concepts are accepted, reflecting Japanese "ambiguity tolerance" in spiritual matters.

Some domestic ancestor rituals, especially during Obon, involve burning incense on the *butsudan*, or domestic Buddhist altar, and offering small dishes of rice to the souls of the family's ancestors. Seven days after death, the soul is given a *kaimyo* ("death-name") that is inscribed on one of the *ihai*, or ancestral tablets, kept in the *butsudan*. The same ancestral souls are also revered as Shinto *tama* (see p.502) or *kami*, represented by tablets on the *kamidana* ("household shrine" or domestic "god-shelf"), often directly above the *butsudan*. Offerings are also made to these family *kami*. Most domestic rites are performed in the early morning, a time considered sacred in both Buddhism and Shinto.

As far as most communities are concerned, by far the most important Shinto ritual is the annual (or, in some cases, biennial) local *matsuri* ("festival"). Virtually every Japanese town, neighborhood, village, or *buraku* ("village quarter") has such a festival, which centers on the shrine to the local Shinto *kami*. There are two basic types of *matsuri*. The first, an "ordinary festival," or "shadow *matsuri*," does not directly involve the local *kami*, but is still centered on the shrine, and culminates in the festive procession of a *mikoshi* ("portable shrine"), around the neighborhood. The second type of *matsuri* is a *taisai* ("big festival"), during which the *mikoshi* contains the sacred image of the local *kami*. In both types of *matsuri*, the three groupings that represent the local community—the *shotenkai* ("merchants' association"), the *chokai* ("neighborhood residents' association"), and the *sodaikai* ("shrine elders' association")—present a positive image of the locality, and at the same time reinforce their own sense of social solidarity and local pride.

The *matsuri* celebrated in the 3rd *chome* ("district") of Nishi-Waseda, a northwest Tokyo neighborhood, is a triennial *taisai* in honor of the sun goddess Amaterasu, who is the *kami* of the local shrine, the Tenso-*jinja*. It is one of thousands of smaller shrines to the goddess found throughout Japan, the most important being at Ise (see p.474, p.481 and pp.488–489).

The *matsuri* traditionally takes place over a two-day period in early September. On the morning of the first day, children carry a small *mikoshi* around the neighborhood. In the afternoon, assisted by the local *sodai* ("shrine elders"), the acting *guji* (the senior Shinto priest, as opposed to a *kannushi* or ordinary priest) chants Shinto prayers and purifies the shrine and its contents by

A miko *("shrine virgin"; see p.474) performs a* kagura *dance—one that celebrates the renewal of life.*

waving a *sakaki*, or branch of sacred pine tree. In the evening, there is public entertainment in the grounds of the shrine.

Early the next morning the *guji* removes the sacred (and rarely seen) image of Amaterasu from the inner precincts of the shrine and places it in the waiting *mikoshi*. In rotation, teams of young men and women then carry it along the narrow street, chanting "*Wa shoi! Wa shoi!*" (a cry similar to "Hurrah!"). The procession is led by the *guji* and includes singers, a drummer, a young man impersonating a *tengu*—the guardian of the shrine —and the *sodai*. Once the procession has returned to the grounds of the shrine, the priest removes the image from the *mikoshi* and returns it to its place in the inner shrine, where it will remain until the next *taisai*.

The fundamental purpose of this ritual is to sanctify the neighborhood served by the *jinja* by periodically exposing it to the sacred aura emitted by the divine image paraded in the *mikoshi*, which also, of course, sanctifies the *mikoshi*-bearers. A *matsuri* is therefore a joyous occasion, one in which the participants feel that they partake of the divine essence of the local *kami*. In the process, they may experience feelings close to ecstasy.

In addition to participating in communal household rites and local festivals, a great many Japanese go to temples and shrines individually to seek the blessings of the local *bosatsu* ("enlightened being") or *kami* (see p.443), especially when faced with some personal crisis. Requests might include asking the *kami* to heal a sick infant or ensure the fertility of a marriage.

One of the most common Shinto rites of passage is the birth ritual known as *omiyamairi* (literally "honorable shrine visit"—*omiya* being a synonym for *jinja*), when the infant is welcomed into the community of its family. Some months after the birth, the parents take the child to a shrine to be purified by the *kannushi*. Typically, the child's extended family are also present, and afterward there is a festive meal.

Ritual purification is a highly significant aspect of most Shinto ceremonies (see also pp.473–475). Brandishing the *sakaki* (see p.496) and chanting appropriate *norito*, or prayers, the *guji* or *kannushi* seeks to remove any spiritual pollution contaminating the person, place, or thing. Such pollution can include possession by *oni* ("demons"; see p.437).

Purification of the bride and groom is central to traditional Japanese wedding ceremonies, which are typically performed by Shinto priests. However, for the most part these take place not at shrines but in hotels and purpose-built "wedding palaces."

The Silent *Matsuri* in Yuzawa

❝ The *mikoshi* part of the parade, the *shinko shiki*, consists of the *kami*'s badges of rank, attendants, paraphernalia, priests, escort, shrine maidens, and the *mikoshi* itself, which carries the *kami*'s *shintai* [the sacred image that is placed in the *mikoshi* before the parade commences]. The *mikoshi* of the Atago-*jinja* is a massive structure carried silently through the streets, in contrast to rowdy Kanto practice. It is preceded by boys carrying baskets into which spectators put offerings of bags of rice and coins. The *mikoshi* is followed by the *mikoshi* guardians, two representatives from each of the Go Cho, dressed in *montsuki* (formal traditional dress), and the representatives of the first families who worshipped the *shintai*. The *guji* (chief priest) of Atago-*jinja* and his assistant, a *guji* in his own right of a neighboring village shrine, ride in *jinriksha*, and the other officiant *kannushi* for the ritual follow on foot. The shrine maidens ride flower-bedecked carts, and *sakaki* carriers, *sambo* (footed trays for offerings) carriers, and porters march on foot. **❞**

From *Matsuri: Festivals of a Japanese Town* by Michael Ashkenazi. University of Hawaii Press: Honolulu, 1993, p.57.

Commentary

This account of a modern *matsuri* procession comes from Michael Ashkenazi, a well-known contemporary anthropologist who has studied the festivals in Yuzawa, a small town in northern Japan. He is describing the *gyoretsu* ("parade"), in which the Atago-*jinja*'s *mikoshi* is carried through the streets of the town every year. The order of marching is important, because it reflects the local Shinto hierarchy. Thus, the *mikoshi* is closely followed by senior representatives of the Go Cho, the five neighborhoods that constitute what would in the West be called the Atago-*jinja*'s "parish," while the *guji* (the senior priest) and his assistant come next, riding in rickshaws. Other priests follow on foot. The *miko* ("shrine virgins") ride in carts, a feature that is unique to this *matsuri*. A big difference between the parade in Yuzawa and those witnessed by the author of this book is the silence—quite a shock compared to the loud and rhythmic shouts of "*Wa shoi!*" that characterize *gyoretsu* in the Tokyo area (see pp.494–496). Although the processions held throughout Japan all contain familiar aspects, each *matsuri* also has elements that are unique to its particular location.

CHAPTER EIGHT

DEATH AND THE AFTERLIFE

Unlike most world religions, Shinto—an essentially life-affirming creed—places little emphasis on death and the afterlife. Its followers tend to look elsewhere, primarily to Buddhist conceptions of the afterworld, for comfort when faced with the prospect of death or the passing of a loved one. Indeed, although most Japanese are married according to Shinto rites (see p.497), only a tiny minority, which includes the imperial family, are buried in Shinto cemeteries.

However, according to Shinto belief, the *tama* ("soul") of the deceased continues to exert an influence on the living before it finally merges with the *kami* ancestors from the family of which it was a part. The Shinto conception of the afterlife thus reflects the Japanese emphasis on continuity over the generations and the collective identity of family and clan.

LEFT: Sacred straw ropes and paper cuttings known as gohei, *which indicate that these gravestone markers in woodland are to be treated with reverence.*

Shinto is essentially a "life religion" and is primarily concerned with the here and now, the abundance of nature, and human and animal fertility. Since the advent of Buddhism, specifically Shinto ideas of life after death and the salvation of the soul have become confined to the belief that a person's spirit persists after death and remains effective for the benefit of the living. The *tama* ("ancestral souls") are considered part of the social group to whom one is duty-bound not to fall into a state of shame (see pp.470–471). The *tama* of the newly deceased are therefore nourished with offerings at the *kamidana* ("family shrine"; see p.493); in return, they are expected to bless and protect the living.

Japan's prehistoric religion appears to have had a well-developed concept of an afterlife. A great deal of attention was paid to the disposition of the body, and during the Kofun period (ca. 300–552CE), elaborate tumuli were constructed to house the spirits of dead emperors. Ancient Shinto does seem to have possessed the concept of a Hades-like infernal region, as seen in the image of Yomi in the *Kojiki* (see p.506), but save for the celebrated episode in which Izanagi visits this subterranean realm in a vain attempt to retrieve his dead spouse (see p.453), there is no further mention of the place and it plays no role in modern Shinto theology.

Buddhist ideas have for the most part superseded Shinto concepts of regions of the dead—but not entirely. After thirty-three years, the *tama* is believed to lose its individual nature and to merge with the collective body of family *kami*. These ancestral spirits are said to dwell on a sacred mountain, often situated in the Kumano, Yoshino, or another mountainous region of the heartland of ancient Japan. The amorphous family *kami* are also invoked in ritual, but at a more abstract level than the *tama* of a family member who has recently passed away.

The Buddhist sects introduced a number of afterworld concepts, including paradisial regions presided over by the Buddha himself (the "Pure Land" and Nichiren sects), the Vairocana Buddha (the Shingon sect), the Maitreya, and Kannon. They also introduced the concept of divine judgment, in which, forty-nine days after death, the soul is assessed by a being called Emma (Sanskrit Yama). Depending on his judgment, the soul is assigned either to a paradise, or to one of the demonic regions of Jigoku (hell), or to rebirth as a beast, a deity, or a new human being. However, the most pervasive Buddhist afterworld concept was that of the "Pure Land," a paradise where souls could escape the torments of Jigoku and achieve *nirvana* (see p.472).

Most Japanese see no conflict in embracing both the Shintoist belief in the soul as both *tama* and *kami* and the Buddhist belief that the soul is assigned to hell or paradise and reincarnation, however contradictory the notions may at first appear.

Today the great majority of Japanese choose to be cremated with Buddhist rites and to have their ashes interred in a Buddhist cemetery. Almost all Japanese cemeteries are attached to temples, especially those of the "Pure Land" sects (Jodo-shu and Jodo-shinshu). However, it is possible to be buried according to Shinto rites, and there are at least two Shinto cemeteries in Tokyo. One of them is reserved for the imperial family, whose funerals are traditionally Shinto in form. The most recent was that of the late Showa emperor (Hirohito) in 1989, which was presided over by Shinto priests from Ise (see p.481) and other important shrines.

Shinto also encompasses a widespread folk belief in *obake* (ghosts)—restless spirits who, in life, suffered at the hands of others and thirst for revenge, or who died under less than honorable circumstances. A good example of this phenomenon can be seen in the post-mortem career of Sugawara no Michizane (see pp.444–445), a ninth-century Heian (Kyoto) courtier who was unjustly accused of misconduct in office and who later died in

Mount Fuji is the pre-eminent sacred mountain in Japan and is one of the places where family spirits are said to gather.

exile from his beloved city. His vengeful *obake* caused numerous plagues and other catastrophes until he was enshrined as the *kami* Tenjin.

Of course, not every restless *obake* is enshrined, and most continue to haunt the living as they act out their anger and frustration. Indeed, most contemporary Japanese amusement parks include an "*obake* house," in which ghostly images provide the same kind of delicious thrills one experiences in a Western "haunted house" at Halloween.

The Japanese Realm of the Dead

❝ The old legends that dead souls go to Yomi cannot be proven. Then it may be asked, where do the souls of the Japanese go when they die? It may be clearly seen from the purport of ancient legends and from modern examples that they remain eternally in Japan and serve in the realm of the dead governed by Okuninushi-no-kami. This realm of the dead is not in any one particular place in the visible world, but being a realm of the darkness and separated from the present world, it cannot be seen....

The darkness, however, is only comparative. It should not mistakenly be imagined that this realm is devoid of light. It has food, clothing, and houses of various kinds, similar to those of the visible world. Proof of this may be found in accounts ... in which a person has occasionally returned to tell of the realm of the dead.

After death the soul leaves the body and resides in the area of the grave, a fact attested by countless accounts ... of both ancient and modern times of miraculous occurrences by spirits in the vicinity of graves.... Some say that the soul goes to the filthy realm of Yomi, but there is not a shred of evidence that this is the case. ❞

Cited in *Sources of Japanese Tradition*, edited by Tsunoda, Rusaku., et al. Columbia University Press: New York, 1958,.p.550.

Commentary

Hirata Atsutane (see p.447) here disputes the belief that the souls of the dead go to Yomi, the primordial land of the dead, from which Izanagi vainly attempted to extract his dead wife Izanami (see p.453). Rather, Hirata suggests that the dead remain in an invisible (and non-localized) realm, one that is governed by Okuninushi, the "Great Lord of the Country" (see pp.440–441), but is nevertheless firmly connected to the Japanese mortal realm.

The Shinto scholar goes on to assert that the after-world is similar to the mortal realm and that because it cannot be seen from the mortal world, it is often erroneously thought to be a dark place. Despite Hirata's attempt to describe a Shinto afterworld, few modern Japanese put much stock in the presence of such a realm. Indeed, the overwhelming majority are buried according to Buddhist rites. Shinto, with its emphasis on this world, has never made much of the nature of "life" after an earthly existence. In the *Kojiki* and *Nihonshoki*, the dark and filthy realm of Yomi is associated with the uncleanliness of death—the decomposition and putre-faction that ceasing to exist in bodily form entails. In Shinto, the practical importance of ritual ablutions to restore purity seems to affirm its remoteness from death.

CHAPTER NINE

SOCIETY AND RELIGION

The Shinto faith has undergone some major changes in the modern period: from its status as a state-sponsored cult between 1871 and 1945, it has, since the end of the Second World War, been transformed into what amounts to a congregational religion. In the course of the last two hundred years, it has also given rise to a large number of sects. Some of these, such as Tenrikyo, command the devotion of millions of Japanese worshippers; while others—for example, Shukyo Mahikari—have a mere handful of followers.

Shinto's movement into the modern age is perhaps most clearly witnessed by the increasing number of women being permitted entry into the priesthood, and by the agreement to allow young women to carry *mikoshi* ("portable shrines") during festivals.

LEFT: *A bride poses for her Shinto wedding portrait. The dress is traditional and includes the elaborate hairstyle and the women's overcoat or* uchikake.

For centuries, women have played a relatively minor role in Japan's religious life, despite the existence of high priestesses of Ise (see p.489) and the fact that there were reigning empresses until well into the early historic period. But around 800CE the impact of Chinese Confucianism and its heavily patriarchal ideology effectively put an end to this early equality. Since that time, all emperors and most priests have been male, even though Amaterasu remains Shinto's most revered deity.

In recent years, the women's movement has begun to exert an influence on traditional Japanese beliefs and practices. There has also been an increase in the number of women Shinto priests, in spite of opposition from the more conservative shrines—in the late 1990s, out of 21,091 priests, ten percent were women, compared with nine percent in 1993—and an increasing number of Shinto shrines now permit young women to carry *mikoshi* ("portable shrines") during festivals.

The act of carrying the *mikoshi* during a *matsuri* ("festival"; see pp.494–496) is regarded as a considerable privilege, especially on those occasions when the *mikoshi* contains the image of the deity from the local Shinto shrine. Traditionally, the task of *mikoshi*-bearing was reserved for young men—women were expected to play a supportive role in *matsuri* processions, providing refreshments for *mikoshi*-bearers and cooking dinner after the *mikoshi* had been returned to the main shrine.

However, this situation began to change in the late 1970s, with women gradually gaining the right to join their menfolk in carrying the *kami* through the streets. In the Tokyo neighborhood of Nishi-Waseda (see p.494), this change occurred in 1978. The *guji* ("chief priest") who approved the change, cited as a precedent the fact that there were once high priestesses of Amaterasu at Ise—Amaterasu is also the local deity of Nishi-Waseda.

However, in other areas it has proved more difficult to break from the past: Shinto's former association with the state militarism that existed until 1945 still causes controversy in the context of the Yasukuni shrine in Tokyo. The *kami* enshrined in this *jinja* are the souls of Japan's war dead from the creation of the Japanese Imperial Army in 1871 to the end of the Second World War. The shrine thus continues to be the topic of considerable debate, particularly when prominent members of the government—sometimes even the prime minister—call to pay their respects. (While the Buddhist sects have generally steered clear of politics, they have also been less responsive to the kind of pressure for change that has led to women entering the Shinto priesthood. Japanese Buddhism has few, if any, women priests.)

Although such occurrences at Yasukuni may not be frequent, they always receive significant coverage in the Japanese media. The Left, evoking prewar "State Shinto" and its intensely nationalist ideology, accuses the politicians involved of violating Japan's 1947 constitution, which clearly prohibits the state from involvement in any religion. The Right counters with the claim that the Yasukuni shrine is a private religious institution and that those who pray there do so as private individuals. Complicating matters is the fact that in recent years there have been repeated attempts to turn the Yasukuni-*jinja* into Japan's equivalent of a "tomb of the unknown soldier," a place where visiting foreign dignitaries may lay wreaths. But the sensitivities of the Left on this issue resonate across much of the Japanese political spectrum and, so far, the measure has failed to receive sufficient backing in the Japanese Diet (parliament).

Since the early nineteenth century, Japan has spawned a host of spiritual movements that have collectively come to be referred to as the Shinko Shukyo ("New Religions"). The great majority of these are derivatives of Shinto, although most are heavily infused with ideas drawn from a variety of sources, including Buddhism, Chinese traditions such as Confucianism and Daoism, Christianity, and, in modern times, even Western occultism. Despite occasional excesses and sometimes garbled theological underpinnings, the Shinko Shukyo provide evidence that the ancient impetus to religious innovation is very much alive in modern Japan.

The first Shinko Shukyo arose against the background of growing social chaos that accompanied the breakdown of the Tokugawa shogunate (1603–1867). At this time, a number of successful new sects sprang up,

A procession of formally attired Shinto priests with their distinctive kanmuri *headgear at the Meiji shrine in Tokyo.*

usually led by charismatic individuals. Their success continued in the Meiji period (1868–1912), by the end of which thirteen Shinto-based sects had been recognized by the Japanese government. One of these was the Tenrikyo ("Heavenly Truth") sect founded in 1838 by a farmer's wife named Miki Nakayama (see pp.462–463). Today, from its headquarters in Tenri City, just south of Nara, it claims a membership of almost two million people. Although it is primarily rooted in the Shinto concept of a hierarchy of *kami*, the religion incorporates concepts borrowed from "Pure Land" Buddhism, including the concept of "salvation" and a well-defined afterworld. The Tenrikyo faith has been carried to Hawaii, North America, Brazil, and other countries with sizeable Japanese immigrant populations.

Several movements have also arisen directly from Buddhist traditions, the most influential being Soka Gakkai ("Value Creating Society"), founded in the 1920s by Makiguchi Tsuesaburo (1871–1944) and closely linked to the Nichiren-shoshu sect. By the Second World War, Tsuesaburo and his disciple Toda Josei (1900–58) had only a few thousand disciples before their devotion to Nichiren's teachings led to their suppression. But after 1945 the movement grew rapidly, spurred by the social upheaval of post-war economic growth.

Soka Gakkai's appeal was primarily to those from rural areas who had migrated to the cities and had lost touch with the social networks that are so important to Japanese life. Attendance at a temple or shrine was based on one's *ie* ("extended family"), so newcomers to an area often found it difficult to join a place of worship. Many Shinko Shukyo arose to meet the spiritual needs of such people, and the more "mainstream" ones, such as Tenrikyo, have come to resemble the older Japanese sects in their promotion of "family values." However, a small minority has been accused of imitating the more notorious cults in the West—for example, through targeting susceptible young people. One such was Aum Shinrikyo, an apocalyptic Buddhist-based sect responsible for a deadly gas attack on the Tokyo metro in 1995.

There are thousands of Shinko Shukyo in Japan today, although many have tiny followings. A good example of a smaller movement is Shukyo Mahikari ("Divine Light"), founded in the early 1960s. It emphasizes the power of healing and has an extraordinarily broad-based theology that draws on Shinto, Buddhism, and a host of other sources. Like other Shinko Shukyo, Shukyo Mahikari demonstrates the continuing vitality of the Japanese genius for blending elements of many different spiritual and cultural traditions.

The Education of Women

❝ The outward manner and temper of women is rooted
in the negative (*yin*) power, and so temperamentally
women are apt to be sensitive, petty, narrow, and
jaundiced. As they live confined to their homes day
in and day out, theirs is a very private life and their
vision is quite limited. Consequently, among women
compassion and honesty are rare indeed.... It may be
added that in ancient times when a girl reached ten
years of age, she was turned to a woman-teacher in
order to learn the virtues and duties of womanhood.
Now that practice has been discontinued, and 'study'
for women means only a little reading. Completely
forgotten is the fact that cultivation of the mind is the
essence of all learning. It is because of this that the
question now has arisen as to whether or not learning is
the business of women. It is imperative that this truth
be fully understood, and that great care be given to the
proper education of women, lest they should turn out
to be the cause of domestic discord and family disaster. ❞

From *Toju sensei zenshu II* by Toju Nakae cited in *Sources of Japanese Tradition* by Tsunoda, Rusaku., et al.
Columbia University Press: New York, 1958, pp.380–81.

Commentary

In this passage from the work of Toju Nakae (1608–48), the author makes a plea for the education of women even though he still accepts the Confucian notion that the "temper of women" is governed by *yin*, perceived as a dark and negative principle, and that "compassion and honesty" are rare among the feminine gender. Nevertheless, Toju urges that women's minds should be cultivated in order to overcome these assumed handicaps, with the ultimate goal being to foster an increase in family *wa* ("benign harmony"; see p.470) by creating ordered and peaceful households.

Despite Toju's seventeenth-century male chauvinism—indeed, his plea is easily perceived as an expression of male self-interest—his request for more education to be provided for women might be considered to represent a small step in the direction of gender equality—though it would be more than three centuries before Japanese women would finally achieve legal parity with men, and full social parity is still an illusive goal.

GLOSSARIES

HINDUISM

adharma evil; immorality; disorder; unrighteousness.

artha wealth, success; one of the four aims or *purusartha*s of life.

avatar the descent of a god in bodily form

Bhagavad Gita "Song of the Lord," (within the *Mahabharata*).

Brahma the creator god.

brahman the universal soul which is present in all things.

brahmin the highest of the four classes; the priestly class.

deva, deva a god, goddess; a generic name for gods used in the *Veda*s and later texts.

dharma responsibility; ethics; law; moral and cosmic order. The principle of order that governs the universe and individual lives.

kama love; pleasure; one of the four aims of human life.

karma Sanskrit, "action." The balance of merit and demerit accumulated by an individual, which determines the nature of one's next reincarnation.

linga phallic symbol of Shiva, the erotic ascetic, whose divine energy has the potential to destroy as well as renew creation.

Mahabharata great martial epic of the Hindus which provides guidance on moral living.

moksha release from ignorance and the cycle of rebirths, often characterized as the union of an individual with the divine.

Puranas sacred collection of legends and ritual practice.

*purusartha*s the four aims of human life, namely, *dharma, artha, kama* and *moksha.*

Ramayana a Hindu epic in which Rama, *avatar* of Vishnu, defeats the demon Ravana and is reunited with his lover Sita.

shakti divine energy, personified by the Goddess.

smriti remembering; refers to those authoritative religious texts which are popularly preserved in the Hindu memory; they are composed by humans, although divinely inspired

Upanishads mystical texts of speculative philosophy.

*Veda*s Sanskrit texts that reveal *veda* or sacred knowledge, compiled (ca. 750–600BCE).

Vishnu sustainer of the universe whose *avatar*s descend from time to time to re-establish order in the world of humans

yuga an era of the world.

BUDDHISM

arhant a "worthy one," someone who has attained *nirvana*, has cut ties with *samsara*, and will never be reborn.

bodhisattva Sanskrit, "future *buddha*," "*buddha*-to-be" (literally "awakening being"). In Buddhism, an individual who attains awakening (*bodhi*) but opts to defer *nirvana* (see below) in order to assist others in their spiritual quests, thus epitomizing the ideal of the Buddhist path according to the Mahayana tradition.

buddha Sanskrit, "awakened one." In Buddhism, one who has attained awakening and *nirvana* (see below) by his own means. There have been many *buddha*s—the most recent of which was Siddhartha Gautama—and there will be many more *buddha*s to come. Used as a title ("the Buddha"), the term refers to Siddhartha, the founder of Buddhism.

Chan Chinese *chan* (Japanese *zen*), "meditation," from the Sanskrit *dhyana*. A school of Chinese Buddhism in which the pursuit of enlightenment centers on the practice of meditation.

dharma Sanskrit, "truth," "order," "righteousness," "duty," "justice." The term is used in both Hinduism and Buddhism; as a proper noun ("the Dharma"), it refers to the "truth" about human existence discovered and taught by the Buddha.

karma Sanskrit, "action." The balance of merit and demerit accumulated by an individual, which determines the nature of one's next reincarnation.

mandala a meditational device that is a representation of the Buddhist universe.

mantra a powerful word or phrase that is spoken or chanted in ritual or as an aid when practising meditation.

nirvana Sanskrit, literally "blowing out." In Buddhism, a state free of all ignorance and desire, in which one ceases to accumulate *karma* (see above) and thus achieves liberation from the cycle of death and rebirth.

samsara the beginningless cycle of death and rebirth from which beings strive to gain liberation.

Tantra the name given to ancient sacred texts and the movements to which they were foundational in Buddhism (from ca. 7th century CE). These texts stress ritual, symbolism, and rapid enlightenment involving the concept of "wrathful deities." *Mandala*s (see above) commonly appear in the Tantra.

Zen Japanese *zen*, "meditation," from Chinese *chan* (see above). A school of Japanese Buddhism that focuses on meditation.

Pure Land Sukhavati, the "Western Paradise" where the *buddha* Amitabha reigns.

TAOISM AND CONFUCIANISM

With the exception of the words Tao and Taoism, Pinyin spellings have been used for Chinese.

Chunqiu *Spring and Autumn Annals*, one of the Five Classics.

Kongzi, Kong Fuzi Master Kong; Confucius.

li 1. ritual, ceremony; 2. reason, principle, as in the pre-existing principles behind the world and all the objects in it. (In written Chinese these words are written with different characters.)

Li Ji *Record of Rites*, one of the Five Classics.

Mencius Latinized form of Mengzi, the major Ru philosopher of the 4th century BCE and interpreter of Confucius's ideas

Neo-Confucianism Confucian revival under the Song Dynasty, which incorporated elements of both Daoism and Buddhism.

qi vital matter; the material of which all things are made.

ren goodness, humaneness, magnanimity, the supreme virtue of a superior person (*junzi*).

Ru the school of philosophy founded by Confucius; Confucian scholar. From *ru*, meaning "weak' or "yielding."

Shi Jing *Classic of Poetry*, one of the Five Classics.

shu reciprocity; closely connected with the idea of *ren*.

Shu Jing *Classic of Documents*, one of the Five Classics.

Taiji the all-embracing *li* of the universe, the Great Ultimate.

Tian Heaven; emperors were believed to be mandated to rule by Heaven.

xiao filial piety; the cornerstone of family, and therefore social, order.

Xunzi a major Ru philosopher of the 3rd century BCE.

yang the aspect of *qi* that is light, masculinity and movement.

yi righteousness, honor, loyalty.

yin the aspect of *qi* that is darkness, femininity and quiescence.

Yi Jing *Classic of Changes*, one of the Five Classics.

zhong sincerity, the sentiment from which reciprocity (*shu*) springs.

Zhu Xi the 12th-century CE philosopher who expounded the revivalist movement known as Neo-Confucianism.

zi master

SHINTO

gohei paired strips of paper, each torn into four parts, that symbolize the presence of divinity; can also be made of metal.

guji the chief priest of a shrine.

hokora small sanctuary in the landscape created to honor *kami*.

jinja Shinto shrine.

kami "beings of a higher place," a life-energy recognized by Shinto as existing in all things, both animate and inanimate; the name given to a Shinto deity, god, or spirit. Belief in their existence and according them respect is central to Shinto.

magatama a wondrous jewelled fertility necklace worn by Amaterasu; it is one of three talismans of imperial sovereignty with a sacred mirror and a sword discovered by Susano.

matsuri annual or biennial shrine festival.

miko "shrine virgin," or "altar girl"; in ancient times *miko* were shamans.

mikoshi portable shrine carried around a neighborhood on the shoulders of young people in a *gyoretsu*, or procession.

norito ritual prayers; liturgies.

obake ghosts; restless spirits.

oharai ritual purification prior to worshiping the *kami*.

sakaki sacred pine branch with which purification rites are performed by a *kannushi*.

shirukume a rope made from rice straw which is used as a marker of the presence of *kami*, also called a *shimenawa*.

sodai lay member of a committee that oversees a neighborhood Shinto shrine.

taisai major Shinto shrine festival, in which an image of the *kami* is placed in the *mikoshi*; held every second or third year in most neighborhoods.

tengu benevolent bird-man trickster and guardian; often impersonated to offer protection to the *mikoshi* during a *matsuri*.

Tenno title given to the reigning member of the imperial family during the seventh century, meaning "Heavenly Sovereign."

torii the sacred ceremonial gateway marking the entrance to a Shinto shrine, comprising two slanting upright supports and two cross-pieces, often made of wood and painted vermilion.

wa the concept of "benign harmony," in opposition to chaos.

GENERAL BIBLIOGRAPHIES

HINDUISM

Baird, Robert D. (ed.) *Religion and Law in Independent India*. New Delhi: Manohar, 1993.

Basham, Arthur L. *The Wonder That Was India*. 3rd ed. London: Sidgwick and Jackson, 1967.

Danielou, A. *Hindu Polytheism*. New York: Bollingen Foundation, 1964.

Doniger, Wendy and Smith, Brian. (trans.) *The Laws of Manu*. Harmondsworth: Penguin, 1991.

Eck, Diana L. *Darsan: Seeing the Divine Image in India*. Chambersburg, Pennsylvania: Anima, 1981.

Erndl, Kathleen M. *Victory to the Mother*. New York: Oxford University Press, 1993.

Hart, George. *Poets of the Tamil Anthologies: Ancient Poems of Love and War*. Princeton: Princeton University Press, 1979.

Hawley, John S. and Wulff, Donna M. (eds.) *Devi: Goddesses of India*. Berkeley: University of California Press, 1996.

Hawley, John S. and Juergensmeyer, Mark. *Songs of the Saints of India*. New York: Oxford University Press, 1988.

Hiriyanna, Mysore. *The Essentials of Indian Philosophy*. London: Allen and Unwin, 1960.

Kane, P.V. *History of Dharmasastra*. 5 vols. Poona, India: Bhandarkar Oriental Research Institute, 1953–1974.

Leslie, Julia. (ed.) *Roles and Rituals for Hindu Women*. Rutherford, NJ: Fairleigh Dickinson University Press, 1991.

Miller, Barbara Stoler. (trans.) *The Bhagavad Gita: Krishna's Counsel in Time of War*. New York: Columbia University Press, 1986.

Narayan, R.K. *The Ramayana*. New York: Viking, 1972.

Narayan, R.K. *The Mahabharata*. New York: Viking, 1978.

Narayanan, Vasudha. *The Vernacular Veda: Revelation, Recitation and Ritual*. Columbia: University of South Carolina Press, 1994.

O'Flaherty, W.D. *Hindu Myths: A Sourcebook*. Baltimore: Penguin, 1975.

Olivelle, Patrick. (trans.) *The Upanisads*. New York: Oxford University Press, 1996.

Pandey, Raj Bali. *Hindu Samskaras: Socio-religious Studies of the Hindu Sacraments*. Delhi: Motilal Banarsidass, 1982.

Peterson, Indira Viswanathan. *Poems to Siva: The Hymns of the Tamil Saints*. Princeton: Princeton University Press, 1990.

Singer, Milton B. *Krishna: Myths, Rites, and Attitudes*. Honolulu: East-West Center Press, 1966.

Waghorne Joanne P., Cutler, Norman and Narayanan, Vasudha. *Gods of Flesh, Gods of Stone: The Embodiment of Divinity in India*. Chambersburg, Pennsylvania: Anima, 1985.

BUDDHISM

Aung San Suu Kyi. *Freedom From Fear and Other Writings*. rev. ed. New York: Viking, 1991.

Bechert, Heinz and Gombrich, R., eds. *The World of Buddhism: Buddhist Monks and Nuns in Society and Culture*. New York: Facts on File, 1984.

Conze, Edward, ed. *Buddhist Scriptures*. New York: Penguin, 1959.

Eckel, Malcolm David. *To See the Buddha: A Philosopher's Quest for the Meaning of Emptiness*. Princeton: Princeton University Press, 1994.

Gombrich, R. and Obeyesekere, G. *Buddhism Transformed: Religious Change in Sri Lanka*. Princeton: Princeton University Press, 1988.

Gombrich, R. *How Buddhism Began: The Conditioned Genesis of the Early Teachings*. London: Athlone, 1997.

Horner, I.B. *Women Under Primitive Buddhism: Laywomen and Almswomen*. London, 1930; repr. Delhi: Motilal Banarsidass, 1975.

Kitagawa, Joseph M. *Religion in Japanese History*. New York: Columbia University Press, 1966.

Lamotte, Etienne. *History of Indian Buddhism from the Origins to the Saka Era*. Translated by Sara Webb-Boin. Louvain-la-Neuve: Institut Orientaliste, 1988.

Nakamura, Hajime. *Indian Buddhism: A Survey With Bibliographical Notes*. Delhi: Motilal Banarsidass, 1987.

Rahula, Walpola. *What the Buddha Taught*. New York: Grove, 1974.

Snellgrove, David and Richardson, Hugh. *A Cultural History of Tibet*. Boulder, CO: Prajna Press, 1980.

Suzuki, Daisetz T. *Zen and Japanese Culture*. Princeton: Princeton University Press, 1959.

Tambiah, S.J. *Buddhism Betrayed? Religion, Politics, and Violence in Sri Lanka*. Chicago: University of Chicago Press, 1992.

Tambiah, S.J. *World Conqueror and World Renouncer: A Study of Buddhism and Polity in Thailand against a Historical Background*. Cambridge: Cambridge University Press, 1976.

Tenzin Gyatso, the fourteenth Dalai Lama. *Freedom in Exile: The Autobiography of the Dalai Lama*. New York: HarperCollins, 1990.

Trainor, Kevin, ed. *Buddhism: The Illustrated Guide*. London: Duncan Baird Publishers, 2001.

Tweed, Thomas A. *The American Encounter with Buddhism, 1844–1912: Victorian Culture and the Limits of Dissent*. Bloomington: Indiana University Press, 1992.

Williams, Paul. *Mahayana Buddhism: The Doctrinal Foundations*. London: Routledge, 1989.

Wright, Arthur F. *Buddhism in Chinese History*. Stanford: Stanford University Press, 1959.

Zwalf, W., ed. *Buddhism: Art and Faith*. London: British Museum, 1985.

TAOISM

Baldrain, Farzeen., Lagerwey, John., Magee Boltz, Judith., and Barrett, T.H. "Taoism" in *The Encyclopedia of Religion* (ed. Mircea Eliade), Vol. 14., pp.288–332. New York: Macmillan, 1987.

Chan, Wing-tsit. *A Source Book in Chinese Philosophy*. Princeton: Princeton University Press, 1963.

De Bary, William Theodore., et al., eds. *Sources of Chinese Tradition*. Vols. 1 and 2, 2nd ed. New York: Columbia University Press, 1999.

Graham, A.C. *Chuang-tzu: The Inner Chapters*. London: Allen & Unwin, 1981.

Graham, A.C. *Disputers of the Tao*. LaSalle, Illinois: Open Court Publishing Company, 1989.

I Ching. Trans. by Richard Wilhelm, and from German to English by Cary F. Baynes. 3rd ed. Princeton: Princeton University Press, 1967.

Jordan, David. *Gods, Ghosts, and Ancestors: The Folk Religion of a Taiwanese Village*. Berkeley: University of California Press, 1972.

Kohn, Livia., ed. *The Daoist Handbook*. Leiden: Brill, 2000.

Kohn, Livia. *The Taoist Experience*. Albany: State University of New York Press, 1993.

Lao-Tzu. *The Tao Te Ching*. Trans. by D.C. Lau. Baltimore: Penguin, 1963.

Lau, D.C. and Ames, Roger T. *Yuan Dao: Tracing Dao to its Source*. New York: Ballantine Books, 1998.

Maspero, Henri. *Taoism and Chinese Religion*. Trans. by Frank A. Kerman, Jr. Amherst: University of Massachusetts Press, 1981.

Overmyer, Daniel L. *Religions of China: The World as a Living System*. San Francisco: Harper & Row, 1986.

Overmyer, Daniel L.; Alvin P. Cohen; N.J. Girardot and Wing-tsit Chan. "Chinese Religions" in *The Encyclopedia of Religion* (ed. Mircea Eliade), Vol. 3., pp.257–323. New York: Macmillan, 1987.

Paper, Jordan. and Thompson, Laurence. *The Chinese Way in Religion*. 2nd ed. Belmont, California: Wadsworth, 1998.

Pas, Julien. *Historical Dictionary of Taoism*. Lanham, Maryland: The Scarecrow Press, Inc., 1998.

Robinet, Isabelle. *Taoism: Growth of a Religion*. Trans. Phyllis Brooks. Palo Alto, California: Stanford University Press, 1997.

Saso, Michael. *Blue Dragon, White Tiger: Taoist Rites of Passage*. Washington, D.C.: The Taoist Center, 1990.

Stepanchuk, Carol. and Wong, Charles. *Mooncakes and Hungry Ghosts: Festivals of China*. San Francisco: China Books and Periodicals, 1991.

Thompson, Laurence. *Chinese Religion: An Introduction*. 5th ed. Belmont, California: Wadsworth, 1998.

Welch, Holmes. *Tao: The Parting of the Way*. Boston: Beacon Press, 1966.

Wong, Eva., trans. *Seven Taoist Masters*. Boston: Shambhala Press, 1990.

Wu, Ch'eng-en. *Monkey*. Trans. by Arthur Waley. New York: Grove Press, 1943.

CONFUCIANISM

Birrell, Anne. *Chinese Mythology: An Introduction*. Baltimore: Johns Hopkins University Press, 1993.

Chan, Wing-tsit. *A Source Book in Chinese Philosophy*. Princeton: Princeton University Press, 1963.

Chu Hsi. *Learning to be a Sage*. Berkeley: University of California Press, 1990.

Confucius. *The Analects*. (D.C. Lau, trans.) New York: Viking, 1979.

De Bary, William Theodore, et al., eds. *Sources of Chinese Tradition*. Vols. 1 and 2, 2nd ed. New York: Columbia University Press, 1999.

Fingarette, Herbert. *Confucius: The Sacred as Secular*. New York: Harper & Row, 1972.

Fung Yu-lan. *A Short History of Chinese Philosophy*. New York: The Macmillan Company, 1948.

Graham, A.C. *Disputers of the Tao*. LaSalle, Illinois: Open Court Publishing Company, 1989.

I Ching. (Richard Wilhelm, trans., and from German to English by Cary F. Baynes.) 3rd ed. Princeton: Princeton University Press, 1967.

Jordan, David. *Gods, Ghosts, and Ancestors: The Folk Religion of a Taiwanese Village*. Berkeley: University of California Press, 1972.

Martin, Emily. *The Cult of the Dead in a Chinese Village*. Stanford: Stanford University Press, 1973.

Mencius. *The Mencius*. (D.C. Lau, trans.) Harmondsworth: Penguin, 1970.

Overmyer, Daniel L. *Religions of China: The World as a Living System*. San Francisco: Harper & Row, 1986.

Overmyer, Daniel L.; Alvin P. Cohen; N.J. Girardot and Wing-tsit Chan. "Chinese Religions" in *The Encyclopedia of Religion* (ed. Mircea Eliade), Vol. 3., pp. 257–323. New York: Macmillan, 1987.

Paper, Jordan and Thompson, Laurence. *The Chinese Way in Religion*. 2nd ed. Belmont, California: Wadsworth, 1998.

Pound, Ezra. *The Classical Anthology Defined by Confucius (The Shi Jing or Book of Songs)*. Cambridge, Massachusetts: Harvard University Press, 1954.

Stepanchuk, Carol and Wong, Charles. *Mooncakes and Hungry Ghosts: Festivals of China*. San Francisco: China Books and Periodicals, 1991.

Thompson, Laurence. *Chinese Religion: An Introduction*. 5th ed. Belmont, California: Wadsworth, 1998.

Tu Wei-ming. *Confucian Thought: Selfhood as Creative Transformation*. Albany: State University of NY Press, 1985.

Waley, Arthur. *The Analects of Confucius*. London: George Allen and Unwin, 1938.

Waley, Arthur. *The Book of Songs*. Boston: Houghton Miflin, 1937.

Waley, Arthur. *Three Ways of Thought in Ancient China*. London: George Allen and Unwin, 1939.

Yang, C.K. *Religion in Chinese Society*. Berkeley and Los Angeles: University of California Press, 1961.

SHINTO

Ashkenazi, Michael. *Matsuri: Festivals of a Japanese Town*. Honolulu: University of Hawaii Press, 1993.

Aston, W.G. (trans.) *Nihongi, Chronicles of Japan from the Earliest Times to to A.D. 697. Vol 1 and II*. London: Kegan Paul, Trench, Trübner & Co. Limited, 1896.

Blacker, Carmen. *The Catalpa Bow: A Study of Shamanistic Practice in Japan*. London: Allen and Unwin, 1975.

Earhart, H. Byron. *Japanese Religion: Unity and Diversity*. 3rd ed. Belmont, California: Wadsworth, 1983.

Hardacre, Helen. *Shinto and the State, 1868–1988*. Princeton, New Jersey: Princeton University Press, 1989.

Hori, Ichiro. *Folk Religion in Japan: Continuity and Change*. Chicago: University of Chicago Press, 1968.

Kageyama, Haruki. (Christine Guth, trans.) *The Arts of Shinto*. New York and Tokyo: Wheatherill, 1973.

Kato, Genichi. (Christine Guth, trans.) *A Historical Study of the Religious Development of Shinto*. New York: Greenwood Press, 1973.

Littleton, C. Scott. "The Organization and Management of a Shinto Shrine Festival" in *Ethnology 25* (1986): pp.195–202.

Littleton, C. Scott. (ed.) "Shinto" in *Eastern Wisdom: An Illustrated Guide to the Religions and Philosophies of the East*. New York: Henry Holt, 1996.

Mason, J.W.T. *The Meaning of Shinto: The Primaeval Foundation of Creative Spirit in Modern Japan*. New York: Port Kennikat Press, 1965.

McFarland, H. Neil. *The Rush Hour of the Gods: A Study of New Religious Movements of Japan*. New York: Macmillan, 1974.

Nelson, John K. *A Year in the Life of a Shinto Shrine*. Seattle: University of Washington Press, 1996.

Ono, Sokyo. *Shinto: The Kami Way*. Rutland, Vermont: Charles E. Tuttle, 1962.

Philippi, Donald L. (trans.) *Kojiki*. Princeton, New Jersey: Princeton University Press, 1969.

Reader, Ian. *Religion in Contemporary Japan*. Honolulu: University of Hawaii Press, 1991.

Tsunoda, Rusaku, Wm. Theodore de Bary, and Donald Keene. (eds.) *Sources of Japanese Tradition*. New York: Columbia University Press, 1958.

Sadler, A.W. "Carrying the Mikoshi: Further Notes on the Shrine Festival in Modern Tokyo" in *Asian Folklore Studies 31* (1976): pp.89–114.

A Short History of Tenrikyo. Tenri, Japan: Tenrikyo Kyokai Honbu, 1958.

Spae, Joseph. *Shinto Man*. Tokyo: Oriens Institute for Religious Research, 1972.

INDEX

Page numbers in **bold** refer to major references; page numbers in *italics* refer to illustrations

ACKNOWLEDGMENTS

Unless cited otherwise here, text extracts are out of copyright or the product of the author's own translation. The following sources have kindly given their permission.

HINDUISM
All the text extracts were translated by the author.

BUDDHISM
Origins and Historical Development, p.130: from *The Life of Hiuen-tsiang.* Translated by Samuel Beal. Kegan, Paul, Trench, Trübner & Co. Ltd: London, 1911, p.105.

Sacred Texts, p.150: from the *Samyutta Nikaya* LVI.11, edited by M. Leon Feer. Pali Text Society: London, 1898. Translated by Malcolm David Eckel.

Sacred Persons, p.160: from *Mi la ras pa'i rnam thar (texte tibétain de la vie de Milarepa)*, edited by J.W. de Jong. Mouton & Co.: Dordrecht, 1959, p.55. Translated by Malcolm David Eckel.

Ethical Principles, p.62: from the *Samyutta Nikaya* XLVII.18, edited by M. Leon Feer. Pali Text Society: London, 1898. Translated by Malcolm David Eckel.

Sacred Space, p.180: from *The Journey to the West*, Vol 1, translated by Anthony C. Yu. University of Chicago Press: Chicago, 1977, p.185.

Sacred Time, p.190: from *Sources of Japanese Tradition*, edited by Wm. Theodore de Bary. Columbia University Press: New York, 1958, p.225–26.

Death and the Afterlife, p.200: from *Japanese Death Poems*, compiled by Yoel Hoffmann. Charles E. Tuttle: New York, 1986, pp.51, 67, 85, 82.

Society and Religion, p.210: from *Freedom From Fear and Other Writings* by Aung San Suu Kyi. Penguin: London, 1991, p.183.

TAOISM
Sacred Space, p.278: from *Xingshi yinyuan zhuan [Hsing-shih yin-yuan chuan]* by Xi Zhou Sheng, translated by Glen Dudbridge in Susan Naquin and Chün-fang Yü, eds. *Pilgrims and Sacred Sites in China*. University of California Press, 1992, p.46.

Sacred Time, p.290: from the *Heart-Mirror of Mnemonics and Explanations from Writings on the Elixir*, translated by Nathan Sivin in N. Sivin, "Chinese Alchemy and the Manipulation of Time" in N Sivin, ed., *Science and Technology in East Asia*. New York: Science History Publications, 1977, p.112.

From *Arcane Teachings on the Ninefold Cyclically Transformed Gold Elixir*, translated by Nathan Sivin in N. Sivin, "Chinese Alchemy and the Manipulation of Time" in N Sivin, ed., *Science and Technology in East Asia*. New York: Science History Publications, 1977, p.115.

Society and Religion, p.312: from *Jiezhou xue huapian* [*Chieh-chou Hsüeh Hua P'ien*] by Shen Zongqian, translated by Lin Yutang in *The Chinese Theory of Art*. New York: G.P. Putnam's Sons, 1967, p.204.

CONFUCIANISM
Aspects of the Divine, p.340: from *A Source Book in Chinese Philosophy* by Wing-tsit Chan. Princeton University Press: Princeton, 1963, pp.497–98.

Sacred Space, p.380: from *Sourcebook of Korean Civilization*, Vol. 1, edited by Peter H. Lee. Columbia University Press: New York, 1993, pp.523–24.

Death and the Afterlife, p.404: from *Chu Hsi's Family Rituals*, translated by Patricia Buckley Ebrey. Princeton University Press: Princeton, 1991, p.5.

Society and Religion, p.414: from *Sources of Chinese Tradition*, Vol. 1, compiled by William Theodore de Bary and Irene Bloom. Columbia University Press: New York, 1999, pp.834–35.

SHINTO
Origins and Historical Development, p.432: adapted from Tsunoda, R. and Goodrich, L.C. *Japan in the Chinese Dynastic Histories* (1951), pp. 8–16, cited in *Sources of Japanese Tradition*, edited by Tsunoda, Rusaku., et al. Columbia University Press: New York, 1958, pp.6–7.

Aspects of the Divine, p.446: from *Kodo Taii* in *Hirata Atsutane Zenshu I*, pp.22–3, cited in *Sources of Japanese Tradition*, edited by Tsunoda, Rusaku., et al. Columbia University Press: New York, 1958, p.544.

Sacred Texts, p.456: From *Kojiki*, translated by Donald L. Philippi. Princeton University Press: Princeton, 1969, p.49 and *Nihongi. Chronicles of Japan from the Earliest Times to A.D. 697. Vol 1*, translated by W.G. Aston. Kegan Paul, Trench, Trübner & Co. Limited: London, 1896, pp.10–12.

Sacred Persons, p.466: Cited in *Sources of Japanese Tradition*, edited by Tsunoda, Rusaku., et al., 1958, p.524.

Ethical Principles, p.476: Cited in *Sources of Japanese Tradition*, edited by Tsunoda, Rusaku., et al., 1958, p.50–53.

Sacred Space, p.488:
From *Nihongi, Chronicles of Japan from the Earliest Times to* A.D. *697. Vol 1*, translated by W.G. Aston. Kegan Paul, Trench, Trübner & Co. Limited: London, 1896, p.176.

Sacred Time, p.498:
From *Matsuri: Festivals of a Japanese Town* by Michael Ashkenazi. University of Hawaii Press: Honolulu, 1993, p.57.

Death and the Afterlife, p.506:
Cited in *Sources of Japanese Tradition*, edited by Tsunoda, Rusaku., et al., 1958, p.550.

Society and Religion, p.516:
From *Toju sensei zenshu II* by Toju Nakae cited in *Sources of Japanese Tradition* by Tsunoda, Rusaku., et al., 1958, pp.380–81.

PICTURE CREDITS

Photos, London/Rene Burri; 174 Magnum Photos, London/Bruno Barbey; 182 Magnum Photos, London/Bruno Barbey; 186 Panos Pictures, London/D. Sansoni; 192 DBP Archive; 197 British Museum, London; 202 Panos Pictures, London/Neil Cooper; 206 Panos Pictures, London/Alison Wright; 212 Magnum Photos/Fred Mayer; 215 Bridgeman Art Library, London/Oriental Museum, Durham University; 220 Art Archive, London/ British Museum, London; 226 Bridgeman Art Library, London/Oriental Museum, Durham University; 230 Réunion des Musées Nationaux/Musée Guimet, Paris/Thierry Ollivier; 234 British Museum, London; 240 Nelson-Atkins Museum of Art, Kansas City. Purchase Nelson Trust #48–17/Robert Newcombe; 245 AKG London/Bibliothèque Nationale, Paris; 250 Corbis/Lindsay Hebberd; 255 Bridgeman Art Library, London/Oriental Museum, Durham University; 260 Getty Images/Stone/Paul Harris; 266 Bridgeman Art Library, London/Oriental Museum, Durham University; 270 Werner Forman Archive, London; 274 Getty Images/ Stone/Keren Su; 280 Panos Pictures, London/Jean Leo Dugast; 285 British Library, London; 292 Art Archive, London/British Library, London; 297 Corbis/ Michael Yamashita; 304 Corbis/ Carl & Ann Purcell; 308 Magnum Photos/Fred Mayer; 314 Hutchison Library, London/Trevor Page; 317 British Museum, London; 320 British Museum, London; 326 Bridgeman Art Library, London/Bibliothèque Nationale, Paris; 334 Bridgeman Art Library, London/Private Collection; 338 Corbis/Dean Conger; 342 Art Archive, London/ Bibliotheque Nationale, Paris; 348 DBP; 352 DBP/John Chinnery; 357 DBP/John Chinnery; 362 Art Archive, London/Victoria & Albert Museum, London; 369 Art Archive, London/British Museum, London; 372 Hutchison Library, London; 376 Hutchison Library, London/Michael Macintyre; 382 Corbis/Mike Yamashita; 386 Panos Pictures, London/ Mark Henley; 394 Bridgeman Art Library, London/Private Collection; 399 Panos Pictures, London/Mark Henley; 406 Art Archive, London/British Museum, London; 410 Hutchison Library, London/Michael Macintyre; 416 Adina Tovy/Robert Harding.com; 420 C. Rennie/ TRIP, Cheam, Surrey; 424 Nigel Blythe/Robert Harding.com; 428 Ono Collection, Osaka/ Werner Forman Archive, London; 434 Japan Gallery, London/DBP; 438 Ernst Haas/Hulton Archive, London; 448 B.A. Krohn Johansen/ TRIP, Cheam, Surrey; 452–453 Sian Irvine/ DBP; 458 British Museum, London; 464 Japan

**Captions for the images
introducing Parts One to Five:**

Page 8: A Hindu temple
gopura, or entrance pavilion,
in Malaysia. Hinduism was
reintroduced to Malaysia in the
1880s and Hindus, mostly of
Tamil origin, constitute about
nine per cent of the population.

Page 110: The Mahabodhi Temple
at Bodh Gaya, India, marking the
site where the Buddha, Siddhartha
Gautama, achieved his awakening.

Page 212: A worshipper in a
popular Taoist temple in Taipei.
Religious practices in such
temples are highly localized
and are generally performed on
an informal and individual basis
rather than conforming to set rules.

Page 314: Worshippers lighting
incese as an act of veneration at the
Confucian temple in the ancient
city of Quanzhou. The temple
structure dates from the 12th–13th
century Southern Song dynasty.

Page 416: The Akino Miyajima
Great Torii rises out of the sea near
the Itsukushima shrine, which is
dedicated to the daughters of the
storm god Susano.